Adoption Reunion Stories

by

Shirley Budd Pusey

Adoption reunion stories / [compiled] by Shirley Budd Pusey.
    p. cm.
  Summary: "Collection of stories about the reunions of adopted children and their birth parents, with sections from the point of view of the children and their adoptive and birth parents"-- Provided by publisher.
  ISBN 0-9762224-5-0 (alk. paper)
  1. Birthparents--Identification--Case studies. 2. Adoptees--Identification--Case studies. I. Pusey, Shirley Budd.

  HV875.8.A36 2005
  362.734'092'2--dc22

                    2005024439

Cover design by The Cricket Contrast
Published by Acacia Publishing, Inc.
Phoenix, Arizona
www.acaciapublishing.com

Printed in Canada.

Acknowledgments

In my first book, *Adoption with Love*, I wrote of the importance for adoptees to know about their birth background and for birth parents to learn of the outcome of the adoption plan they made for their beloved baby. It has been a real pleasure for me to play a role in facilitating many reunions, making it possible for that information to be available to these people.

I want to express my sincere thanks to each person who graciously participated in the interviews for this book. They were so willing to share their personal, private thoughts and express their innermost feelings and emotions. This was not an easy task. Because of their cooperation, it is my hope that this book will help the reader to better understand the unique and often difficult challenges that adoption triad members may face as well as the very gratifying rewards that they can gain.

In addition, I wish to offer my deep appreciation to my dear husband, Gene, without whose support and encouragement this book would never have been written.

Contents

About the Author

Shirley Budd Pusey was awarded a B.S. degree in Sociology and a Graduate Certificate in Social Work by the University of Utah. She served as a social worker on a medical research team studying temporal lobe epilepsy for two years.

Shirley and her husband moved to Colorado where she joined the Denver Department of Child Welfare as an adoption counselor for two years.

Later, in Phoenix, Arizona, she continued her career as a counselor in the adoption field with a private agency for over thirty-two years. During those combined thirty-four years, she was involved in the placement of over 700 babies, mostly newborns.

In 1993, the Confidential Intermediary Program was launched by the Arizona Supreme Court. She became the agency representative to that program to serve as an intermediary. This program trains and certifies persons who are interested and qualified to do adoption searches for any adult member of the adoption triad -- adoptee, birth parent, or adoptive parent. Intermediaries have access to sealed adoption files to facilitate their searches.

Adoption work pretty much filled her time while at the agency, but she did complete a few searches, which she enjoyed very much. So when she retired in 1998, she opted to continue as a "C. I.," and has completed more than 100 searches, most of which resulted in reunions.

It is noteworthy to mention that many of those involved adoptees, birth mothers and adoptive parents are people with whom she had worked at the agency.

Shirley has conducted numerous adoption-related workshops and has presented talks to various groups. Her book, *Adoption with Love*, about her experiences as an adoption counselor, was published in October 2000.

Shirley is married, has two daughters and five grandchildren. She currently resides in Scottsdale, Arizona.

Shirley Budd Pusey

Introduction

For some time the practice of adoption, to some extent, was shrouded in mystery and/or secrecy. So, too, were members of the adoption triad. We have all heard about some of the many kind-hearted, unselfish and concerned people who have adopted older children or children with emotional or physical health problems. In most of these situations, the motivation is primarily benevolent. Friends and family are aware of the details. Ultimately, most of the parents gain a great deal of satisfaction and fulfillment in taking on such challenges, and the children, of course, benefit greatly.

Some of us have known married couples who have adopted normal, healthy newborns. Many of these adoptions are motivated by the fact that the couples have experienced problems with infertility, and have very painfully grieved the loss that infertility represents. Many of these couples are not comfortable in sharing this fact even with close friends and relatives. In addition, birth mothers have, in the past, kept the fact of their out-of-wedlock pregnancy hidden from most of the people they knew, even parents and best friends. These are some of the reasons that there has been some secrecy in relation to members of the adoption triad (birth mothers, adoptees and adoptive parents). Some adoptive parents have even been reluctant to share the fact of adoption with their adopted children. However, in some way or another, the children would eventually learn how it was that they became part of the adoptive family. This knowledge would often lead to some resentment toward their parents, feeling that they had been betrayed and lied to. Further, it often has a very negative effect on their self-image, thinking that there must be something bad about being adopted, since the fact had been hidden.

It wasn't until the late sixties and early seventies that adoption counselors started emphasizing the importance of being truthful with adoptees about their origins, acknowledging their right to know these facts. We have found this a much healthier way to deal with this matter.

Continually, through the years, progress has been made in handling the facts regarding adoption, in a much more open and honest manner. Adopted children are hearing the word, "adoption", at a very young age and the total explanation and circumstances are emerging in a very natural way. In this manner, there is no cause for negative feelings to surface.

As adoption has become more open, we have seen the positive effect it has had. Today, in many of the United States, a confidential intermediary program has been instituted. They vary from state to state in their procedures, rules and regulations. In Arizona, the intermediaries have access to closed adoption files and can do searches for any adult member of the triad when another adult member has requested a search. Ultimately, a reunion may take place (with the written consent of both parties) or there may only be non-identifying information exchanged through the intermediary – such as updated medical history, etc. Age exceptions can be made for earlier contact if there is a medical problem, but only with a court order. Some people may question the advisability of such contacts, but, in by far the majority of cases, they have proven to be comforting and healing for all involved.

Alex Haley once said, "In all of us there is a hunger, marrow deep, to know our heritage, to know who we are and where we came from. Without this enriching knowledge, there is a hollow yearning. No matter what our attainment in life, there is a disquieting loneliness."

It is my belief, after forty years of working in the field of adoption, that the birth mother (and sometimes the birth father) and the adoptee go through life with knots in their stomachs due to many unanswered questions. For the birth mother and/or father: Did I make the right decision for my child? Has he/she had a good life? Is he/she still alive? Does my child hate me for the decision I made? Will I be forgiven when he/she understands why I did it?

For the adoptee: Why was I placed for adoption? Wasn't I wanted? Who do I look like? Where are my birth parents now? What is my medical history? What were the circumstances of my conception? What was the relationship between my birth mother and birth father? Were they married or did they eventually marry each other? Are they still living? Do I have any birth siblings? Am I like my birth relatives?

Obtaining answers to these questions is the only way to untie those knots, for the adoptee to learn just who he or she really is, and for the birth parents to have the comfort of knowing the outcome of her/his very important and loving decision.

There has been a lot of questioning about adoption reunions. Are they really good? Or do they just create problems? Why is it necessary for there to be a reunion? Shouldn't we just leave well enough alone? Well, if we do, just how will those knots get untied? How will all those questions be answered? Well, they won't!! That is why we have broken down some of the barriers and opened some of the doors. Now adoptees have the same rights as others: to know who they really are, what their heritage is, and to know they have always been loved, not rejected!

With today's adoption practice many of these problems may never arise. Often, the birth mother (and, on occasion, the birth father) will have the opportunity to choose the adoptive family, perhaps by viewing profiles or even by interviewing potential couples. Communication (directly or through the agency) between the two sets of parents ensues with letters and pictures being exchanged. In some instances, there are even face-to-face contacts. Such adoptive relationships remove the mystique of the unknown and most often result in very emotionally healthy situations.

But what of those reunions that take place years and years later? Arizona started its Confidential Intermediary Program in 1993 and it is administered by the Supreme Court. I have been certified with that program since its inception and have facilitated many reunions. I wondered how those reunions had fared over a long period of time and began some time ago to interview members of the triad to obtain their impression.

The motivation for this book was to tell the stories of reunions. There are many different outcomes. Some will delight you. Some may make you sad and bring a tear to your eye. But all kinds of people become members of the adoption triad so there is no set pattern established for the reunion results. Nevertheless, some of those concerns may be allayed and some proven valid. But one way or another, questions about reunions may be answered.

In the course of putting this book together, I conducted ninety-six telephone interviews. Each one was recorded with the knowledge and permission of the interviewee, knowing that the information was being obtained to print in my upcoming book.

Since I did many of the adoptive placements as well as all of the searches, there are references to, "I called 'you', meaning that the interviewee talked with me.

I certainly hope that this book will help you see how meaningful reunions can be for members of the adoption triad. Yes, the adoptive parents, too, gain rewards, even though they may have some initial reluctance. Their curiosity about the birth mother (oh, yes, they do have a lot of that) is satisfied. They often receive her acknowledgment of gratitude for taking on the responsibility for which she was not prepared, and for providing well for the child to whom she gave birth. Further, everyone can obtain updated medical information.

Frequently, during these interviews, other interesting information surfaced, often about childhood problems and challenges that the adoptive parents faced. I have included much of that information as well. It furthers a more complete understanding of adoption in general and how it is similar and different from birth families.

Most everyone has little, if any, concept of the very different and difficult challenges triad members face.

In each story I have touched on the manner in which the child was told of his/her adoption. I strongly believe that it affects their self-image.

It is very important for all triad members to face and accept all the challenges that adoption presents and to embrace fully all aspects of the love that it has to offer.

There are occasional references to "closet birth mother." This is a birth mother who has shared the fact of her out-of- wedlock pregnancy and subsequent adoption plan with no more than one or two people. In other words, she has not "Come out of the closet."

It is extremely important to note that whenever there is a reunion of an adoptee with a birth parent, the adoptive parent(s) have some very strong emotions about it. They may be supportive, but they still may feel somewhat threatened or even resentful. In almost all of the reunions that I have facilitated (well over one hundred) the adoptees have told me that although they gained a great deal of satisfaction as a result of the reunion, they still felt a closer bond with their adoptive family.

Note some abbreviations throughout the book: ISRR – International Soundex Reunion Registry is an organization in Carson City, Nevada that facilitates reunions between adult triad members if they are registered. CIP – Arizona Confidential Intermediary Program.

All names have been changed to protect identities.

Shirley Budd Pusey

To Give the Gift of Life

By Patty Hansen
(An excerpt from the book *Chicken Soup for the Woman's Soul* with permission of the author)

You had your eyes open a little while ago, but now you just want to sleep. I wish you would open your eyes and look at me. My child, my precious, my angel sent from heaven... this will be the last time we are together. As I hold you close to me and feel your tiny body warm against my own, I look at you and look at you... I feel as if my eyes can't hold enough of you. For a human being so small, there is a lot of you to look at... in such a short time. In a few minutes, they will come and take you away from me. But for now, this is our time together and you belong to only me.

Your cheeks are still bruised from your birth – they feel so soft to my fingertip, like the wing of a butterfly. Your eyebrows are tightly clenched in concentration – are you dreaming? You have too many eyelashes to count and yet I want to engrave them all in my mind. I don't want to forget anything about you. Is it all right that you are breathing so rapidly? I don't know anything about babies – maybe I never will. But I know one thing for sure – I love you with all my heart. I love you so much and there is no way to tell you. I hope that someday you will understand. I am giving you away because I love you. I want you to have in your life all the things I could never have in mine – safety, compassion, joy and acceptance. I want you to be loved for who you are.

I wish I could squish you back inside of me – I'm not ready to let you go. If I could just hold you like this forever and never have to face tomorrow – would everything be all right? No, I know everything will only be all right if I let you go. I just didn't expect to feel this way – I didn't know you would be so beautiful and so perfect. I feel as if my heart is being pulled from my body right through my skin. I didn't know I would feel so much pain.

Tomorrow your mom and dad are coming to the hospital to pick you up, and you will start your life. I pray that they will tell you about me. I hope they will know how brave I have been. I hope they will tell you how much I loved you because I won't be around to tell you myself. I will cry every day somewhere inside of me because I will miss you so much. I hope I will see you again some-day – but I want you to grow up to be strong and beautiful and to have everything you want. I want you to have a home and a family. I want you to have children of your own someday that are as beau-tiful as you are. I hope that you will try to understand and not be angry with me.

The nurse comes into the room and reaches out her arms for you. Do I have to let you go? I can feel your heart beating rapidly and you finally open your eyes. You look into my eyes with trust and innocence, and we lock hearts. I give you to the nurse. I feel as if I could die. Good-bye, my baby – a piece of my heart will be with you always and forever. I love you, I love you, I love you...

Shirley: Could this birth mother possibly not be thrilled to have the opportunity to meet with this child once she has become an adult? Seems very unlikely. What reassurance and comfort she would hopefully have about the decision she made for this child's future.

Julie

Julie's adoptive parents had already adopted a son when she was placed with them. They were told that their birth mothers were unable to take care of them and so they wanted them to have a mother and father. Then when Julie was nine years old, they had a birth daughter. The fact of their adoption had never been secret as all their friends and relatives knew. It probably helped a lot that they had two friends who had adopted at about the same time. Their son had blond hair and the other members of the family had dark brown hair. They dealt with a lot of questions regarding it. His hair did darken as he got older. Julie looked a lot like her adoptive father.

When their son was about eight, he expressed a desire to have a picture of his mother. They explained they would be unable to get one at that time, but told them that when they were eighteen they would help them find their birth mothers if they wanted.

Julie, viewpoint:

"Life really changed for me and my brother when the new baby came. The baby became the real center of attention, taking much more of my parents' time. She seemed to be showered with material things. I never felt that we were deprived of anything, we just didn't get absolutely everything that we asked for, as did the 'baby' of the family. The baby had a learning disability. The indulgence continued throughout our lives. In spite of that my brother and I have a close relationship with this sibling. I believe that my mother and the baby always had a much closer bond than my adoptive mother had with me. That sister has recently married and so for the past year a great deal of family activity has been centered around her. She and her new husband plan to leave this country for the next year and I see this as an opportunity for me and Mom to strengthen the bonds that we have. My dad and I have always been close and share a lot of the same interests. He is a super guy!

"I had a few friends who showed me their family photo albums. They pointed out the family resemblances. That was not true when I looked through our family album.

"When I was in my twenties I went into the service and met a man with whom I became infatuated. As a result, I became pregnant. Briefly, I considered adoption for my child since I'd had a stable and secure life with my adoptive parents. As the pregnancy progressed, I began to feel life and knew then that I would not be able to go through with an adoption plan. My daughter is now eleven years old and we are best friends."

Shirley: Many years later, Julie came to my office to get as much information about her birth family as she could. She had been curious for a long time and her adoptive parents had been understanding and supportive of her need to know. At that time, I was only able to provide her with non-identifying information. That satisfied her for the time. Years later she heard of the CIP and contacted me right away to launch a search for her birth mother. Her birth mother had been married a number of times and it was a challenge to locate her, but I did find her still living in Arizona. She was pleased about the contact and open to a reunion with Julie. It was only a short time before arrangements were made and the two of them met.

Julie felt that the meeting answered so many of the questions that she'd had most of her life. She finally knew who she looked like. She and her mother bear a strong resemblance. She admitted that there were some disappointments for her in the meeting. She had visions, when younger, of a beautiful fairy godmother-like person. She learned a great deal about her birth parents' relationship, her birth father, siblings, etc. She now has pictures of many of her relatives. Her birth parents did marry for a period of time and had another girl. She and Julie look a lot alike.

Julie has been able to meet this sister, see pictures of her birth father, learn of his interests and aptitudes (construction), has met her maternal grandmother and has met one of her half brothers with whom she has a very close relationship. Her two mothers have met. During that brief encounter, each was thanking the other profusely – her birth mother for the adoptive parents taking over the responsibility for which she was not prepared and the adoptive mother for the birth mother giving them the chance to be parents to such a wonderful daughter. Julie said that this expression of gratitude went on and on and she finally told them, "Okay, okay!" She hasn't continued to have contact with her birth mother because she felt that she was anxious for Julie to help them out financially. Julie has just started her first position since completing her degree, has bought a condominium and is in no position to help her with support money. Julie and her fiancé (they plan to wed in a few months) will sell her condo and buy a larger home.

Julie feels that her adoptive parents and siblings are her family. She is very glad that she was adopted. Nevertheless, she carries pictures of several members of her birth family to whom she bears a strong resemblance, especially her sister who was born to the same parents – a full sister. Incidentally, her birth father died several years ago. He was a very moral man who probably urged her birth mother to consider adoption for Julie since she had been conceived out-of-wedlock and adoption would mean she could be raised in an intact, established family.

Julie's adoptive mother feels that she was always comfortable about a search because she found herself curious, too. Further, she and her husband always felt so grateful to the birth mothers for giving them the opportunity to have the parenting experience. It was because of them that they had children! She did have some fears that the birth mothers would not want contact. They surely did not want their children's feelings hurt. Their son never expressed any interest in actually doing a search as Julie did. She feels that Julie's mother is a very nice person, but they do not have a close relationship. She does not feel that the reunion changed Julie. She is still a strong member of the family and always will be. She is frank in admitting that she has a very different relationship with each of her two daughters and attributes this to the fact that they have very different personalities, and that the younger one has learning difficulties. She feels that they have to be handled differently.

Maureen, birth mother of Julie would like us to know:

"At the time of this pregnancy, I was married to my first husband and had one son. However we had separated due to marital difficulties and I was struggling. My parents were caring for my son and I became involved with Julie's birth father and became pregnant. I did share this fact with my mother, but had to keep it a secret from my father. He would have been very upset with an out-of-wedlock pregnancy. I didn't want to disappoint him. Since my husband was the legal father, he also signed the adoption papers. I later divorced him and married Julie's father. We were together for ten years and had another daughter, but he developed a drinking problem and we divorced. He was the real love of my life.

"After I signed the papers for the adoption, I was very depressed for a year and I went downhill for that amount of time. Over the years I've had periods of depression especially around Julie's birthday and holidays, always wondering where she was and how she was being cared for. I never told anyone else about the pregnancy so those close to me always wondered about the reason for my depression. On some occasions I sought medical help and was put on medication. Julie was thirty-four when I met her again.

"When you told me that she was wanting contact with me, I immediately began worrying about how I would let my family members know. I felt I needed to tell her sister first as she always thought that she was my oldest daughter. I told her husband and had him tell her as I knew that she would likely need his support when she found out about it. I was worried about how she would react. She is still having to go through some adjustments over this although the two of them have a good relationship.

"I don't have frequent contact with Julie. We haven't talked for a few months. I did get a letter from her a few weeks ago, telling me that she plans to marry. I haven't been told of the details and have not been invited to the wedding. The whole thing has been a huge adjustment for me.

"Over the years, I had thought of doing a search for Julie. I have called the agency on a number of occasions to leave information about deaths in the family, etc. I had hoped that the information would be passed on to Julie. In the mid-90s, I got a packet from the Supreme Court's CIP to do the search, but somehow I never got around to proceeding with it.

"I got a lot of incorrect information about the adoption. I was told that she would be placed with a doctor and his wife and that she would be placed right away, but she was in foster care for about three months. I thought if she was with a doctor she would be fine. I am comfortable with the kind of life she's had and the way she turned out. She seems to be well-adjusted and has been loved throughout her life.

"I met her adoptive mom. She is easy to talk with and I like her. I asked her a lot of questions and she confirmed that Julie was not placed with them for three months. When I met Julie, I felt an immediate connection and we shared affection. I called her fairly often to begin with, but she is so busy, she was just starting her job. She and my other daughter struck it off very well to begin with, but then Julie just dropped out of sight and my other daughter's feelings were hurt. She wonders now if she should have ever met her."

The Richards

Louise and Frank Richards had experienced one miscarriage and then decided to adopt. They adopted Tara and then Brad. After placing Tara for adoption, her birth mother, Pauline, found herself pregnant again out of wedlock and wanted to place her second child for adoption with the same family who had adopted Tara. The agency felt that this would work out well as the Richards had expressed a desire to adopt two children. So Brad was adopted into the Richards family, too. It became apparent as he grew that he was part Afro-American, a fact that the Richards hadn't known before. Presently, Tara is at college and plans to marry soon. Brad is in high school.

Pauline:

"I placed these two for adoption as I was not prepared to raise a child and I thought it would be best for them. I was adopted myself and I thought it was the right thing to do. I never regretted my adoption decision because I knew in my heart that they were okay. They have different fathers. I didn't name either father and I am not in touch with them.

"The children were nineteen and seventeen when we had the reunion. When you (Shirley) tried to contact me I was scared to death. You left a message that you had some very important information for me. I was afraid it was about some family member. I thought I wouldn't call you back, but then got the courage to pick up the phone. When you told me what it was about I was shocked, excited, overwhelmed and felt a lot of peace. I had blocked the whole adoption thing out of my mind. It was the last thing I had ever thought of. In about two months I actually met with the parents for about a four-hour conversation. Now we are all friends. I occasionally go to their house for dinner and I call Louise once in a while. We have a very positive relationship. At first it was a little tense but we now know each other and I feel very comfortable with them. I have a daughter who is sixteen. She only learned about Tara and Brad when we had the reunion. She was shocked at first but then was very excited that she has two half siblings. She thinks it is pretty cool and they are friends.

"The reunion satisfied my curiosity about the children: how they were, what they looked like, how they feel about being adopted, etc. They are happy. Meeting the parents was even greater because they are awesome people. They are the most loving, perfect family. Tara and Brad call me Pauline, not Mom. But sometimes Brad jokes around, he'll say, 'Hey, birth mom.' He is pretty funny and has a sarcastic twist and so do I. The reunion gave me a lot of comfort about my adoption decisions. It made me feel whole. It completes the circle. I realized that what I did was right. It made me feel good that they searched for me. We all have the same sense of humor and look a lot alike. All three of the kids are very musical and talented.

"Louise and Frank have been a tremendous support to me because I have been having marital problems. They are Christian. They bought me a Bible and made a list of verses for me to read to help me through this time. They've been great – the neatest people you would ever want to meet."

Shirley: Frank and Louise had moved clear across the valley for the benefit of Brad. He had been in residential treatment for about five months. When he came out they made the move to change his environment and put him with a new set of friends and it has worked well. He is staying on his medications and is still at home. He wants to be a musician and spends much time practicing on his drums. He is taking lessons from a well-known jazz drummer who feels that he has promise. He has been doing well.

Frank and *Louise* say:

"As we raised the children, we talked about the fact of adoption at a very early age. We had taken a terrific class about adoption that had been very helpful and we followed the guidelines that were laid down. We answered every question that came up until their curiosity subsided. We always let them know that their birth mother loved them and that it was a very hard decision for her to make. As they grew older, we told them that God chose them to be in our family. Tara was always curious and always said she wanted to meet her birth mother. There was a period of time when Brad would not own up to the fact that he was adopted. He did not want to discuss it. We think there is a certain part of Brad that was a little angry. He was different. When he was two, he was called 'nigger' by some neighbor kids. Good cause for anger. We got a lot of crazy looks once he was older and you could definitely see the Afro-American. He seems to have taken the best features from both sides – both nationalities and both ethnic groups. He has beautiful coffee-colored skin, his features are fine. He is a beautiful young man. Girls have called him since kindergarten.

"We always told Tara that when she was old enough she could look for her birth mother. Because of a quirk, we knew Pauline's name and social security number. When Tara was eighteen we gave her that information and she didn't comment for a long time. At that point, I think it made her a bit nervous. She never had a problem with having a mixed-race brother. I'm sure there were occasions when they were out together that she would get strange looks, much like we do when we're out with him. She never voiced any negative feelings about it because Brad is her brother and there is no doubt about that. They are half blood brother and sister.

"We were always comfortable in talking with them about it. It just wasn't an issue. Tara was our daughter and Brad was our son. Their birth mother's relinquishment was an act of love, not abandonment. She felt they would be better off in a home with two parents. We emphasized three things: she loved them, she was not financially stable, and this is where God planned for them to be. Tara asked questions like, 'What do you think she is like?' When she got older, the discussion was a little deeper. We told her that if she decided to search, she should not allow her expectations to be too high or low. We think she probably fantasized about her. She wanted to know her ethnic background more than anything. Frank is part Italian and the birth mother is part Italian and Tara is very proud that she has some of the same ethnicity as Frank.

"In knowing Pauline, we have learned there are things in her background that are directly related to Brad's problems. He has inherited her illness. She has never been officially diagnosed bipolar (Brad's diagnosis) and she says she is not, but we feel that she is. She has depression and high anxiety and takes medication for both. We also learned that she had been in counseling for some time. We didn't know that until after we adopted Brad. In fact, close to the time of the reunion. We had several pieces of paper with things blacked out, but we could read it if we held it up to the light. We'd never tried that until Tara expressed concern that she might develop it later on or be a carrier to her children.

"It appears there is a strong genetic strain. Pauline, too, was adopted. She has made contact with her birth mother and has learned that she suffered with severe depression. If we were to adopt now with the knowledge of the medical history, both of the children would have been considered at-risk. At the time we adopted, people did not consider bipolar a genetic illness. We don't know if Brad's came from his birth mother or birth father. Through a series of mistakes, we have the birth father's name and know that he is now in the southeastern part of the United States. We had considered doing a search, but felt that it could be a disruptive factor in his family life. He is not even aware of Brad's existence.

"We've had some very challenging times with Brad. We never knew what he was going to do next. He made three suicide attempts. He has lost more in his nineteen years than most kids have ever lived in their nineteen years. He has been to hell and back with his illness. He was on the wrong medication for two years. The day we put him in the residential treatment center was the worst day of our lives. We will never forget it. Now that he has been correctly diagnosed, he is being treated effectively. He's done so much on his own. He fights this thing every day. We are so proud of him for what he is right now. He has done unbelievably well. We don't think there is anything he cannot do. He is such a good guy.

"Tara met Pauline about a week after we did and wanted to meet with her on her own. It was about a month before Brad met her and Louise went with him. Pauline's daughter was with her. Both of the kids felt a certain closure after that. She was very open with them and answered all the questions they had. Since we had met with Pauline before, our confidence was pretty high that things would go well. We had some concern about Tara's impressions and how they'd compare with her expectations.

"Sometimes Pauline will call and talk to me for two hours. We have tried to help as much as we can with some of the problems related to her divorce. We do feel that it is more important for the kids to develop a relationship with Pauline than it is for us. Tara talks with her about every one to two weeks. She seems to feel that Pauline wants to have a deeper relationship than she is ready for. She's occasionally overwhelmed. Once in a while she calls Tara for moral support and with Tara's schedule of school, part time work and a fiancé, she feels that she is not always prepared to provide it. We have offered help, but she wants to handle it herself.

"Pauline has a lot of friends, but at times she needs a lot of support and she sees us as a stabilizing factor. We like her and she is an interesting person. She is fun and easy to talk to. The kids like that part of her more than anything. We feel that Pauline sees us as perfect people. We have been married for twenty-eight years, we have a fairly stable life and she puts us on a pedestal. She views us as the perfect family and we are just like any other family. The problems we do have in our relationship with her have to do with her not understanding boys. Sometimes it appears that she is playing favorites with Tara over Brad. There have been a couple of occasions when Tara came to town and she invited her to dinner, but not Brad. He didn't get a Christmas gift from her until February. Brad never says anything. He is a pretty tough guy and very forgiving. He doesn't make a big deal of it. We don't know if it hurt him or not. He's an extraordinary young man.

"We have gained as a result of this reunion and certainly not lost anything. We are planning to have Pauline sit in the mother's pew with Louise at Tara's wedding. It is because of her that we have a daughter. Tara feels very strongly that I will always be her mother and Pauline will be her friend. We would absolutely do the search again. Our whole family has gained a friend and the kids have gained someone else who loves them very much, a stronger love than you would have from any other relative. Pauline is very concerned about the kids and would do anything for them. She has made a broader support net for our children. She is someone else to love them. You can't be loved by too many people. In addition, the kids have a half sister. This has been a positive experience for all of us."

Tara wanted to add this:

"I think I always knew I was adopted. I always felt comfortable talking about it. It made me feel more special than anything. I was in the second or third grade when I realized the concept of being born to someone else and that my brother and I were real brother and sister, but we had different dads. There was some comfort in knowing that we both came from the same woman. My parents were always very positive about it and we thought it was cool that she wanted us to be in the same family. I have always been curious. Aside from my brother, there was no one that I looked like. So my mom told me that when I was eighteen, I could try to find my birth mother. Even though I was not born to them, my adoptive mom was my mom and my adoptive dad was my dad. I wondered what was going through my birth mom's head when she got pregnant but mostly I was curious about what she looked like. That sounds a little shallow, but I had already put together the type of person she was and knew that she had gone through some rough times.

"I found that I do look like her. We have the same eyes, the same smile, similar skin color, similar hair color. That was a good feeling. Comforting. It was harder with my brother. First of all, he is male and half Afro-American, so it was hard to see myself in him. They told me that she placed us for adoption because she wanted us to have a healthy upbringing and a stable family. It was an act of love, not rejection.

"I felt pretty comfortable about sharing my curiosity with my parents except sometimes I feared Mom's feeling – that I was looking for another mother. I would always reassure her that she knew our relationship was strong enough that she did not have to worry. They'd always respond to my questions with support and encouragement and tell me as much as they could. I was nineteen when a decision was made to do the search. We were concerned because of Brad's bipolar illness. I wanted to know for my sake and my children's sake. It was definitely important information.

"When I first met Pauline, I was nervous, excited and a bit scared but pretty comfortable with it. Now we talk on the phone every three weeks and I see her about every three weeks. I talk with Mom and Dad about twice a week, more now because of the wedding plans. Pauline sees my parents as a source of strength. They serve as some support for her. I am happy about their relationship. They met her before I did and they were positive about it. They called me that night and told me that she was a great lady and wanted me to meet her. If I ever had a child before marriage I would definitely consider adoption. I feel much closer to Mom and Dad than I do to Pauline. I have met her daughter and she is going to be a bridesmaid in my wedding. I am glad that the search was done and I would do it again. The challenge now is in defining our relationship and making it a positive one. We have to make an effort to do that just as you do with any relationship. She has a lot going on in her life and always has. It is sometimes overwhelming because she looks to me for support and it is just too much for me. I go back and forth on how much I want her in my life. It is hard, but overall it is a very positive thing."

Brad's letter to Pauline before they met:

"I've been waiting to tell you that I couldn't be any more grateful for the loving, caring, and considerate family I was placed in by you, and with that information alone I'm beyond comfortable in saying I LOVE YOU.

"There's one thing I've wanted to know for as long as I can remember. Do you know all the ethnic backgrounds of my birth father? In other words, besides the English/ Irish that's in me, do you know the other ethnic backgrounds from my birth father?

"If you ever have to ask me what I'm thanking you for, it's for showing me that you care about me by putting me in such a great and loving family, and for taking the time out of your life to write me and telling me that what you have done have all been acts of love, not rejection.

"Thank you for loving me, but most importantly for giving me life. You are greatly appreciated!!

"LOVE,

Brad.

"P.S. Please feel free to write back whenever you want. I would really like to hear from you, and your daughter if it's all right with her."

Shirley: An appointment was made for me to talk with Brad on the phone, but he preferred not being interviewed. I think his letter expresses his feelings very well.

Janice

"My parents always told me that they chose me so I felt that being adopted was being somebody special. Some of my friends at school would tell me that I looked nothing like my brother and I would simply tell them that I was adopted. My parents referred to my birth mother as my real mother or the lady who gave birth to me. My parents had no birth children. One time we had a school assignment to trace our family history. It made me wonder what my birth history was. It was then that my mom took me to the agency and you (Shirley) gave me all the non-identifying information, like age, weight, height, coloring, interests, etc. You told me about ISRR and said I could contact them when I was eighteen. I felt very frustrated. You had my file across the desk from me and you couldn't give me the information I wanted. I wondered why you couldn't just walk out of the room for a minute and I could look at the file. Now, as an adult, I understand. It would have been against the law for you to give me any more information. I was mad at that restriction. I was glad to know that her giving me up was an act of love.

"My mom was very accepting of my curiosity as I think that she was curious, too. I didn't really talk much to Dad about it, but he was always supportive of whatever I wanted to do. After that I went off to college, got a degree in Sociology and now work as a social worker. I thought about a search again after I had my first child. But it was more my husband than me. He can't stand not knowing something. I didn't feel there was anything missing in my life. My parents had been there for me even when I was an idiot teenager. My husband was the one who searched out the CIP. Occasionally, I had looked in yearbooks to see if there was someone who looked like me – maybe a sibling. Then our first child was born with a hole in her heart, and the doctors asked what my medical history was. I didn't know. Finally I decided to search.

21

"I told my parents that we were going to do this. Mom and Dad were excited about it. Once you got my birth mother's number for me, I was hesitant to call because I had some concerns about how my mom would feel. I called Mom and talked to her for quite a while. She assured me that nothing was going to change as far as we were concerned, and she encouraged me to call Mary. I may have had some guilt feelings. Mom said it was silly. Okay, I will.

"I'd never made any other real attempts to find her. My husband found the CIP because he is a private investigator. He brought home the book and we went through it. I thought, 'Oh my gosh, that's Shirley Pusey, she was the caseworker who handled my adoption.' So I contacted you to do the search.

"Now I talk with Mary quite frequently. She comes here on vacation and the children and I went over last summer and spent two weeks with her. I have met her whole family. We have been together about seven or eight times. I usually call her every week.

"I have also talked with my biological father. Mary gave me his name and my husband located him in Colorado. He had not been supportive of Mary when she got pregnant. He was very defensive at first when I called him. He thought we wanted his money. We told him that we were not doing anything funky here. We just wanted him to know that he had a daughter. He then mailed pictures. There is a resemblance. We haven't been in touch for over a year now. He is very different from me and I am very much like Mary – not in looks, but tone of voice, expressions, sense of humor, quick speech, sarcastic tone, and a smart aleck mouth. Mom is not at all like that. She is a neat lady. Mom and Dad are the best. I was raised well with good values. I was very fortunate.

"My parents are glad that I did the search. When my dad met Mary, he said that he now sees where I get it. My mom and I are great friends, but my dad and I have a terrific relationship. My relationship with Mary is very different. I call her Mary, and my kids, ages ten and eight, call her Grandma Mary. She told me that her parents made the adoption decision and that she never saw me.

"I was shocked when I learned that she had never had another child. Her husband had a vasectomy before they married. She just couldn't bring herself to have any more kids after losing me. She didn't marry until she was thirty."

Mary's viewpoint:

"It was definitely not my plan to relinquish for adoption. My parents said that this is what I was to do. I had no choice. In those days you did what your parents told you to do. The birth father denied paternity then, even though he doesn't now. I waited a long time for this reunion. Janice was thirty-five years old. I had attempted to do a search for her but was told that there was just no way. The file was closed and we couldn't get any information. I had always hoped that one day I would meet her. I knew before I married that I would not have another child. My husband had been married before and his wife was very fearful of a pregnancy so he had a vasectomy. He encouraged me when I considered doing a search, but he was afraid that I might be opening a can of worms. When you contacted me, I started to cry and thought it was a miracle.

"Janice and I first talked by phone and I learned that she had two children and I am a grandmother. That was hard to take, as I don't think that I am grandmother material. I am only fifty-five. When they came to visit, the children were a bit of a challenge so I really felt like a grandmother then. I gave them candy and stuff like that, which you're supposed to do with grandchildren. It was probably confusing for them having another set of grandparents.

"When we went to her parents' home, we saw the 'Janice Shrine' in the living room. It had been set up for me so I could see what Janice looked like at different stages of her life. We now joke about the 'Janice Shrine.' It made me feel a bit uncomfortable when her dad kept thanking me for letting them raise this beautiful girl. They didn't tell me that she had ever been a problem. They have done a wonderful job of raising her. I am her mother and Ruth is her mom. I can't imagine all the things that she has gone through to make her into such a beautiful girl. I know what kind of a kid I was. I think any mother deserves an award. I am sorry that I didn't have the opportunity to raise her. The most gratifying part of this reunion was knowing that she was safe and sound and had a good life growing up. But I was disappointed that she doesn't look like me. She looks more like one of my five older sisters. If I had kept her, I know that my life would have been different and I likely would not be married to this wonderful man.

"I still have a lot of anger toward my parents. I have wondered what I might have done if I had been in their position, and I am not sure, so it is really hard to forgive them fully. My father had passed away when I met Janice. I think my mother has had regrets since she met Janice.

"If there is anyone out there who is considering a search, I say do whatever you can to try. Be aware that it may not go as well as mine. It could turn out bad. But there is such an empty feeling and such concern if you don't try. I've never stopped thinking about her all those years. It is a part of your life. So my advice is to go for it and use every possible means and don't worry that it might be impossible. If I had known then what I know now I would have pursued it strongly. I have a niece who has two children and their names are the same as those of Janice's two children. It is really weird!"

Ruth, Janice's adoptive mother adds:

"We were unable to conceive so we felt quite comfortable with adopting and talking with Janice about the fact that she had come from another woman. We never explained why she was given up and she never asked. She did ask for our approval to do a search after they were asked to write a history of their heritage in school. She was confused – should it be about us or her birth mother? We were happy for her to do the search. She was only fourteen and learned that she couldn't do a search until she was of age. I was very comfortable with her curiosity because if I had been adopted I would want to know. Once she got the identifying information she called me to say that she didn't want to call right then. She didn't know what to say. I told her that I thought she should call and it would all come naturally. She called the next day. Apparently, it worked out okay. Mary came to our house soon after and I had all of Janice's childhood pictures out so she could see them.

"She and Janice have a close relationship and talk about once a week. I think that's fine. Janice and I are very close too. The reunion has not had any effect on our relationship. Some people tell me they think I'm crazy. I never feared I would lose a thing."

Karen

"I was seventeen when my parents separated. I was aware that they were having problems as my friend had seen my dad with another woman. He denied it. Then he deserted the family about ten years ago. It hurt a lot. My parents read a book to me called, 'Why Was I Adopted?' It helped me understand that my parents couldn't have children so someone else had a baby and gave it to them so they could have their own family. I knew that applied to me and my brother who is three years younger. I never really felt different from others. I knew that I had another family somewhere, but my adoptive family made me feel so loved. I was curious about my birth background almost all my life. I was anxious to get medical history and know where I came from. I questioned what they looked like, who I looked like and if I had any personality traits like them. They assured me that my birth mother loved me. She was only sixteen at the time of the pregnancy and couldn't offer me anything so she wanted me to be with a family who could provide for me and care for me.

"My mom and I are very close and I told her about my curiosity – she was very supportive. Dad told me to do what I needed to do. He was not overly enthusiastic about my finding my birth parents. I was only twenty when I contacted you. I had a baby girl when I was twenty and married her father when I was twenty-four.

"My parents were disappointed but then Mom became more supportive and started going with me to the doctor appointments. Dad wanted me to give the baby up for adoption. He kept telling me that someone else made the decision to give me up for adoption and I needed to do the same. I just told him that I was nineteen, living on my own and supporting myself. Since I had been told I could not have a child, I would never forgive myself for giving this one up in case I couldn't have any more. My doctor and his staff were pretty shocked that I was pregnant. To me, that was a sign that I needed to keep her. Dad never knew that I was going to do a search. The last time I spoke to him, I was eight months along. I haven't seen or talked to him in years. My mom was disappointed over my pregnancy. Her plan for me was to finish college, have a career, get married and have children. It didn't work that way but she told me that whatever I did she would support me one hundred percent. What a relief! I'm not sure I could have handled my mom not speaking to me.

"I tried to contact you because you had done the adoption and your name was part of my vocabulary for as long as I can remember. At the time of the first contact with my birth mother, I was very nervous. I didn't know what to expect. It was unreal. I couldn't believe that after all these years it was really happening. I called her and we talked for about an hour. After I talked with her, I was really excited. I called my mom and everybody I knew – all my friends and close family. They all knew that I was adopted and had always wanted to find my birth mother. We planned to meet just a few days later. I wanted my mom and my husband to go with me and Connie, my birth mother, wanted her other daughter, JoAnn, to go, too.

"As the time approached, I had butterflies in my stomach and my heart was pounding. I started to feel nauseated. At one point in the car I couldn't feel my legs and I was numb. When we got to the restaurant I needed to go to the rest room and when I did I told myself that they would come while I was gone and sure enough as soon as I walked out, they were there. I was in shock, it didn't seem real, it seemed like a dream. We were both in instant tears. My mom was crying and it was just a huge relief to finally have it done.

"I have seen her a number of times since. I went to JoAnn's birthday party and they came to mine. They have met my grandmother and my aunts and uncles as well. This seems to be comfortable for Mom. She knows that I am not looking for a replacement and is glad that Connie and I are getting along so well. Connie and I speak almost every day. I talk with my mom every day, too. She works with me and we carpool together. I feel good that I have a positive relationship with both of them. I have positive feelings for JoAnn, too. She and I are still learning about each other. My mom, Connie and JoAnn only have contact at family gatherings.

"Mom thanked Connie for giving me up for adoption. She has been wanting to tell her that for a very long time and Connie says that she doesn't know what she would have done if she had not made that decision. She also thanked Mom for taking such good care of me and for being such a positive influence in my life. I do feel closest to my adoptive family. I have been with them for twenty-six years and they have never made me feel like an outsider because I was not blood related. So I'm very glad I did the search and would definitely do it again. I have met Connie's mother and her husband and a few cousins and an aunt and uncle. They have all been very accepting of me and I feel we will be life long friends. I feel my life is fuller now. I have more family around and have always said, 'The more family, the better.' I have a much bigger support system now. It has made a huge difference in my life. It's like coming full circle. I was not able to finish college. My dad was paying for it and when I refused to give up my daughter for adoption, he refused to talk to me and stopped paying for my education. At that time I could not afford it. I work in a dental office now and in another year I will be office manager."

Connie, Karen's birth mother:

"Two years after I gave Karen up I had another daughter, JoAnn, who was born before my first marriage. She lived with me and had a son before she was married but the father is an involved parent. My niece was born the same year as Karen so I was able to envision Karen in the same stage. Karen is really neat. She is a pretty girl. She is everything I thought she would be.

"I knew that I would never have an abortion so I was glad for a good alternative. I knew it was the right thing to do. The birth father signed papers, too. I told Karen that I would help her find him if she wanted to, but she said she doesn't really want to. She has reason to be angry at men at this point, especially father figures. She said maybe later. I assured her that he was a nice man.

"I have a lot of admiration for Gwen, Karen's mother. She is a lovely person. It is strange because a lot of the situations are the same between our two families. The day that you called me was the day I knew would come. I knew that I would be ready for it, but it about blew me over. It has given me a lot of comfort to know that she understands. I feel that we were all meant to be where we were all through our lives. Her mother really wanted children and couldn't have children and I really could not have taken care of Karen. Time has shown that it was the right thing for everyone.

"When we first met, they brought pictures of her growing up and her wedding. When we saw each other, we knew. We look a lot alike. JoAnn has known about Karen almost all her life and she has said many times that she wanted to find her. I told her when she was ready she would find us and that would be the right time. It was like I knew her before I even met her. I've realized that there has been something missing all my life and now it's not true any more. My husband says it's like I am whole now. I never realized I didn't feel complete. I'm glad everything was just the way I thought it would be. I'm so glad it turned out well for us. I don't think she could have had a better mom. It seems it was meant to be that way. And now Karen knows how much she is loved on both sides."

Gwen, Karen's adoptive mother:

"When we learned that I would not be able to conceive a child, adoption seemed the natural step to take as we both wanted children. We adopted our son, too. We read about adoption to the kids. It was one of those things you talk about and you don't even realize that they understand, until one day they say something to you. The book explained that they had grown inside someone else. Then when they were in their early teens, I explained the relinquishment and adoptive process. You had called with an update of Karen's birth mother. That was easier, because our son's mother was older and had one child that she kept. It was hard for him to understand why she could keep that child and not him. It seemed to be a matter of progression that when questions came up, we just handled them. We gave them simple answers to their questions until they got a little older, and then we gave them all the information that we had. We told them it was a difficult, loving decision for both of their birth mothers, and I was very lucky that they chose the option they did. There may have been a time when they thought of their decisions as betrayal, but I am sure in their hearts they knew it wasn't. Our son thought it was odd that Karen wanted to find her birth mother. He may be angry at his birth mother – she had one child, then placed him for adoption. I explained that she was unable to take care of two children. I would think he'd be interested in knowing about his sibling.

"In their preteens, things came up in school about different family members and that sparked their curiosity. We always had the little sheet with the background information on it and they often looked at it. He was always asking why and Karen wondered what her birth mother looked like. She felt tall and wondered if

her birth mother had been tall – will I be tall? I really did not feel
uncomfortable in talking with them about it. Our son feels
betrayed because of his adoptive father, with good reason, and
may feel the same about his birth mother. I think he feels that he
would betray me by doing a search. He often asks how I feel about
Karen's search. I was behind her 100%. When she told me that
you had found her I was really happy for her. In the restaurant, I
knew exactly who she was when she walked in the door. I was a
little unnerved meeting them for the first time. I would be lying if
I said that I was completely relaxed.

"She is a wonderful person. She has been wonderful to the
family and to Karen and me, but I would probably be lying if I
didn't admit that I had some uneasiness or discomfort – not that I
think Karen is going to love me any less. She told me that she was
going to do a search at eighteen, but she waited. I had known for a
long time that she wanted to do a search, so it was not a surprise.
I was surprised at how fast it happened. I had an odd feeling and
was very nervous when she asked me to go with her to meet Connie. I wasn't surprised that she wanted me to go but I thought she
might change her mind and I would get out of it. I thought for sure
I'd be crying and very upset, but I wasn't. Karen and I are very
close. We call each other when we get home from the office in the
evening. We are very different personality types. She is very independent, very A-type personality. I would not say this to her face,
but she is very much like her father. She got his traits being the
firstborn. I am more of a laid back, tell-me-what-to-do-and-I'll-do-
it type person.

"We had some of the typical teenage problems with Karen and
we occasionally locked horns. When she got pregnant before she
married I was not happy about it and I knew that she would be
adamant about keeping the baby – I was the same – at least about
an abortion. I just don't believe in it. Because of her adoption, I
knew that was the way she would feel. Of course, that was the
downfall of her relationship with her dad.

"This was after he'd left home. I found he'd had different
affairs for about fifteen years. He said some cruel things to Karen.
He told her that her adoption was my idea, which meant that he
really didn't want her. That's the way she took it. I have to admit
that I briefly thought, 'Like mother, like daughter' when she got
pregnant – oh, dear, she was following in her mother's footsteps.
But that was a fleeting thing and now I wouldn't change it for the
world. I knew it was going to be hard. She would not be able to go

to school like she wanted, and I am so proud of her for all that she has accomplished. She is very, very smart. She has proven to be responsible at work and a good mother.

"She was living with her husband-to-be when she got pregnant. Her dad was opposed to that, too. He had moved out and I had moved to a different house. Between the two closings we had to live in an apartment for a month. Karen said she wanted to stay in the apartment. Her dad said that he would move in with her. He moved in for a week and left, so her boyfriend moved in with her. She was eighteen and our son was fifteen when their dad left home. Difficult time. It was hard on both of them. I don't know what they felt, but they were both rejected. Their dad remarried the last woman he was involved with. She can have him.

"I think that this reunion has been fine. My relationship with Karen is the same. I think it has been good for Karen. She has learned so much about her birth parents. And she has met her sister's child and now her daughter has a cousin – cute little cousin. She has gained knowledge of things that might have been troubling her if she had any questions or doubts. Now she can ask directly. Connie has been great and it is fine that they keep in close contact. I just don't want her to take advantage of Connie's guilt feelings for giving her up. I think Connie is trying to make up to Karen by giving her things or baby sitting. I am glad they haven't had any more children. This one is enough for me until our son gets married.

"I don't feel slighted or fear that she is going to pick that family over me. I admit that I was nervous, as this was the woman who gave birth to my child. There is a little pain in that since I was unable to have a child – a little envy in that she got to deliver her and I couldn't. But then I had the pleasure and displeasure of raising her all those years. Ninety-nine percent of it was wonderful."

JoAnn, Karen's half sister who was born to Connie and was raised by her:

"Meeting with Karen has been a great experience. I think I was in kindergarten when Mom saw a girl that she thought might be that daughter, so I have always known that I had an older sister. I had always wanted to find her. Mom called me as soon as she got the letter from you. She knew that I would be excited, too. She was very excited. It has been great since we met. For Halloween, we took our kids out to a pumpkin farm to get pumpkins. We E-mail to keep in touch. Her girl and my boy enjoy playing together. I am so glad to finally have a sister. We also look a lot alike. She looks more like Mom than I do.

"Having been an only child and then not being an only child anymore, I was kind of nervous. It hasn't been a problem at all. Finally getting to know her is like filling in missing pieces. All my mom knew was that Karen was adopted by someone in Arizona and they really wanted to have a child. It seemed that they would be good parents. She didn't know a whole lot, as she didn't want to be too involved. I asked questions of any one in the right age group who might have been my sister. I met her the first time when Mom did. It probably relieved some of the nervousness because we were all going through it at the same time so we were support for each other. I was totally involved in everything that was going on, from the first phone call.

"Now we talk almost daily, almost more than Mom and I do. They have a great relationship too. It's nice for me as I have some-one to talk with. I know that my mom is still going to love me as much. Mom told me that she did not consider adoption for me because of the position she was in. She was a few years older and she was more stable and had more support. It was a much better time for her. Mom was married twice while I lived at home and that was to the same person. He was my step-dad. My biological father was not involved much through my whole life. I have not met Karen's father, but I am curious to see what he is like, too.

"I think this reunion has been great for Mom. She's always wondered if she made the right decision, and this was confirma-tion that she did. I don't think she ever regretted the decision. Now seeing how Karen's life has been, she feels that she got the best care possible – better than Mom could have provided. It is just nice to be able to share life with her now. There are some real coincidences. Her husband used to be good friends with my boy-friend, and they were in the same social group. We have known a lot of the same people, but have never been in the same place at the same time. We just kept missing each other. We both live on the same street, just ten miles apart – a twenty-minute drive. Nothing has changed between me and my mom since we met Karen."

This Was a Couple's Plan

Pete and Marla, the unmarried birth parents, were surprised to find that she was pregnant. What to do! They knew they didn't want an abortion.

Pete, viewpoint:

"We figured that it would take someone else to take care of this baby. They would be able to offer a more stable environment for her. Our fathers got together and helped us out. They thought adoption was the best solution. I have never regretted making that decision. The only thing I regretted was waiting so long to find out what happened to her. We both signed papers for the adoption. I am still in touch with Marla. We are still good friends and I saw her not long ago. She was married, but is divorced. She has turned out to be the best mother in the history of the United States. She has two of her own and two stepchildren and now she takes care of little kids for her work. She was a good mother when she decided on the adoption plan, too, because she decided what was best for her baby. That was a tough thing to do. I never got to see the baby when she was born. I was separated from the situation because of the fact that I loved Marla and went along with the plan for her to be in a home for unwed mothers.

"Susan, our daughter was thirty-two when I found her. Our first contact was by phone and I was so relieved and happy. She is coming to my stepdaughter's wedding. She visits me often. Marla sees her when she comes over from California.

"I first thought of doing a search about five years ago after Marla called me. She told me she was divorced and so was I. We went to lunch and talked about it. Then nine months went by and we talked again. She said she'd found an agency that finds adopted children. She had registered so I registered and donated some money to the cause. A year went by – nothing happened. I was sitting in the office one day and decided that I was going to find her. I picked up the phone and called Phoenix, the CIP and I found your name (Shirley) and you made it happen. It was that easy! I just had to make the serious move to find out if she regretted it, if she was dead or what. I had to know something before I left this world. When I mentioned to other people what I was doing, they shook my hand and told me they thought it was the best thing I had ever done in my whole life. All my friends knew about it. They've all got families and I'm walking around with nothing. I have no other children. I do have my stepdaughter, whom I have raised since she was eight years old, but I never adopted her. Now she is thirty and getting married.

"I decided that even if I had to borrow money I was going to find her. I didn't have to borrow money when you did the search for me. It was less than I thought it would be. I'm used to dealing with lawyers and paying big fees. For what you get with the CIP, I would say it is the best deal in town.

"Susan is gorgeous. You should meet her sometime. My stepdaughter knew about Susan when she was nearly an adult. They are best friends, but they are in different parts of the world. I am in touch with Susan by phone very often. When she visits she stays at my house and we have a blast. This search has satisfied my curiosity one hundred percent and the reunion has absolutely given me comfort about my decision to place her for adoption. I haven't met her adoptive parents. I understand they are quite old and don't like to travel. They know about the reunion and are okay with it. Susan calls me Pete, but occasionally calls me Dad in a funny way."

Susan was happy about the reunion, too:

"I was seven when Mom and Dad told me and my older brother that we were adopted. We were riding in the car. They had planned for some time to tell us together. I don't know why – they didn't want us to run away or something. I had a different reaction than my brother. I was shocked so I crawled over the seat to the very back and stared out the window. It was hard for me to grasp at that age, but I was thankful. I was born to another woman when all along I thought I had been had been born to my adoptive mother. It was hurtful because I was never very close to my family. In a way it made me feel a little better. That's why I have never felt a close connection with my family – I'm adopted!

"My parents were reserved, a little older, conservative, of a different era, but nice – little show of physical affection. I had an older brother and sister who were their birth children. They were fifteen and sixteen so they baby-sat me a lot. It was just like a houseful of people all the time. Maybe that helped to make us not feel so close. People were in and out a lot. Not the cohesiveness of most families. The older siblings were very loving to me. I think the parents did a good job of treating us all the same. My older siblings prefer to differ – they thought my parents were much more strict with them. I was envious of friends with younger, prettier moms. I often would look at other pretty dark-haired women in drug stores or elsewhere and fantasize that they might be my mom.

"The subject of adoption was not brought up much after we were told. They gave it to us in one whole story. But then they didn't talk about it much. My brother took it harder than I did. He treated me very badly, was cruel to me. He was jealous of me because I was younger and the baby. He was very intelligent. You know how very intelligent people are sometimes – weird. He was troubled, I think. When they told us the story, it was kind of a tension time. My mom was nervous, high strung by nature and on medication. So that situation was clearly not an easy thing for her to do. She'd lost her first child at age sixteen as the result of a brain hemorrhage.

"I was always curious about my birth background and my mom brought the subject up one other time, asking me if I wanted to find my birth mother. I really didn't want her to help me. I wanted to do it on my own – more like when I was in college. I called the hospital and the agency and they told me that the records could not be opened out of curiosity. It had to be for medical reasons and I would have to get a lawyer. I didn't have any money so I thought I would just let it go. I was also afraid of hurting my adoptive parents. Basically, I had the piece of paper, front and back which were all of my papers – birth certificate, slight description, psychological information, very short There was a paragraph about Pete and Marla and their homes. That was it. When my adoptive parents explained the reasons why I had been given up they conveyed a feeling of love, not abandonment, by the birth parents. They spoke more of how much they wanted me and how much I meant to them. They wanted me to feel comfortable and reassured. I feel in my heart that they have always tried to do their best. Because they are a bit older and different, it was hard for me to relate to them. I didn't feel free in sharing my curiosity with them and I never made any other attempts to do a search. I took it as far as I could at the time.

"When you contacted me, I wasn't really surprised. I always felt it would happen. So when you called, I was fairly calm. I was in Central Park and you had told me they would be calling me. When I heard Marla's voice for the first time I remember a chill going down my spine because her voice was so similar to mine. I froze. It hit me that it was reality. I went to the park because I wanted to always remember when I first talked with them. I talked to Marla first because I have very close relationships with my girl friends. I hadn't anticipated contact with Pete. I was floored when I learned that Pete had initiated it and started the ball rolling. I had thought more about her.

"I flew to meet Marla two weeks later and as soon as I saw her it was an indescribable feeling. We look somewhat alike – shape of face, eyes and voice. We hugged and both started bawling – very emotional – crying because we were so happy. We talked and talked and she stayed the night with me in the hotel room. It was a long first meeting and I didn't want her to leave. The next day we went to her brother's house. She has a large extended family and I met everyone – my stepsister and brother, her two sisters, two of three brothers, her father. It was a little weird. I felt like I was on display. They kept staring at me. They had all known about me. It was a wonderful thing for them – like finding the missing piece of the family. They were all so nice to me. I had made them a little photo album of me at different ages for both Marla and Pete – pictures of my adoptive parents, too. I was there for the weekend.

"The next weekend I went to visit Pete. We'd had several phone conversations. He was okay with my meeting Marla first. He'd sent me some photos so I knew him immediately. I look more like his side of the family. It was a similar weekend to the previous one. We got along very well. We are similar in nature – very independent, social, easygoing people. There is a very different dynamic in the two relationships. She is more emotional and asks a lot of questions, is more sensitive and nurturing in nature. With Pete, he is a guy, more like my friend and that is fine because it would be more uncomfortable for him to be emotionally exposed. I cried when I met him and he teared up. We just sat and stared at each other. The next night, the whole family came over and Marla came too. I was thankful for that. I was wrung out after those two weekends. They went very well. My parents had cautioned me not to have high expectations. They were nice and supportive and told me that they were proud of me and knew that Pete and Marla would be proud of me, too. They said they would be excited meeting me and seeing how I turned out. It was six months later when I saw them and told them all about it in detail.

"It was wonderful meeting the extended family. My mother has virtually no extended family and my father very little. So all of a sudden I have a big family. I have a good relationship with each of them. I have visited each one about four times and they have visited me once. It is easier for me to visit Pete for financial reasons. He sometimes pays my airfare. He has renovated a room for me to stay with him. He is very sweet and I feel very comfortable with him. I have never stayed with Marla and haven't seen as much of her. She is very busy. When I went to Pete's for the wedding, so many of his friends and relatives approached me and told me that I had made such a difference in his life. He seems to have a better outlook. It seems to have been good for both of them because they have had guilt about this. Marla sent my parents a thank you. They both want to meet my parents, but my mom is a bit intimidated. It has given all of us closure. It has helped me be a little more independent and has added a lot to my life.

"In this situation I think they made the right choice. I was brought up in a good family. They took care of me. I think adoption is wonderful, but I could not go through it again and so I could never give up a child. I'm old enough now that I could take care of it. I definitely feel close to Marla and Pete in the short time that I have known them. It is a very different relationship than I have with my adoptive parents. They are very good people, but as I said, I have never been very emotionally tied to them."

Marla wants you to know this:

"I made an adoption plan for Susan because I was fifteen at the time and I knew I was too young to keep a child. My mother had raised six children and I don't think my parents were terribly willing to help me. It would have been a selfish decision to keep her. I felt that with adoption, she would have a good home. I only regretted the fact that I missed her every day of my life until I met her. I was truly sad about her always. Thirty-three years passed. I contacted Pete because I needed to put closure to it. We were together off and on before we made the decision to find Susan.

"I'd thought about a search many times before. I was going to do it when she was twenty-three, but I felt that I wasn't getting cooperation from those around me. I was married and my children were ten and twelve. I wanted to contact her for all the right reasons – she was a young woman and I thought she would understand and maybe she would need me. She might be getting married, having children and I wanted her to know her background. I had wanted to know her all my life. When Pete contacted me and told me that he could get this done, I felt absolutely elated. She and I now have a very nice relationship. She is a busy career person and I would like to be in her life only as she would like me to be. There is a plan for me to meet her adoptive parents. My children are now twenty and twenty-four and I have two step-children. They are curious about her, too. They are all so happy for me.

"The search gave me extreme comfort about the decision I made and it changed my life for many reasons. I'd felt such a hole in my life forever, not knowing her, not knowing if she was okay, where she lived, what she was like. It brought closure to something that was raw in my life. It gave me immense peace. It took the word shame away and it turned into a celebration. All my family members love her so much and she was so happy to meet them. She was as comfortable and poised as anyone could be. She is an amazing young woman so you have to feel good about the way she was raised. We are so grateful. Every minute was a miracle.

"When I first heard her voice I couldn't believe it – she sounded just like me. I was thrilled that she wanted to meet us as much as we wanted to meet her. She called me on Easter morning and we were getting ready to go on a picnic and I was making potato salad. I had not yet told my children about her. But I stopped everything and pushed myself into a closet so I could have some privacy. My son was pushing me and asked what I was doing. I told him that he had to give me a few minutes, he had to understand, I had to take this call. She told me that she couldn't thank me enough for the decision that I made for her. She said she'd had a great life and that she is a very happy person. Hearing that was like the end all to end all because it meant everything to me. It was so clear that she had been given a wonderful upbringing. She is a total blend of Pete and me. The first time we met she called me Mama Marla for a while. She is more like me in her habits and interests than the children I raised. Her career is in interior design and I have this huge knack for decorating. It is an absolute treasure to have had this reunion. I think she and I have always been looking for each other – in the people on the street, in a store, wherever! I love her more than life!"

Roger, Susan's adoptive father:

"My wife and I had three children and our oldest died at the age of sixteen due to a malformation of the blood vessels in her brain. My wife had a hysterectomy, but we still wanted more children so we filed to adopt. Some people thought that we were trying to replace our daughter, but that was not the case. We first adopted a boy, and had hoped for a family of four children so we let it be known that we would be interested in another child. Two years later we adopted Susan right out of the hospital. Everything from that point on was very normal because we never felt any difference in our feeling for the two adopted children and the two that had been born to us. All of our children now live in different states. It is our feeling that the adopted son is the closest to us. We had thought that probably one of our birth children would maintain the strongest attachment, but it did not turn out that way.

"Susan was intent upon doing some studying and then followed her interest in becoming a decorator. She does extremely well, especially for her age. We feel no different than we ever did. The strange part is that she has two moms now. As a result there's some stretching of feelings. We know that both birth parents married and are divorced. Now, through your intercession, she finally did meet her birth parents, whom she did not know until this came up about two years ago. She's become close friends with both of them, and they are both single. We see her a few times each year. It is sad for us, although it affects my wife much more, because Susan doesn't literally have a married mother or father. This complicates who is Mom and who is Dad – that kind of thing. We haven't met either of them. That hurts some. If you are looking for a scenario, it is not the typical one. That's pretty much the whole story. If she hadn't found them, she would probably progressively become more involved in her own life and, with her not being married, we would likely see her less as she put her roots down in Texas. She may see them more than she sees us. But this is happening with all the children. We see them less as they get older, but we keep in contact with them. They call and visit with about the same frequency."

Roberta, Susan's adoptive mother:

"At about six or seven we took them away from home one day to tell them they were adopted. We didn't want them to associate it with home. They were very upset and, of course, they went through the stage, 'You aren't my parents.' I didn't explain to them that they had grown inside another woman. I just told them that we'd had them since they were born, that we loved them and they were very special to us. I think they had more attention than the others. When we visited my husband's family, they'd ask if these were the adopted children. I was so angry with them. You can't stop it, so many people knew. There are other adopted children in the family who did not find out until they were older, and they were very upset. The agency told us we had to tell them, but we didn't hammer it into them. I wasn't comfortable talking about this as it suddenly separated them from us. They felt that they were not quite integral members of the family. I didn't feel it was my job to go into the part about their birth mother giving them up. They didn't ask why. Susan wanted to see who she looked like and what the circumstances were. I can understand why she was curious. I really don't want to talk about it because it upsets me. I am happy for her, but I feel we have lost her to a great extent.

"On Mother's Day she called me for about five minutes She had just returned home from visiting her birth mother. She used to send us cards for birthdays and stuff, but she doesn't any more. They were at least a sign of affection that she is thinking about us but we are like outsiders now instead of being part of the family. She once mentioned doing a search and I never objected to it. We had given her all the information that the agency gave us. I didn't try to keep anything from her. Our son never asked any questions. We are his parents and that is that. He calls us every week and is so close to us. Susan said that we would always be her mom and dad. After she met them she asked us for pictures of her growing up. We sent about forty pictures as our gift to them. I don't want to go on about this anymore. There is too much hurt there. It may be selfish on my part but I don't know what to say. We have lost a lot as a result of this reunion, but then that is life. We loved all our children dearly. You can't change or govern their lives. You just have to stand by and watch. Sometimes it is hard to sit on the sidelines."

Michelle

"I think I always knew that my sister and I were adopted. For a long time I felt that it was like when you go to the bakery and look through glass and pick out what you want. I thought the babies were all bundled up and my parents picked me out of that bakery. I had a lot of questions, mostly relating to the total scenario – how old was I? What did the house look like that you brought me home to? How long did we live in that house? How old was my sister when you got her? Then I would ask questions about who my mom was. I looked a lot like my adoptive dad so I really didn't feel different until I was older and personality traits started to come out. My sis is three years older than I am. There were no birth children.

"When I reached puberty, emotions started to run high. I wondered what my birth mother was like and if I had any brothers and sisters. I really wanted a brother. No such luck! My sister and I did not get along very well. There were big personality conflicts and I was the problem child. At least I was labeled that. I probably was. I was given the impression that I was born at a time in my birth mother's life when she could not take care of me, but she loved me very much and wanted the best for me by placing me with people who could take care of me. My parents were those people. It definitely wasn't that she didn't want me.

"My questions increased as I grew into my teen years. But they were mostly questions that they could not answer. Nevertheless, I continued to share my curiosity with them. I told them when I decided to do a search and actually, my mother took the initiative and put me in touch with Search Triad and they put me in touch with ISRR. They were always very understanding of my curiosity and were very cooperative. My mom had always done the very best she could to handle my questions with what she knew.

"As soon as I was old enough to go on the list at ISRR, they put me on. They immediately put us in touch with each other. I had never heard of the CIP. When I first got the call from the Registry, I thought I had won something as they asked about my birth date, so when I learned they had found her, I was in complete shock 'cause I didn't expect it to be so quick. I imagined it usually took longer. So when Virginia called me I was somewhat uncomfortable – but not in a bad way. The first time we talked was only about fifteen or twenty minutes as she was at work and on her break. We made arrangements to meet the next day. We went to lunch. It was like it was not really happening. We gave each other big hugs. I showed her all my baby pictures.

"Our relationship is good now and was good at the beginning, but it was one of those trial and error things. We all went through a hard time. I needed things from her that she could not give. When we first met, she was very angry about her decision to give me up. She was hurt when I showed her baby pictures and tried to include her with the people in my life. She didn't want to hear it because she wasn't there. She felt she had missed out and was angry.

"I had so much to share with her that she didn't want to hear. That was frustrating for me. It made me feel that she didn't want to be a part of my life. I didn't understand why. There were times when we really didn't talk much. It was in 1996 that we first met. Right after that, my boyfriend and I and our son moved in with her for about six months. We moved out of my parents' house. This boyfriend is now my present husband. He is African American and she was dating an African American at the time. She was the type of person with whom anything goes. My parents were more traditional. She was like the cool mom. That was the kind of person I related to because that's the kind of person I am.

"I couldn't handle the way her boyfriend was treating her and how she put up with it. It was time to move out. We saw each other once in a while and she came to my daughter's first and second birthday parties. But we were pretty much on the outs. We didn't know how to deal with each other – until she had her heart attack. Then things changed. In December of 2002, she was in Kentucky – long period of alienation. I was angry at her and she wanted to pretend that I didn't exist or that the situation didn't exist. There was a lot of weirdness – uncomfortable tension. I would still talk to her sister all the time – she and I were really close from the beginning. We spent a lot of time together. I grew up differently. We are different people and it is hard for me to see her go through all that she goes through. It's just one of those common sense things, you should know better. My dad always treated my mother well. I don't agree with the relationship she is in now. It is the same kind of pattern. I just have to remember, it's her decision.

"After her heart attack, she came back here to live with us for a few months – my husband and me and our children. She wanted to spend time with me. She wanted to get to know me. She wanted us to be close – on a really deep level. Things were good but we would cry all the time and it was kind of a healing situation for both of us. But she is very bullheaded. It is just crazy – the genetics. Even though I was not raised with her, we still have a lot of similarities. That is one reason we have trouble, as we are both very set in what we believe. We don't want to hear what anyone else has to say. I think that is our problem. I just have to take her with a grain of salt and realize that she is an adult and she can take care of herself. I should enjoy the time that I spend with her because obviously she is in my life and I met her for a reason.

"There are times when I don't know if it's worth it – I get so upset and hurt. It is really uncomfortable for me to feel like a little kid again. When she doesn't want to spend time with me I think she doesn't care or love me. It is different to be around her as compared to my mom – a different atmosphere. I was always worried about my parents being disappointed in me, if I did something wrong. I am still worried about that. They were actually very supportive of my marrying a black man. They paid for his divorce, and are paying for his child support.

"My husband is nine years older than I am. We've been through a lot and survived. I think it has to do with growing up with a strong foundation. My parents have always been there for me. When I met Virginia, I actually became closer to my parents because I had a deeper respect for them. When I was younger it was like, 'I hate you, I don't want to live here, I want to go live with my birth mother, she would be nicer to me.' You just have this image of what you think it would be like and it really isn't like that at all. I don't say I'm disappointed. I really love Virginia. I think she is a wonderful person and she has a huge heart. She is not the person that I fantasized about.

"I still hold my parents up on a pedestal in that they do no wrong. It is hard because I thought I would feel the same way about Virginia and I don't. I was torn because I felt guilty for loving her so much. I felt that I was taking something away from my parents. I still struggle with it. Virginia wants me to call her Mom and I can't do it in front of my parents because I don't think it is respectful. I can do it when they are not around. I have a different relationship with each one. Virginia, I can tell anything, it doesn't matter what it is. I don't worry about her thinking less of me or being disappointed. With Mom and Dad I think there is a deeper respect. I talk to Virginia more, but I still feel very close to Mom and Dad. Perhaps it's because they are more moral than she is – higher standards.

"My mom and Virginia spoke at my wedding and that was awesome. Virginia thanked my mom for the great job she did raising me and Mom telling Virginia thanks for giving me up so they could have the opportunity to love, raise and take care of me. We all just sat there and cried. It was a big moment. Now I don't see Virginia as often as I would like, but we do talk almost every day.

"I talk to Mom when I need guidance in child rearing or whatever. If I am sad or have a bad day I will call her. She is more my guiding light. Virginia brought me into this world. She is more like a friend. I feel uncomfortable when the two of them are together. I feel that I am betraying my loyalties. There is no basis in their behavior that should make me feel that way. I feel that I shouldn't care about Virginia as much as I do.

"The search has answered a ton of questions. I would surely do it again. I feel better about having placed a child for adoption myself. I feel better about the prospect of meeting him some day. You never really know how things will work out. I was always the odd ball – loud, rambunctious, out spoken and nobody in my family is like that – even my adoptive sister. When I met my biological family, it all made sense – that's where I got it from. I have met a number of members of Virginia's family. I grew up in a very reserved family. I was not married when I had the son that I have now and I did consider adoption for him, but the situations were different. I thought 'I can't do this any more.' There were heartaches in giving up one child just ten months before so the wounds had not completely healed. I just could not go through it again. I was determined to make it work.

"I am still in touch with the birth father of my first child. I try to keep tabs on him so if the child ever wants to know him I can give him the information. He was not married, but engaged to a divorcee with kids. He had built them a house and they were living together.

"Virginia and I have been on the same beam since January of 2003. I love her dearly. We have a blast together and I am glad that she is a part of my life, but there is some heartache that I carry with it. She has a sharp tongue. Sometimes I don't think she means quite what she says but I understand her point. She knows that I am a very emotional and verbal person – in the way that I feel about people.

"I am very physical. My Mom played with me, bounced me and all when I was younger but as I grew older it diminished. With Virginia I still have that kind of contact. Mom is more reserved. I think that's how she was raised. She is not affectionate with my sister either, but my sister really doesn't like to be hugged. Virginia and Mom are totally different people and there are certain things that I get from each of them that I need. I really feel blessed to have both of them in my life. The loss of Mom would be the hardest on me. She is the one I call when I am sick. She is the one I call to go to the store to pick up things for me.

"Virginia's daughter is two years younger than I am and she is a lot like Virginia. We are jealous of each other. I am because they have all these memories together and I feel like an outcast. At first it was fun because at the big family functions I was the big phenomenon. Everyone wanted to get to know me and see who I looked like, whose ears and hands I have, etc. Then that goes away and I don't feel that I have this history with them, even though they like to include me in all the functions. At first with her daughter, I took her out and got her hair and nails done and was the big sister, which was fun, and we connected as she has two boys and one was the age of one of ours. I sat her kids and vice versa for a while. But she is into different things. She didn't grow up like I did. She lived and lives in a different world than I do."

Sylvia, Michelle's adoptive mother:

"We knew that we wanted to have a family right from the start and when it appeared that there wouldn't be a child born to us we comfortably turned to adoption. It was easy to talk about it with relatives, friends and the children themselves. I think Michelle figured it out on her own. One time she said, 'Well, you're not my real mother. Another woman had me.' I don't recall that she was particularly upset with me at the time. She was just thinking about it. I'd told them their mothers were not in a position to care for them so they made the best plan they could. I didn't paint it as an act of betrayal or love. It was a situation they were in and adoption was the logical solution. Whenever they asked questions, I told them whatever I could remember of the information that you (Shirley) had given us.

"Michelle, at about fourteen, was being so rebellious and hard to manage. She talked of her real mother – that she would have been better off if her birth mother had kept her. I got tired of it. So I looked into it myself – contacted Search Triad and ISRR. I decided I should register them both since I was doing it. They were able to be registered but not actively until they were eighteen. I was surprised when my other daughter decided to do a search. She always wanted to see her half brother. When she went to high school she kind of looked around to try to see someone who might look like her. She would check at the bus stops, too. She now thinks there is some physical resemblance between her and her mother. When she found her mother, she learned that her brother had died just the previous year of cancer. It was very sad that she missed that opportunity.

"I've met Michelle's birth mother. I felt fine, but she felt very uncomfortable. She's never felt comfortable around me. She used to come to the kids' birthday parties, but she has not been to one for a long time. She was very anxious to meet me, but after two minutes, she wanted to leave. I know that she and Michelle talk often, but I don't know if she sees her much. Michelle doesn't tell me. Right now, Michelle and I talk about once a week, sometimes more.

"I do feel that I have lost a little as a result of this reunion. I feel like I am sharing her and it isn't exactly what I would like. Most mothers don't have to share their daughter with somebody. We still have the same feelings for each other. I am thankful for her, although she still has a lot of growing up to do. She has grown up enough that she can appreciate her parents. I have handled all the crises. Even now there's one crisis after another and my husband thinks I have become resigned to it. They moved in with us before they were married. That was terrible, but we did finally insist that they sleep in separate bedrooms. Then they would go to a friend's together every so often. They were here until their daughter was three. We bought a town house for them and they got married shortly after. That's where they are now. It is in our name and they are supposed to pay us rent, but they're not too good at it. So we are still being tested. We had to get his divorce from his wife. He was in special classes in school and never graduated. He doesn't read or write well, but does some math. He has some talents. He can sing wonderfully, is good at art and is personable.

"Michelle fell for him right away. I was disappointed and told her she could do better. They now have all his children with them. He'd wanted to get custody for some time as his former wife had remarried and the stepfather abused the children. We, of course, paid the attorney fees. Sometimes I wonder what I am doing – but I am doing it, I'll admit it. This is very hard for me to talk about (crying) 'cause Michelle is taking care of children that she didn't give birth to.

"She is so good to them. My assistance to them may not encourage them to do their best, but it's not going to last forever. Her husband has a hard time finding work and he hasn't liked almost any job he's had. He's also had some physical problems which limit what he can do. I'm thankful when he is employed. Michelle is a very good talker and persuasive. She does her job well and has won prizes for her accomplishments.

"We are both close to retirement although we have used some of the money that we had saved. We have had a lot of challenges and have had a great deal of joy as well. Our other daughter is a real source of pride for us. She is in touch with her birth mother but has not met her as yet."

Virginia, Michelle's birth mother:

"I was only fifteen when I got pregnant and delivered at sixteen. I did not like the idea of an abortion and my stepmother insisted that I could not keep the baby. I stayed with a cousin and was there until after the baby was born.

"When Michelle was eighteen, she registered with ISRR and then I registered when I came back to Arizona in 1995. They matched us and it was good because it was quick. She was twenty and I was thirty-six. When we talked and made plans to meet the next day, I was really scared. I was afraid that she would criticize me for placing her for adoption. It didn't turn out that way at all. When I met her it was just unbelievable, I can't explain it – I was happy!

"Now we talk every day. We call each other. She calls on her breaks. She is busy with kids and I am busy with other things. I had put information about me in her record. I never told my dad that I wanted to search for her. He knows now and goes to the kids' birthday parties. When I wanted to find her my cousin said not to do it because I would ruin her life. I told her that I had to do it even if we would not have a relationship. I wanted her to know I loved her and never forgot her. It was important to me and important to her. Yes, thank God, it was. This was the best thing in the world.

"My other daughter is two years younger. I wasn't married when she was born. I kept her and that was hard after giving Michelle up. I am not married now, but I have been married three times. The guys were all wrong and I never had any children with any of them.

"When I contacted Michelle, my daughter was thrilled. She had always known that she had a sister and that we would find her. She was great with it until they met and then jealousy set in. They are not close and I am caught in the middle. I tell each of them how the other is doing. I was with my daughter's dad for a couple of years. I don't have a relationship with Michelle's adoptive mother. I see her at birthday parties and things like that. We never call each other. The children call me Grandma and they call her that, too. So they have two grandmas at the parties, and great grandma and grandpa – my parents.

"When Michelle got married, it was the first time Sylvia and I had really talked and I told her she had done a beautiful job of raising her. I, of course, feel closer to the daughter that I raised than I do to Michelle, because I have had her all my life. Michelle and I have a different kind of relationship because she was an adult and she has a different kind of personality. You just can't go back. I am very glad that we've had a reunion. I feel complete – like everything is straightened out and I've met my daughter, as I always wanted. I have come full circle. The contact has satisfied all my curiosity and answered all my questions. I would do it again."

Janet

This search was a very challenging one since the birth mother, for whom I was looking, had made several different moves over a rather short period of time – all here in the Valley, but to different homes.

Janet:
"My mother was the one who gave me most of the pertinent information about adoption in general and my background specifically. Dad never really talked about it much. He was very casual about it. I became curious at about fifteen and learned that I had to wait until eighteen to do a search. Mom was supportive and encouraged me to find out about my birth family. She initiated the search for me. My parents had also adopted my older brother and some people had told me that he and I look alike, and we also had some comments about similarities between Mom and me. That made me feel good, but it didn't take away my curiosity about my birth mother and whether I looked like her.

"Mom contacted the CIP and the search was done. Our first contact was by phone and we talked about fifteen minutes. We made arrangements to meet at a restaurant. My boy friend went with me and she had other people with her, too. It was rather uncomfortable to begin with but got much easier as time went by. I recognized Alice, my birth mother, as soon as she walked into the restaurant because we look so much alike. She told me that the reason she gave me up was because my biological father gave her a hard time. They were not married. Later I met my birth siblings. They are all younger than me.

"Presently, we have no relationship at all. I don't feel much of a connection to her. I don't really know her and my adoptive mom is my real mother. I think Alice is a very nice person, but I don't

Shirley Budd Pusey

feel comfortable having a relationship with her. I don't think my adoptive mom would care but I am not motivated to contact her anymore. She has not met my adoptive parents, but my mom called her recently to see how she was doing and found that she has terminal liver cancer. I have little concern about that, as she doesn't take good care of herself. She continues to smoke and drink even though she is sick. In her younger years she did a lot of drugs. That was not while she was pregnant with me, but before and after. She could have had a much better life if she'd taken care of herself. She has three other children – two boys and a girl. I don't have any contact with them, either. My main concern was for health information on that side of the family and it has been satis-fied. My mother wants me to do a search for my birth father so we can get his health information. Alice gave his name to my mom, but I don't really want to contact him. Mom would likely do the search for him. It would be nice to have a full health history, but I don't want him knowing anything about me.

"There are some coincidences in all of this: Both Alice and I have worked as waitresses, she for several years. We have a lot of the same tendencies, both strong-willed, fairly independent, same sense of humor. I am more motivated than she is. She's had a lot of chances to better her life. I'm the kind of person who would take any chance to better my life instead of just blowing it away."

Alice, Janet's birth mother:
"With my liver cancer diagnosed one year ago, I was given two to five years to live. The reason I planned adoption for Janet was because her birth father threatened to steal her at any time, and that is just not what I wanted for my daughter. I put him out of my life forever. It took a lot of strength to give her up. Did I ever regret it? I still do (tearfully).

"When you called me, I was very excited. I'd hoped it would happen and had dreamed of the day. I had considered doing a search, but I didn't know how to go about it. Right after you called, I immediately called her and we talked for some time. We have a lot in common; she has my personality. You can definitely tell she is my daughter. When we met in person, we talked for about two-and-a-half hours, and there were big hugs and lots of tears. My other children had always known that I placed a child for adoption. I never hid it from them. They were okay with it and wanted to know why I did it. I told them it was because I loved her and thought that was the best I could do for her. I married two years later and told my husband right away. It has been very hard through the years worrying about her. I wanted to know what she looked like, how she was doing in school, if she liked her parents, if she was healthy, if she was being treated right. The reunion answered all my questions. I know now that the adoption decision was the right thing. I really like her mom and dad. They are wonderful parents.

"Presently we are not in touch very much. I sent her a card for her birthday and I try to contact her, but seldom get her. I don't get cards from her on my birthday. Her parents gave me scrapbooks for every year of her life – her achievements, her graduation, what she looked like at different ages. It still hurts to know that I had to give her up. I will always have regrets about it. I surely hope that we stay in contact in the future."

Marilyn, Janet's adoptive mother:

"Alice has always been so appreciative of the way that we raised Janet. I have tried to get Janet to be closer to her, but I have to let her do her thing. She may be fearful of hurting my feelings, but I have told her that it does not matter to me. Janet and I are very close and that is not going to change. Alice told me that she thought it was great of me to let them meet without me there. I had to do it for Janet because she is the one who wanted it. To know all of her background is very helpful even though it is scary as hell. Alice is only forty-two years old – much too young to be in a situation like this. We were told that she picked us out of five couples. Some information they gave her was not particularly true, but now she is very happy that Janet has us for parents.

"The reason we adopted in the first place was because I am diabetic and we wanted to stop diabetes in our family. Basically we have two healthy children. Janet is going to marry in the spring and I would like Alice to come to the wedding, but with her condition, she may not even be around by then. Janet is not particularly interested in having her there. We have discussed this with other people and some say that we should do what we want to do since we are paying for it and others say that Janet should make the decision. I keep telling Janet that without her she would not be our daughter. It took a lot of love for her to give Janet up and all her life she wondered about her. When we adopted, we were told that the birth mother could search or we could search and if both of us put a letter in the file to that effect, they would put us in touch with each other. We would call to check to see if she had put a letter in the file, but they never told Alice that she could write a letter.

"Our children really understood the whole relinquishment process and adoption placement when they were three or four. They did understand that they came from someone else's tummy and not mine. It probably took a period of years for them to grasp the full understanding of the whole process – it developed over a period of time. None of it was a secret. I told Janet that she was given up because her birth mother could not provide the things that she would need. That was all written out in the letter that she wrote to Janet. She has read the letter over the years. Many people have read it and it has made grown men cry.

"Janet was about eight when she started asking questions. She wanted to know if her birth mother was around here and what happened to her. She talked about searching for her. I was okay with it. I understood that she would want to see her and know about her. She wanted to know what she looked like. I think she wanted to see a mirror image of herself. We did try a few places on the Internet, but that would not work since Alice never had access to a computer. I'm not sure if we registered with ISRR. We also did some research at the library. When I got off the phone with you and you had given me her number, I went to Janet and said that you had just found her birth mom. I started crying and gave her the number.

"Then Alice called Janet instead. Janet was going to wait until the next day. When she took the phone, she did her little pacing back and forth, back and forth like she does and she told Alice about it. Alice said she does the same thing. She never sits still when she is talking, just paces back and forth between the kitchen and the living room. They laughed about that. I cried because I was happy for her. She finally got what she wanted – to find her. Alice has sent her a card a couple of times but hasn't for some time now. I call Alice every now and then, but I talk with her mother more, about every three or four months. That is because we have a closer bond, I guess, and she is kind of a go-between. It is hard to reach Alice as her number has changed so much. If I need any information, I call her mother first.

"Neither Alice nor Janet has tried to make a contact in over a year, even though I encourage Janet to do it. I think we have gained a lot as a result of this reunion. Janet realizes the better life she has had because of the adoption. It is so good to know about Alice's health history. She has had a total of thirteen pregnancies – the children she has plus several miscarriages. Her mother keeps us up to date on what is happening. We have really become quite close to her parents. They will definitely be invited to the wedding. I think Janet feels very sure she has the right family."

The Carlsons

Carol and Glen Carlson adopted after trying for some time to have a child. They both wanted to be parents and went through considerable testing. They felt that they needed a new dimension to their relationship. Since she was infertile, she was afraid he would not stay married to her so she was very relieved when they started the process. Ultimately, they adopted a girl, Hannah, and then a boy, Greg.

Hannah had been an easy baby and would tell the cashiers in the grocery store that she and her brother were adopted and her father was a doctor. They had used the word "adoption" around them from a very early age. Carol expressed the feeling that she was such a beautiful child, such a gift, so easy to get along with. She didn't feel she deserved the right to have her.

Greg was more of a challenge – a crier, spit a lot and not as easy-going. The children began asking questions at about the age of eight and understood at that time that they had been born to other women. Carol gave them the information that the agency had provided – physical description, education, etc. She encouraged both of them to do a search at the appropriate age so they could learn more of their background. Carol always felt that Hannah had low self esteem relating to being adopted and in her teen years she had a lot of problems: out-of-wedlock pregnancy (she miscarried), skipping school, etc. They put her in a private girls' school and she did very well there.

I was able to find Hannah's closet birth mother, who was married and had four other children. Her husband knew of the adoption, but her children didn't. She and Hannah wrote letters to each other and Hannah sent pictures, too. But there was no further response from her birth mother. This was an extreme disappointment for her.

Greg was very curious as to why his birth parents gave him up. He knew that they were a married couple, but Carol depicted it as an act of love. Greg said that his parents seemed comfortable in talking about the adoption, but he feels that children learn to see more than that by the look in their parents' eyes.

Greg learned early on that his birth parents later had relinquished another male baby for adoption through the agency. He was extremely set on finding that brother and had a search done so they could meet. He'd always wanted a brother. He also learned that his parents had given birth to a girl before he was born and he understood that the grandmother was raising her. He feels that now when he talks about meeting his grandma, or his sister or his birth mom, it makes Carol feel uncomfortable, but she acts like she is okay with it.

Greg met his brother, Jesse, when Jesse was twenty-one and it was close to Christmas time. They met at a café and the reunion went very well. They spent the whole day together. He could see that they had the same mannerisms and sayings.

Greg said:

"Wow, he has existed all this time and I hadn't known or had the connection that I had always wanted. I felt nervous and confused when I first saw him like when you go to take a test and you don't have any of the answers. A brain lapse. That was three years ago. Now we have a very good relationship. We call each other two or three times a week, and hang out together. We're like brothers, good friends. My parents are quite fascinated with him.

"We both were raised by strict fathers. Jesse reminds my folks of the way I used to be – sorta irresponsible, the black sheep of the family. He is younger than I am and not quite as mature. Both Mom and Dad were supportive of the reunion. He has more interest than I in searching for our birth parents. I would like to be in touch with our sister first. Our birth parents were not having a very easy time in life. They were moving around a lot so they may be difficult to find. I don't want to find them in ruins. Jesse and I were both lucky in that we ended up in affluent families. My Dad provided well materially and my Mom provided well emotionally. Both of us raised Cain when we were teenagers so we are a lot alike.

"Ever since I knew I had a brother, I thought about him daily, and it was him I wanted to search for, not my parents. I did try but had no luck. It drove me crazy until I found him. When I did, and

55

we talked on the phone, I felt like I was talking to myself. He sounded just like me. The only word we could really say was, 'Wow!' and we said it about a hundred times in that conversation. We met the next day. He is like a mirror image of me and is now my best friend. We have so many things in common. We both enjoy sushi and went out for sushi almost every day the first month. We have agreed that we want to meet our sister first, but we will do the search together."

Shirley: Greg feels that he and Hannah had a good relationship as they were growing up. He feels he has a different bond with Jesse, but equally as strong, even though he has so much more background with Hannah. Greg is very glad that he did the search for Jesse.

Hannah adds this:

"I always knew I was adopted, but when I got older, 10 or 12, we talked about it more. I wondered why I didn't look like my parents. They gave us all the information they had about our birth parents. Mom always made us feel special because we were chosen. At sixteen, I began asking questions. I wanted to know why I was put up for adoption.

"I was just as curious about why Greg had been placed for adoption – his parents were older. My birth mother was only thirteen when she had me, but it didn't seem to me that his parents should be in the baby relinquishment market. Then they had another child they placed for adoption. I don't recall ever feeling rejected, but it is possible that I did – I learned in counseling. As I was growing up I felt closer to my mom, but now I feel closer to my dad. He has more in common with me and my husband.

"I've had a lot of anxiety all my life – diagnosis is panic disorder. I had many problems in my teen years. I was institutionalized for three weeks and then went into a girls' home for two years. I didn't like the home but I think it did me more good than the institution. It helped to make me the person I am today. It also helped me to respect my parents. I missed them so much. Now that I have a son (3 ½) I appreciate them even more. His birth was a real big deal for me – he is the only blood relative I know. To see him looking like me and resembling my baby pictures is wonderful.

"Dad and I talked about doing a search some time ago, but I was too young. I was probably seeking a new set of parents who would be more lenient. Later when I thought about it I was afraid of upsetting Mom, but then she thought it would be a good idea. I was twenty-six then. In fact when my birth mother said she might want contact, I called Mom before I made the decision. I surely didn't want to cause trouble, upset or hurt in the family. I mainly wanted medical information. Mom felt a great appreciation for my birth mother. She wouldn't have had me if it hadn't been for her.

"I told her that I wanted to write letters at first and then talk on the phone, but it ended with just letters and my sending some pictures of me as a baby. I haven't heard from her since. I wrote again and said if this was too hard for her and she didn't want contact to let me know – no response. It was almost like being abandoned at that point. It was a difficult way for it to end. I made it clear to her from the beginning that I understood that her family didn't know and I did not want to cause any problems. She made it clear in her letter that she didn't want contact even though initially she had. She seemed confused. She leads a busy life with four children, and working as a hairdresser. They live in an apartment so they must be dependent on her income. If she doesn't want contact, that's fine, but if she ever came back, I would have to be pretty certain that she was going to follow through. What she did really sent me into a tailspin. My counselor feels things have been worse since this happened. I had given possible contact a great deal of consideration and consultation, preparing emotionally, and then nothing.

"Her letter to me was pages long. It didn't say why she placed me for adoption, or anything about her present life. She did tell me not to try to contact my birth father – she thinks he's crazy. I'm beginning to think that I have more of him in me than her – not that I am crazy, but as far as emotional problems go.

"I was fifteen when I became pregnant. I was scared, didn't want to tell my parents, and didn't know what to do. My grandfather suggested abortion, but I was absolutely against that. So we planned adoption, but then I miscarried. I didn't feel that I could have taken care of a baby. It's the same now – probably scary for everyone the first time. I don't want to have any more. There were complications after my son was born. I lost fifty pounds. We have talked of adoption, but my husband is absolutely against it. That upsets me since I was adopted. I'm very glad that I did the search. I have more medical information now. There is always a risk in doing a search, but if you don't do it you will always wonder. I told my birth mom that she made a selfless decision and thanked her for giving me the life she did."

Carol, the adoptive mother:

"Raising children proved to be a challenge for us. Greg had a lot of problems – he got involved in drinking. He is doing well now and is training to be an instructor of 4-to-6-year-olds. Hannah has always had trouble with her sense of self worth. She ran away from home, lived on the streets and told police that she had been abused and we finally had to deal with Child Protective Services. Then she was sent to Girl's Ranch. She's now married to a very nice man. She lives in New York and is very involved with her in-laws. But she is still having panic attacks, which have increased since her birth mother cut off all contacts. She may be a bit of a hypochondriac.

"At an early age, the children knew they had grown inside another woman. We had a book about how a baby is born. We told them that their mother loved them a great deal and wanted them to have a family. At about the age of eight they started asking questions and I shared the information from the agency with them. They referred to that information many times. It is all a part of the history of who they are. Regarding searches, I encouraged both of them. That would answer some of the questions we could not answer – Who do I look like? Why am I different? I was glad when you (Shirley) found Hannah's mother.

"I've had no contact with the birth mother. I am curious, but not overly so. She must have taken care of herself in order to have such a healthy baby. Greg's parents were interviewed on television as they signed the adoption papers. I tried to watch it but couldn't bring myself to – a married couple giving up a child. You called us to let us know that they had relinquished a second son and we told him right away. They look like twins – same eyes, same smile, same wonderful no-cavity teeth. I don't feel I have lost anything as a result of Hannah's reunion but I have concern about Hannah's well-being."

Jesse, Greg's birth brother:

"Adoption was a familiar word at a very early age. I knew it applied to me and it didn't make me feel different. Simply, Mom and Dad were Mom and Dad. When I did understand it, I used it against my parents by accusing them of not being my real parents. I had an adoptive sister two years older. They showed us the papers they had about our background information. Since I realized why my birth mother gave me up, I've had a lot of respect for her, especially now that I am a father. Mom explained that times can be tough for people and when they don't use protection, things happen that they can't control. They may have had financial or mental problems. They respected me enough that they gave me to someone who could give me the life they wanted me to have.

"I tried to do a search for my brother at eighteen, but was too young. So I was really glad when Greg found me. We met the next day. My parents were excited for me. Greg and I see each other about twice a month.

"I am so glad that we are reunited. I'd have searched for him if he hadn't found me. We both enjoy guns and shooting and have been out to the range a lot. We both enjoy sushi. My parents are health nuts and so is Greg. I have a lot of common interests with his dad. There's a good relationship all the way around. That's really cool."

Marlene

Marlene is the birth mother of Dan. At one point Dan was willing to make an appointment for an interview, but he failed to keep the appointment. Although he has been in touch with his birth family for a few years and has been in fairly frequent contact with them, his adoptive parents are not aware of this reunion. Apparently Dan feels they would strongly oppose it and be very upset with him for becoming involved. The birth parents are married to each other and they were the ones who requested that the search be done.

Marlene tells her story:

"It was on my high school graduation night that I became pregnant with Dan. Neal, the father, still had a year of high school to go. We had been dating for some time. When I missed my period I told him – we were both scared to death. We proved that you CAN get pregnant the first time! We went to a doctor to have a test and I turned my class ring around so it would look like a wedding band. We told our parents. His folks, whose youngest child was only two, said that we could live with them and keep the baby in their small home. We knew that it would present a hardship for them financially, but we longed to keep the baby. My mom was very, very upset and asked me not to even touch her. It was like I had some horrible disease. She made it imperative that we give the baby up for adoption. So arrangements were made for me to go to the Florence Crittenton Home, a home for unwed mothers. Dad was much more sympathetic and understanding. I had a younger sister who was the perfect child. She was quiet, and obliging about everything. I went with the wild group and yet didn't get involved in most of their dangerous activities. I was very outgoing and involved in a lot of extracurricular activities.

"I knew that this was going to be a big disappointment to our parents. His parents tried to come up with solutions. Mom said that it would kill my dad. She acted like I had leprosy. I laid my head in her lap and she said, "Don't touch me!" The plan was for me to go to college and I knew that I would not be able to enroll that year. Later my dad came to me and told me not to worry about anything. He said that everything would be just fine. I kept apologizing and he would reassure me. I always felt closer to my father. Then my mom took me to a gynecologist. I asked her not to come in with me, but she did and she asked the doctor if he could tell her how many times I had done 'it'. I covered my face. It felt like it was burning. There was no sympathetic edge from my mom. The doctor told her about the Home. I was about four months along when they took me there. We were not really in a financial position to do that. Mom and Dad would bring Neal up about once a month. We didn't realize that we could have a say in it.

"In order to help out financially, I took one of those jobs where you work in a home tending kids or helping out. It was awful. I couldn't lock my door and the parents slept in so the kids would come into my room first thing in the morning. I was so tired. The woman really took advantage of me. Also she'd give me a bad time saying she couldn't see how anyone could give up a baby. It got worse and worse. I called the Home and they decided they would never send anyone there again. I was doing a lot of work that I shouldn't have been doing. I gave my folks all the money I earned there. I lost all my confidence and self esteem during that time. I felt like some type of alien – they were so ashamed of me.

"When I had the baby, they put me completely out and when I woke up I was surprised that it was all over. The doctor said some hurtful things to me as well, related to the fact that my parents would not be paying all of the bill. I always felt that I was a disgrace to everyone and like people were trying to hide me. Neal and I had not decided what the plan for the baby was going to be. But between Mom and the caseworker they said there was no other way. The caseworker said that she had a wonderful family waiting and we needed to do what was best for the baby. We did try to look at the practical side. We didn't have money to pay for a pediatrician or shots. I finally called Mom and said I was going to bring the baby home. Her one word was, 'No' and she hung up. We talked about it and realized that his parents' home was already crowded and it was not really fair to them or the baby. They would have to be financially responsible for us. Mom kept saying how unfair this was to the baby. He would not have nice clothes, and kids would make fun of him and, of course, we did not want this to happen. We were overwhelmed and finally started to think they were trying to do the best for us.

"By then our parents were not speaking. Mom had called Neal's mother and told her not to write to me anymore and give me false hope about keeping the baby. When I didn't hear from her anymore I wondered if she had changed her mind and they were not going to be able to help us. The agency told us that they would do their best to put him in a home that we would approve of. They brought him in for me to see. He was dressed in such a nice little outfit. They asked if I wanted to hold him and I said that I couldn't because I wouldn't be able to let him go. They took some pictures. So I have three Polaroid pictures of him. Several times I regretted our decision and we even checked to see if there was a time period that we could wait to sign the papers. I said I needed more time. They said that the family had everything ready and were so excited and that he would have the best of everything. I signed the papers at the Home and Neal signed in a lawyer's office. One day in church I could hear the babies crying at the back and I started crying. My mother nudged me and said, 'Stop that right now!'

"We married three years later. We wanted to wait until we could be totally independent. I had a good job in a mailroom and by the time we married I had worked up to supervisory training. About a year and a half later our next son was born. We had a daughter two years after that. Even with these two wonderful children, we never stopped thinking about Dan. In fact, every year we went to the state fair for the sole purpose of looking for a child that looked like us or like our other son. We searched the face of every little boy who would be about the right age. We took in a lot of fairs! We did not tell our children about Dan until you let us know that you had found him and he was open to meeting us. He was thirty-three years old. We told our children that we had something important to tell them. I wanted to do the talking, but then my tongue would not work. Our daughter said, 'Mom, you are not pregnant, are you?' I told Neal to take over and he did a great job. We told them we had promised to keep this a secret and that's why we had not said anything before. Then we told others and we were so happy that we could now share this with everyone. Neal's siblings had not known about it and we told them.

"Dan told you that he would call us at a certain time. We waited for him to call and he didn't. I know that it would have been a very hard phone call to make. Later he called and we talked for the longest time. You wouldn't believe all the parallels in our lives. Dan was thrilled to death that he had a blood brother and sister. His parents had been given a lot of incorrect information. They had been told that we had gone to college, which was not true at the time. We wanted to make sure that he'd had a good life. He sounded just like our other son on the phone. I thought it was him at first.

"After the next phone call, we made arrangements to meet him in a hotel. Before he arrived we went through the worst case scenario – what if he was on drugs? etc. He arrived late and we were so nervous. When we opened the door the anticipation, the anxiety, we had never felt anything so big. That was a big step for him to take, as he didn't know what we would be like either. He was the spitting image of Neal. He came into the room and he hugged me and it let loose so many emotions that had been bottled up. We had been living all those years with a lie and now we could let it all out. Neal hugged him and I got more emotional. We were so excited! We had picture albums with us and we all looked through them. I couldn't turn the pages – my hands were shaking. He was calm – just like Neal and our other children. They are all laid back, but I am not. I wear my heart on my sleeve.

"He had lots of questions. He saw a picture of our grandson and he said that he and his son could be twins. Our children were so anxious to meet him and did soon after. He and his son came to visit and it was amazing how much his mannerisms were like our other son's. They had similar grades in school and similar interests. You'd definitely know they were siblings.

"We had considered searching for a long time. Every time we heard of an adopted child being abused, we would be so upset. Then we read about the CIP in the paper. That is how we got in touch with you. Dan had divorced some time ago and he shared custody of his son. We now see them about every two months. We have big get-togethers with lots of food. We feel that we gave Dan his heart and soul and the adoptive family nurtured it. It just has to be something that we passed onto him for him and his brother to have so much in common. He had far more than we could've given him. He had a car in high school. Our kids worked in high school. I gave them a little spending money.

"We are so glad that we did the search – it has given us comfort that he had a good life. He calls us Mom and Dad and called us on Mother's Day and Father's Day. That means so much to us. I would surely do this all over again. I hope that his adoptive mother would not be able to tell from this story that it is about Dan. They still know nothing about our reunion. After we started telling everyone, my mother was not at all happy, but now she is very proud of Dan and his son. Dan said that he had considered looking, but he was frustrated because he had no names to start with."

Shirley: In talking with Marlene about her mother's strong reaction to all this, I wondered if there had been something in her mother's life that elicited such a negative response. She told me that her mother has had some strokes and she is surprised at some of the things she says now and what she doesn't remember. One day her mother told her that she and Marlene's father had played around out in the cornfield.

However, I talked with her a few months later. She feels that her mother has softened considerably and is now a much nicer person. Further, her mother has developed a very close bond with Dan and is glad that he is now part of their lives.

Jim

"My mother, Nancy, was afraid she would lose me when I did the search for Natalie, my birth mother. I assured her that I had no question about who my mother is, and that is the woman who raised me. I can't remember a time when the word adoption was not familiar to me. I was always told that I was chosen. I was seven or eight when I really understood that I was born to someone else before they became my parents and I realized that my brother and sisters had different birth parents. All of us were adopted. I was first, then a sister, a brother and another sister. My mother went out of her way to make me feel special, so I did feel a bit different.

"All the information I had about my background was one and a half pages the agency gave them and there were a whole lot of blackouts on them. Not a lot of information. When I asked who my birth mother was, my mom told me, 'She was a lady who had you and placed you for adoption so we could adopt you. She couldn't take care of you and we really didn't know why. We just know that we had an opportunity to have you!' My mother seemed a bit uneasy when I asked about my birth mother. My parents had no birth children. She told me that my birth mother couldn't afford to keep me or the guy she was with didn't want her to. I know now that it was very hard for her to do. I feel that she loved me – it was a very unselfish act. I've never harbored any ill feelings at all.

"I asked questions off and on through my childhood. Since I knew so little, I took on my adoptive parents' information, and that is what I would tell people if and when they asked – like what did my grandfather do? I talked of my adoptive grandfather. When others talked of their family history, I thought I really didn't know mine, except that of my adoptive family. I kept a lot of my curiosity to myself. I didn't tell my adoptive parents about it until I moved out of the house. They told us they had some information we could have when we were ready. I didn't feel a need for a while after I moved out. I thought it would make my mother nervous. Even when I got it, it took me years to figure out what to do with it. Then it took me years to find you.

"I contacted the ISRR and did spot checks on my own. I really thought it would never happen. I finally got frustrated with that and decided, 'Let's do it!' So I called the agency and they referred me to you. They told me that the records were sealed and they could not give me any information. I didn't tell my parents until after I contacted you. I then thought there might really be a chance to meet her. I was a radio announcer then and I thought that we might have a reunion on the show. There had been many reunions on the Maury Povich show and others so we thought it would be great to do it on our show. My mother was rather upset about it. I think that if Mom agrees to be interviewed by you that there will be some family discussion. I really have not been encouraged by anyone in my family to do a search."

Shirley: Just about an hour after I talked with Jim, his mother called me to make an appointment for an interview. She told me that her cousin had given up a child for adoption and just had a reunion. The cousin called me the next day and said she would like to participate in the activity.

Jim continues:
"I am now forty and have no children. I always said I would never like to have a child like me, but if there was ever a chance for me to adopt, I felt I owed it to the world. In my youth, I created all kinds of havoc. I was diagnosed as being ADD, placed on ritalin, and I guess that worked for a while. I was involved in lighting fires – lighting the neighbor's lawn on fire, putting it out and then lighting it again. There was always some kind of problem and as I got older, the problems got bigger. I was into drugs, too. There were four adopted children, all from different families, all exhibiting signs of alcoholism, diagnosed as ADD, and with drug addiction. We all have addictive problems and signs of attention deficit disorder – especially if the father and mother were both addictive, alcoholic or ADD."

Shirley: I pointed out to him that what they all definitely have in common is, they were reared in the same family and they had each been relinquished by their original family.

Jim said:

"Oh, that's a new thought. Whole other story. Food for thought.

"When I first talked with Sarah (the birth mother) I panicked when she said, 'Hey, man, how are you?' I sometimes use that phrase as a greeting to people and out of the blue I heard her say it and I dropped the phone. What? That is exactly what I would say. I had thought about this day for a long time. You had warned me that she might not want contact, or might be unable to be found. But here she was and she sounded like me and talked like me and some similar interests came out. There were a lot of connections and about twenty minutes into the two hour conversation, I told her that I wanted to say this to her, 'I understand that you chose to give me up for adoption, and whatever the reason was behind it, it doesn't matter to me. What matters is that you gave me up for adoption and I turned out fine. I just want to thank you. I harbor no ill feelings.' I think she's wanted to hear that for as long as I've wanted to say it – or longer.

"There's been no contact between my birth and adoptive parents. I did tell my dad about my contact and he was interested, but I didn't tell my mom until just this week. I told my dad the story that she told me and he was just blown away that she had two daughters older than me. They don't know about me. She never told them and that is why she has apprehension about a reunion. Her husband knows. When she became pregnant, her mother didn't want her to have me. She gave her money to go away and 'take care of it.' but then her grandmother heard about it and she gave her money to go to another state and have me and place me for adoption. I don't believe she could have told me that if I had not told her the heartfelt things that I did. She expressed a lot of things that she had been holding inside.

"I always call her on Mother's Day, my birthday, Thanksgiving and Christmas. I thank her for having me. I have to be careful about who may answer the phone. I understand her situation.

They live just a three-hour drive from where I live. It is very disappointing that we cannot meet in person. I sent her a picture of me and my wife, but she has not sent me one of her. When I first mentioned a search, my mom said she didn't want to hear any more about it. This week I told her I had been talking to her. She said that she didn't want me to find out anything that would hurt me, and she had just learned about her cousin. I told her that was not happening here, for we were not meeting in person, by Sarah's wishes. I told her I was learning things about myself, and getting to know me better."

Nancy, the adoptive mother:
"I am very proud of Jim. I have always loved children and wanted to have six. I believe that children are a gift from God, no matter who has them. The child has no say in it. It was easy to turn to adoption as a method of having a family. I prayed to God to choose my children – the ones he wanted us to have so we could love and raise them. We have four adopted children. Jim is the oldest. Three of them were infants. The fourth one was placed when he was six years old. He had been very abused and mistreated and tortured – head held under water, hand in scalding water, etc. He had been in a number of foster homes. Each of my children have had his or her own problems along the way – health wise, addictive, emotional – and I found it difficult to discipline them the way they should have been because I was so afraid that since they were adopted it might trigger feelings of not being wanted. I did whatever I needed to do for each individual child.

"There were only five years between the four of them. I told them stories about adoption when they were little, read them adoption stories and sang them songs about being adopted. They loved them. I made them up. They wanted to hear them over and over again. I wanted it to be a familiar enough word that it would never be a surprise to them. Whenever it would come up, we talked about it. I wanted them to feel secure and stable and not different. I think by seven they understood that they were born to someone else. Actually, I can't remember their ever bringing it up, although I am sure they did. The second boy just wanted to wipe the whole thing out, didn't want to talk about it. The others felt so secure like this is where I have always been and this is where I belong and am supposed to be. I think that God has a plan for every person and this was His plan for them. So the birth mother was just God's means of getting them to me and into our family. They really didn't wonder about it a lot. My oldest daughter did ask what her birth mother looked like and if she looked like her. She is quite tall and the rest of us are short. I wasn't able to tell her. I told her, 'She was in the navy or some part of the service and she was going to go overseas. She wanted you very much but she had to give you up.' Then she didn't ask anymore. I didn't feel threatened in any way. We got no information on my second son. The hurt feelings that I had were when Jim told me that he had found his birth mother two years ago.

"My first reaction was surprise because I didn't even know that he was thinking about it and then I felt very hurt and my feelings changed to jealousy. He is so considerate and thoughtful. He never said another thing about it until about two weeks ago when he told me that he had talked with you and he wanted me to talk with you, too. I said no at first because I wouldn't know what to say, but as I got thinking about it, I thought that maybe there is something I can say that would be helpful to another adoptive mother. I decided that the purpose of this book was to help people understand what happens in reunions. I was hurt because he had searched out his birth mother when from birth they were my children. It was not like they were adopted children. They were mine and I didn't think they would think about another mother. We didn't talk about it any more so I didn't think he was pursuing it until just recently. Two of my children, the six-year-old boy and one daughter – have both said that they want nothing to do with their birth families. Whether this is true in their hearts, I don't know.

"My youngest daughter has expressed some desire to find her birth mother and has asked if she has any half brothers or sisters. I know that all four of my children love me in spite of any mistakes I may have made. They know I love them in spite of some of the problems they have had along the way. I would now encourage it if they have a need to do it. I feel that God gave me these kids for a reason and He gave me the best and they deserve the best. My other son who wants nothing to do with his relatives would still like to go back to the town where he lived as a child. I do know that his birth mother didn't want him. I don't know how she would receive him if he did look her up. Whatever he wants to do, I will help him do it, but it could be an ugly scene for him. He's already had too much ugliness. He's married, has children and is not a very good father – has to control all of the family. I never really knew why Jim's birth mother gave him up until he found her. She told him there was no father so she had to give him up. I've found that no matter what you tell a child about their mother giving them up out of love, they still have a feeling of abandonment or rejection. They feel unwanted. I wanted all four of them to feel very loved and I told them that they were loved and were not aborted. Their birth mothers loved them but couldn't take care of them so they found a family where there would be two loving parents and a good home that they weren't able to provide.

"I was always comfortable in answering their questions because they came up so rarely. I told them everything that I knew. I haven't had any contact with Jim's birth mother and I have no desire unless Jim would want me to. Since the reunion, my relationship with Jim has not changed. He appreciated my willingness to talk with you. He and his birth mother have gained since he told her he was okay and he has great adoptive parents. I didn't want her to feel guilty. I was glad she didn't have an abortion. Jim told her he didn't blame her. I think it is wonderful if they both want the reunion. My cousin's reunion answered a lot of her questions. It was a real fulfillment for both of them.

"All parents can have children who turn out good or bad – adopted or not. My brother and I are different as day and night and we had the same upbringing."

Tommy

Tommy was born with his right forearm missing. His birth mother, Jeneal, kept him until he was six months old and then decided that the challenge was more than she could handle and that there would have to be a couple who could handle it better.

Jeneal:

"From the moment I knew that I was expecting a child, I planned to place it for adoption. At the very last minute, and just before he was born, I planned to keep him. My girlfriend was pregnant at the same time, but she got married and had family support. I was in her shadow. She was also telling me not to give him up. If she got to have a baby, I wanted one, too. I'd been in counseling with you (Shirley), and had been picking out what I would want in adoptive parents. Religion didn't matter, as long as they believed in God. When he was born with a deformity, I felt extremely responsible for it. I was kind of numb. It didn't look like it would be a big problem. They thought he had a thumb, but it turned out to be only cartilage. The doctor said that it was not genetics, but his position in the womb – there was pressure there, and it didn't allow the bone structure to develop right. I felt so guilty because I had not taken care of myself as a young person, and then I tried to hide my pregnancy from my father. I was only 15. Once it was confirmed, I was already five months along, and I had worn my clothes really tight. I was in denial. I had in my mind that only bad girls got pregnant. Here I was an older adolescent and I'd had training about this in school. I didn't take it all in, and thought you could only get pregnant when you were married. Sounds hard to believe that I didn't think what I was doing with my boyfriend could create another person.

"I was really glad that I had not given him up at birth. I may have never seen him or known anything about him. I'd never want Tommy to think that he was not wanted because he had a deformity. In a way, I felt very thankful that I had not gone through with the adoption. As hard as it was, it still made me feel better that I kept him for six months. It was a rough six months. I cried all the time and was a very nervous mother. I felt that he was not getting enough nutrition. He cried all the time. Until we supplemented my breast milk with formula, he had to eat every two hours. He had an immature digestive system. Every week, I had to take him to get a new cast on his arm to accommodate the growth.

"My brother was like a surrogate father. He was a big influence in my decision to finally place him for adoption. One day he told me that I would never have a future, that I would be a welfare mother for the rest of my life and Tommy wouldn't have a chance at ever having a family – a mother and father who love him. He said I was making a big mistake. Maybe I was a zombie for lack of sleep. Well, my friend's parents had divorced and her father had remarried. He and his new wife agreed to take Tommy for a trial period and I was not to come around their house. He really flourished while he was there. He gained a lot of weight. My friend decided she didn't like the idea of it all, so she took me over there one day. I told her I wasn't supposed to do it, so I waited in the car. She brought him out to me. They found out and they returned Tommy to me. They were crying and all upset. I was full of emotion and very confused by the whole thing. For three days, I rocked that baby and cried and knew that I was going to consider adoption again. I took him back to the agency, so emotional I don't remember anything about it.

"I started trying to find Tommy when he was twenty-one, but gave it up because I became homeless. I was going to college and living in a car. Before long, I married, was divorced and then married again – had two sons and a daughter. I later started the search again and found him when he was thirty-one. The search papers went through the day after 9/11 – September 12th, and it took a year to find him. When I told others that I was going to search, they encouraged me. I had decided to do a search because I wanted to tell him that he was not given up because he had a deformity.

"When we finally met I did tell him – he smiled and we hugged. Now he calls me all the time – at least two to three times a month. He came out and spent last Thanksgiving with us. He came early and stayed into December. He has met most of his half-siblings. I'm so glad that I did the search. I got to meet his parents during the summer of 2002. I really like them. They had me to dinner and it was wonderful. I never had any regrets after I finally placed him. When I made my final decision, it really was final. It's given me a great deal of comfort. I know it was the right thing for sure. He is going to school now. He calls me Mom. We kinda laugh and he calls me Jeneal, too. He is a happy person. I love seeing the pictures in the photo album that his mom made for me – one when he was just a little guy, running alongside the pool into his dad's arms. That made me feel so good. They explained to me all the conscientious medical work that had been done. He had received the best medical care for his arm. He was written up in a medical journal. His arm is a bit shorter than his other arm. It's thinner and he is missing one finger. They moved his index finger to replace his thumb. He loves playing the guitar and is good at it. His friends call him Little Hand Tom – a term of endearment. He likes that.

"I've had some real traumas in my life: when I was 12, my mother committed suicide; at 16, I had a child out of wedlock and the following year I was brutally raped and left for dead. I felt that I didn't have much of a future. When I finally did the search, his mother said that it was perfect timing because he was not ready at the age of twenty-one. He really is a great person, and he has great parents. I think the world of them."

Earl, the adoptive father, E-mailed me (Shirley):

"I thought that before we talk tomorrow, I'd E-mail you some random thoughts I have regarding adoption, and specifically our adoption of Tommy. First and foremost – we love Tommy very much and have no second thoughts about having adopted him. When we adopted Tommy, we knew precious little about his background. We only knew that his natural parents were very young and that his handicap made it difficult for his single, teenage mother to keep him. What we did not know was that Tom's mother had a family history of mental issues. I seriously doubt that knowledge of this background would have prevented us from adopting Tom, but it would have conditioned us for what happened during his early teen years, and we might have been better prepared to deal with it. It might also have affected how the doctors handled the many surgeries to reconstruct his arm and hand. They kept him on painkillers for extended periods, and it has occurred to us that it may have had an influence on his later problems. He got into drugs and we dealt with that, but not with the deeper issues we didn't know about. Most of his friends who were into drugs with him got over it and are now leading productive lives. He has made some progress with his addictions, but he has yet to become a truly self-sufficient member of society. He does, however, seem to be happy and lives for the moment.

"When we adopted Tom, I believed that the environment outweighed genetic issues. So I felt that we could put him on the right path by providing a good environment. He was raised in a Christian, healthy, normal home environment. He was taught proper values at home and attended good schools. We set good examples for him in the way we led our daily lives. He stole from us to support his addictions. It was shocking when we met Jeneal. She and Tom are almost carbon copies. Their personalities, problems, thought processes, are virtually identical. So much for my theory that environment outweighs genetics. I think our case shows the need to provide all of the information possible to adoptive parents. Had we known everything about the background, we would have sought help much earlier. I don't know if that would have resulted in anything different for Tom in the long run – we'll never know.

"Another conclusion that may be of value is that even with all we've been through, we love Tom as we love our birth daughter. The bond we formed with him as an infant, the joy we experienced as he grew up, is so strong that we will always regard him as our child. We don't know why God put him into our hands, but we've always done the best we could for him, and we always will.

"As for my wife and me, we have been greatly affected by Tommy. We spent years agonizing over his condition and what we could do next to try to get him on the right path. It was a great strain on our family and obviously also affected our daughter. Somehow, we made it this far. Our daughter is doing well and has her own family. Gloria and I have moved on to retirement and are enjoying this phase of our lives more than any previous phase. We're deeply involved in our church. Gloria pursues her quilting, and I enjoy mission work (Habitat for Humanity, tutoring school children, helping senior citizens repair their homes, etc.) and golf. We still worry about Tom and pray for him constantly – but we somehow are now able to keep him in the back of our minds rather than constantly obsessing over him as we did for years. He knows that we are always there for him and calls when he needs help."

Earl, retired military officer's phone interview:

"Somehow we knew that Tommy's placement with us was meant to be and so we were happy to have that opportunity. It has been a big challenge, totally changed our lives and still does. We go as long as three months without hearing from him or knowing how to reach him. Then he will suddenly call and say, 'Here I am and I'm okay.' AND, 'I need help – send money.'

"The military almost entirely paid for his medical care, but we paid for some. The reconstructive surgery was done in the Jewish Hospital in Louisville, Kentucky. It was a leading team who did the surgery. They made his index finger into a thumb so he could have prehensility. He gained a lot of use with that thumb. It was very successful. They took bone out of his arm area to make a wrist, which is stiff, it does not bend like yours and mine. That arm is considerably shorter than the left arm and is very small. He writes left-handed out of necessity not out of dominance. He is extremely well coordinated and very athletic. When he was young, he and I played catch all the time. He would throw and catch with the same hand. He'd put a glove on his left hand, catch the ball and very quickly put the glove under his right arm, get the ball out and throw it back to me. He grew up not knowing any different so he is extremely versatile with the arm. His body strength is not particularly good which keeps him from getting some of the jobs he applies for. For example, working in a restaurant, he can wash dishes, but he could not carry heavy trays.

"He got a high school degree and that was a struggle with his getting into drugs. We started him in college, but he got into drugs right away and did not complete a semester. He has picked up classes along the way and now is close to a two-year degree. We had paid for his schooling all along the way, but he now has a deal with the state of Colorado where they are paying for his schooling and he is also getting Social Security Disability Insurance. He went for years without a driver's license. We gave him several cars over the years and all of them ended up in the trash heap and he lost his license. Recently he was able to get his license reinstated in California, and so we gave him another car. We hope he gets by with that. We are supplementing his Social Security check. This challenge will never end for us. I wonder if he will ever be self-sufficient. We've told him over the years that we never want him to be homeless and without something to eat.

"He has such a beautiful personality and gets along well with people. Now he's in Santa Barbara going to a community college. When we go for a long time without hearing from him and suddenly the phone rings and he says, 'Hi, Dad, how ya doin'?' Like nothing was wrong. We fuss at him a little and tell him to not ever let us be without a number where we can reach him. According to him, he was told he had a diagnosis of schizophrenia. He was getting his medical care through the state of California and has seen a psychiatrist numerous times. He will be here for the holidays this year.

"Our daughter and Tommy are about six years apart and they were extremely close until he was about twelve. It was a marvelous fit. Tommy got straight S's in school. He was absolutely tops in everything. She was so proud of him. She baby-sat for him. They got along great as brother and sister and then he started to get into his problems. That drove a wedge between them. She distanced herself from him. The man she married had some drug problems some time before and they thought maybe he could help him. So Tommy went out to stay with them, but it just did not work and they kicked him out of the house. Gloria went out to stay with them for a few months to see that he graduated from high school – he did. He came back with us and we put him in college but he couldn't handle it. Ever since then he has been in and out of the house, with our knowing or not knowing where he was. He's had psychiatric evaluations and nothing was ever mentioned about schizophrenia. They just called him a hard-core case. With his personality, he can convince anyone he is okay and doing fine. People are drawn to him and put their trust in him. But he will lead you down the primrose path and you will soon learn that he is using you. Only through him did we learn that he was schizophrenic.

"Jeneal told us that she was schizophrenic and told us the whole story of her mother's suicide and when she was a teenager she had problems due to her mother's problems. There were moments when we wondered if you (Shirley) knew anything about all this. But we remember very distinctly your telling us that you had given us all the information you had and that you knew very little about his background.

"In Tommy's later years, we told him that if he ever wanted to try to find his birth mom we would help him. He never expressed interest in it until you called. If he ever felt anger toward her, he never expressed it. We told him that his birth mother was very young and was in no position to take care of him and that it must have been extremely hard for her to let him go. But she did what she knew was the best thing for him. The only time it was talked about was when we brought it up, and we didn't frequently. Once in a while we would mention it to see if he was ready. He never took the bait.

"It would be great if we could channel all his energy and intellect into a positive channel. He's extremely bright. His IQ is phenomenally high, but he is unable to focus on something and stick to it and that has been Jeneal's background, too."

Gloria, Tommy's adoptive mother:

"Jeneal had Tommy when she was a child. She was only fifteen and the birth father was fifteen also. She had a difficult life. I think it continues to be difficult for her.

"We adopted because we had been advised not to have any more children because of a physical problem I had. It flared up when I was pregnant with our daughter. I think Tommy understood that he was adopted from the day we brought him home. He started talking in sentences at about a year old and the word adoption was familiar to him from day one. Every year we had a 'Celebrate Adoption Day' on the anniversary of the day we adopted him. So he knew that adoption applied to him. His sister was jealous because she didn't get one – only her birthday was celebrated. Tommy had two celebrations every year. We always made sure that she got a little gift on that day, too. We were very comfortable talking with Tommy about his adoption. Being military, we had several friends who had adopted children from overseas and they were all familiar with the word adoption. Tommy actually understood at about ten or twelve that he grew inside someone else. He realized that his sister grew inside of me and he didn't. He never asked any questions. Whenever we brought up the subject of his birth history, he would just say that it didn't seem real to him, so he never got excited about doing a search. He wasn't about to think of anyone else as his parents except for the ones he had.

"I was really glad when you contacted us that Jeneal was searching. I had given him every bit of information that we had. As a matter of fact, I was curious to learn more. When you contacted him he seemed interested. His concern was that it would upset me, like maybe he would be trying to replace me and that would be the last thing he would want to do. I reassured him that I had no problem with it. Then he was okay with it. After he met Jeneal, he got very curious about his half brothers. I actually think the reunion has had a positive effect on him. With all his problems, he saw himself as a single person with all these problems and didn't quite understand where they were coming from. I think he saw so many similarities in other members of his family like drug abuse. Some of Jeneal's other children had problems with drugs. Mental problems. Schizophrenia. All of her other children have had problems of a sort. Children with problems sometimes feel that it is something they have done to have such negative tendencies and now he knows that he has come by it naturally. I still believe that it is a choice. I see a lot of people who come out of just terrible backgrounds and they are able to get over it. Some people just have stronger power than others.

"We have met Jeneal. She came to Colorado and stayed for a week. She came over to the house and we talked and got along beautifully. When we met I did not at all consider her mentally ill. Her life style is fairly unusual. The man she is living with sounds like he is a fairly good influence on her. We had quite a bit of contact right after the reunion. I tapered it off myself. I feel that Tommy is an adult now. Since he is a grown man, their situation is between them and I don't care to be in the middle anymore. Right after the reunion, I think she went into a period of depression. I got a lot of E-mails and calls from her. I had to taper it off. Now we only E if necessary. There doesn't seem to be any reason for us to have a close relationship.

"Tommy met his birth father in California one evening. There doesn't seem to be a real strong desire for a relationship. He has younger children – maybe a second marriage. Tommy said he was very nice and he has the musical talent that Tommy has. They played guitar and had a nice evening, but he has not contacted him since.

"This reunion has helped me gain a lot of relief, knowing that it wasn't just all bad decisions on our part. We know a lot of his problems could not have been helped. That was of great benefit to me. I'm with Earl in feeling that things are passed along through heredity more than I ever did before. For years I wondered if I had caused any of his problems – maybe choosing the wrong counselors or something. You have to let it go or it will make you crazy. Tommy is very closely attached to the family. He doesn't want separation at all for which I am so grateful. He really is not that dependent on us anymore. He pretty much takes care of himself. Not too often do we have to get him out of a pinch. We did send him a couple hundred dollars to register the car. When Earl writes to him, he pops a twenty in the envelope, but that's nothing. He takes care of himself and we are happy about that. When he was younger, we pulled him out of many, many spots. His Social Security helps a lot. Who knows, he may have been clean for years. I know he still drinks. I think he is past the drug usage. He is in his thirties now. However, Tommy will tell you what he thinks you want to hear, because if you are happy, he is happy. He is so intelligent – he started reading the newspaper at four years of age. You bring up a political issue and he knows all about it. He was in all the gifted programs when he was in school. I hope that intellect won't be wasted. It is what has kept him alive from time to time. He can charm his way out of every situation. He's no more of a challenge than a lot of our friends have had."

Tommy, last, but certainly not least:
"The word adoption was familiar to me for as long as I can remember. When I realized that it applied to me, I didn't feel different from others. My folks had a girl born to them six years earlier and they were wonderful parents to both of us. I became curious about my birth family around thirteen or fourteen and I was asking about what they looked like and wondered why I went to this family and not another one. I was more curious as I got older. They always told me that the decision had been made on the basis of love. I was never made to feel that anyone rejected me. I mostly felt different from others because of my missing arm. I had noticed that other kids looked like their families and I didn't look like mine. Kids can be very straightforward, sometimes painfully so. You know, you don't look like your sister or your parents. I would have no answer. I wouldn't share the fact that I was adopted or tell them about it. It was really none of their business. So I kinda kept it to myself, but it made me feel uncomfortable.

"My parents were very accepting of my curiosity and when I was twenty-five, my mom suggested that I look into it. She was curious, too. I never did anything about a search as I didn't know how to go about it. Jeneal found me about the time I might have started looking for her. I know that I was not easy to find as I am quite a rogue. When you called me and told me that Jeneal was looking for me, I was very interested, curious and a little scared – maybe intimidated. My whole life I have been interested in meeting her. There was quite a jumble of emotions – nervousness, anxiety as well as curiosity. Everything was just fine the first time I hugged her, we just looked into each other's eyes. We didn't say anything, we just smiled and laughed and cried – it was wonderful. We had spoken several times on the phone before meeting. We had several short conversations then she drove out to Colorado to meet me.

"I call her about every three months. We both need someone to talk to periodically and she is not that far from me in age (seventeen years older). No offense to my adoptive parents, but they are considerably older. It is different. We have a little more in common as far as modern problems are concerned.

"I definitely feel that I was placed with the right family. I am in touch with them on a weekly basis. Most of the time I am the one who calls because it is hard to get in touch with me. We are going to try to change that. I am getting a cell phone.

"The interesting things that I learned from Jeneal were that I had brothers and a sister. I've met two of them. Two out of three ain't bad. It was interesting to see how much our lives had paralleled each other. We had actually been dragging right by each other. When my dad was stationed in California, she'd lived in the same town. There are parallels between her dad and my dad. They were both in the Air Force. We had been through similar experiences, just seventeen years apart – very interesting. We had a lot to connect with each other. It was not done on purpose. It was fate. It all helped immensely.

"I'm here with my folks for Christmas vacation for two weeks. I am enrolled in college in California and will go there when I leave in early January. Ironically, it's a school that Jeneal once attended. I'm about ten hours short of an AA and I am working part time and will go on to get my Bachelor's Degree. I hope to have it by the time I'm thirty-five. I think I'll pull it off. I've got to settle down and I think Santa Barbara is where I would like to live. I guess I got my roguishness because my dad was in the military – we moved around a lot. Each place that Dad was stationed was long enough for me to develop meaningful and lasting relationships. Literally, I have fifteen to twenty close friends that I'm in contact with. I'm truly blessed to have so many friends and I can stay with them if I choose.

"My schooling is financed by grants and sometimes when I need it, I'll take out a student loan. I have a 3.0 grade this semester. It's given me some confidence. I will major in communications – I enjoy writing. I have a job offer in Colorado when I get my degree. It sounds good but I'm not really sure about it yet. I'd like to go on to graduate school and become a professor. I'd really like to do that. I'll likely stay in Santa Barbara for a time.

"I had several big questions of Jeneal. Her explanation as to why she relinquished me was that she was too young. I would like to have children some day but I'm not ready now. I can understand why she felt that she could not care for me. I have very strong and loving feelings for her. This experience has been very healing for everyone. I appreciate the work you did in putting me and Jeneal together. It was a long time in coming, but I think everyone came out okay in the end."

A Big Family

Amanda:

"I always knew I was adopted. I had two friends who were adopted so I didn't feel insecure about it. I never felt different, strange or awkward to say, 'Oh, I'm adopted.' I was just one of many. One day the agency called to say they had another baby for my parents. They thought that she would be just perfect because the birth mother and Mom look a lot alike. Today they do look a bit similar to each other.

"I have one adopted sister and there's one birth child – a boy. My sister and I had conflicts. She was very different – a real challenge for my parents to raise, very vocal and physical. They had to spend a lot of time with her. So my brother and I got to be very close and developed a special bond. They treated all of us the same.

"I became curious in my teen years and asked if they knew anything about my birth parents. They told me that she was young, unmarried, and still in school. She did not feel that it was in my best interest to keep me so to place me was an act of love. I first thought of doing a search when I was pregnant with my second child. My sister found her birth mother when she was eighteen and that was a very traumatic event for our family because of the way she handled it. She did it secretively. Then one day she said, 'Oh, Mom, by the way, I'm going to be on the television show, Fantasy, because I found my birth parents.' It took us by surprise. She learned she had a full-blooded sister and brother. The reunion on that show was really glamorized in a sense. Any time after that when she had a conflict with my parents she would say, 'Oh, I'll go live with my real parents.' As she learned more about the biological family she appreciated my parents so much more and realized the kind of life she might have had as compared to the life they had provided. It was awesome to go through it. She really mellowed and matured.

"When this little search buzz came into my head, I was very reluctant after seeing the hurt my sister had put our parents through. I didn't want to cause them another painful situation. I didn't ask them about it. When I got pregnant with my first child, I'd go to the doctor and they'd ask about my family health history – I didn't know. I only knew my husband's family history. It became apparent that I needed to get that information. Maybe if I just find my birth mom and don't meet her it would be okay. So I called the agency and got a little information from them. They said that thirty years ago they got very little medical information so it would not likely be too helpful. One day my dad asked if I had ever thought of searching for my parents. I told him that I had called the agency just to make an inquiry and they didn't have much to say. I asked how they would feel if I did look for my birth parents. They said if I thought it was something I really needed to do, they would totally support me.

"I made no attempts to search on my own. I called the agency again. They gave me your name and you told me about the CIP.

"When I first met Georgia, I was a little apprehensive. We had talked on the phone a couple of times. I wanted to meet her and found that we both lived in the valley, so it would not be a big deal to meet. It was the uncertainty of not knowing what to expect. Wondering – oh, did I get my crooked nose from her, little facial things and physical features? Do I look like her or like my birth father? Uncertainty, apprehension, excitement – it was just a bunch of emotions but I was definitely looking forward to it. Scared.

"Now we talk every two to four weeks. It varies, depending on whether I am consumed with my kids and the activities that I am involved in. I haven't seen her in a while. She waits for me to make contact. I wish she'd call me more than she does. I think she respects where I am and doesn't want to bother me and it works both ways. We see each other about every two months. She and her parents have come to my kids' birthday parties and other events we've had and that's okay with my parents. I think the first couple of times it was a little awkward. The only involvement she has with my adoptive parents is for special events. They were excited and relieved to see that she was a very normal person and a nice lady. We were excited to meet her mom and dad. They live in the valley as well. They are very down to earth. For me it confirmed why I am so normal. I was raised in a normal environment and my birth family was very normal, everyday people. I have also met her brothers and sisters.

"I have three children and one on the way. I feel closer to my adoptive family than my birth family. The reason for my search was primarily for the medical history. But the more I thought about it and prayed about it, I felt that I wanted to thank her for giving me such an incredible opportunity to have such a good life and reassure her that she made the right choice in giving me up and thank her for giving me all the opportunities I have had.

"I am definitely glad I did the search and would surely do it again. I would encourage adopted children to look. I feel like it completes the puzzle and fills in all the blanks that you have wondered about all your life. It really does complete you as a person. It gives you fullness that makes up for the missing link that adopted children have as they grow up. My parents gave me every opportunity and I have been fairly successful in what I have chosen to do. I went to college. I was a teacher for nine years, got my master's degree in education and followed in my mom's footsteps. We actually have a lot of teachers in our family. I hope this book reaches out to people who are in my situation and encourages them to do a search as well."

Georgia, Amanda's birth mother:
"I planned for the first eight months to keep the baby that I was expecting. However, I am not a particularly maternal person, in spite of the fact that all my life I had planned to marry and have three kids. In the last month of my pregnancy, my parents and my doctor convinced me that I should place the baby for adoption so it would have the security and stability of two parents and a financial situation that would allow her many opportunities. I did finally see that's what would be best for the baby, so I made arrangements with the agency to place her for adoption. I admit off and on I've had some regrets about it, but I know that it was the right thing to do.

"Amanda always checks with her adoptive mother before she invites me to any family function. She wants to make sure that her mom will be comfortable with my being there. She often invites my mom and dad as well. I think that's excellent. She is a very thoughtful young woman. I was seventeen when I got pregnant and turned eighteen nine days before Amanda was born. I had a hysterectomy when I was twenty-three, so I never had more children. That is one of the reasons that it was so special when I heard from her. I married for a short time at twenty and divorced when I was twenty-one. We were together about eleven months. I haven't been seriously involved since. I did have a private investigator try to find Amanda's birth father. He succeeded, but I never made contact with him. I managed to get a picture of him from his high school yearbook. She has a lot of his features.

"Amanda was thirty-four when she found me. One of the first things that happens when you place a child for adoption is that you really don't expect to hear from them until they are at least eighteen and then when you don't hear by twenty-five, you think you won't ever hear from them and you don't know if they are alive or well or whether they got hooked on drugs, disease, killed in a car wreck. There is so much unknown – you always wonder and spend a fair amount of time thinking about that little girl. It was so good to know that she was alive and well. I figured her parents had told her she was adopted so you think they have no desire to know who you are – then you think maybe they're no longer living which is a little scary.

"We met the week after you called. Right after you called I went over to tell Mom and Dad. I wanted to make sure they knew what was going on and they were all right with it. I had two brothers who never knew that I was pregnant. I wanted them to find out from me. I talked with both of them before I met Amanda. They took it very well. They and my two sisters have now met her and her kids. She knows my whole family, and I have met all of hers and her husband's family. It gives me such a wonderful feeling. Her mom loves her so much. It gives me a lot of comfort. She is a lovely person, so is her dad and in-laws.

"We met on the fourth of July and spent about three hours together. We both had a lot of questions. When she was expecting her third child, she told her daughter that I carried her inside my belly. It upsets her so much that I don't have any babies in this big house that I live in. Her daughter was two then and she was upset that I don't have a husband. She's a sensitive girl.

"Amanda and the children call me Georgia, never Mom or Grandma. I think her mother gains comfort with time in her relationship with me. I think she was initially nervous about it. But my mom, Amanda and her mom met for lunch one day shortly after I first met her. Her mother brought a rose for me and my mom. I thought that was a precious thing to do. I am just not a maternal person so I am no threat to her. Presently, we talk and E-mail. I haven't seen her now for a couple of months. I usually wait for her to call me. She is very busy with her little girls – one in private school, another in preschool and then a two-year-old at home. One daughter has tennis and golf lessons and another has dance lessons. They are also busy in the church, with their parents. At times I go over and baby-sit the kids while she plays golf or something. Or I'll meet them and we will go to dinner. Baby-sitting is a bit intimidating because I've never spent much time around children. I love them dearly, but they sometimes make me a little nervous. I have no experience. They give me hugs and loves. I always bring them bubble gum and goldfish.

"This reunion really satisfied my curiosity because not knowing was very tormenting. It undid the knot in my stomach. It was so enjoyable to meet her mom and dad and see what responsible care she's had. She has always been secure and has had lots of opportunities in life. She and her husband are wonderful parents, too, and they enjoy parenthood. All in all, the reunion has given me a lot of comfort about the decision I made, and knowing what I know now, I think I would be okay doing it again. If I had kept her, I think I would have stood a better chance of getting married as I would have put more effort into finding someone so she'd have a father to help raise her. I'd have had more of a desire to settle down and raise a family. It has been so nice that Amanda and her family have accepted me and my family into their lives. It has added an unbelievable amount to my life.

"Another thing – most of my friends knew nothing about Amanda and they were shocked. They couldn't believe I could keep something like that a secret. It was one of those things that were not talked about in those days. But I truly have come out of the closet. Shortly after we met, Amanda thanked me for not having an abortion and giving her life. I kinda chuckled and told her that abortion was not really an option back in those days. It's hard for someone of her generation to understand how different it was to be pregnant and not married then. My hysterectomy changed my goals – I just wanted to be successful at my job, so I think I became emotionally distant at that point. It really changed my personality. I get a lot of vicarious satisfaction out of observing Amanda with her family. She is living my dream. The nicest thing that ever happened to me was your (Shirley) calling me a couple of years ago to tell me about her."

Jewel, Amanda's adoptive mother:

"Amanda is very different from my other daughter, Sandy, who is three years older. Sandy is a wonderful girl, I love her dearly, but she was hard to raise. Maybe that is why Amanda turned out so well because it seemed that she was on her own while we were trying to get this one kid straightened out.

"We adopted because of a medical problem. I had diabetes and I had a lot of trouble in my pregnancy with our son. They said that there are a lot of babies out there and suggested we adopt. I had written a report on adoption in high school so I knew about it. I felt that it really didn't matter. So we made the decision to adopt. Our first girl is three years younger than our boy. We read books on adoption and started out early talking with her about it. We told people that this was our beautiful adopted daughter and we used the word quite often when she was a baby. As she got older we decided that it was better to read the book – with Amanda we didn't do that. We just didn't care if she knew she was adopted. She was just our daughter.

"We adopted another girl so they would have something in common and could be buddies. I was comfortable using the word adoption, but it wasn't a word that we felt was necessary to use often. We told them that they grew inside someone else and that person, for some reason, couldn't take care of them so they made arrangements for us to be their parents. That was the end of the story. I don't remember there being questions until they got older.

"Sandy began talking about finding her birth mother. Someone told her that she could be on TV if she wrote a letter to the program when she did. She found her through ISRR, wrote a letter and was on national television. It made me cry because I was not ready for it. There she was on TV with this person she had already met. Isn't it strange that they don't talk about the mother who raised her. It's all about the birth mother. That bugs me. There was an article in the paper about her and they asked me if I wanted to be included in the article and I said, 'No way, I want nothing to do with it!' However, I have had her family here. They came because she was going to get married. The wedding didn't come off but they came anyway.

"That part of it I've kinda gotten over, so when Amanda said, after her second child was born that she really needed to know something about her background, I told her that she needed to look. She went about it in a much different way. She consulted with me and I said okay, but there was still some hurt there, too. (Crying) I felt she needed to do it. It was important to learn the medical history. Georgia and her mom and dad are certainly nice people. They are a lot different from Sandy's family. They are just like us. But still you have the feeling that, oh, dear, there's that other person. I'd invested all these years and, wait a minute, they want to find another mother? I have friends who are adopted and they've said it never occurred to them to look for another family. They don't want another family. My girls are not that way. Why not? Wasn't I a good mother?

"With Sandy, I felt that it needed to be done. With Amanda, it was entirely different. She is a very loving and kind person. She doesn't know that my feelings were hurt when she decided to search. (Crying) You know what? Those people are always at every birthday party. There was one thing that happened that really hurt my feelings and I have told Amanda about it. Amanda's mother-in-law, who is a good friend, saw Georgia and her mother with one of the children and said, 'Oh, that would make a nice picture, I'll get a picture of the grandmas.' I thought, 'Wait a minute, I'm the grandma.' She didn't realize that I was standing right behind her. Anyway, I thought Grandma was a name that was earned. It just bugged me to death. My sister and niece were both surprised by it. There are just little things that happen that you don't expect and you are taken aback.

"When we adopted Amanda they wanted it to be an open adoption, but I didn't want to know. I feared that they would take this baby away from us. From that time on if an older person paid any attention to Amanda, I would quickly go the other way because I was fearful that they might be some birth relative. They could be grandparents of the child. Under these circumstances you feel you don't own exclusive right to motherhood or grandma-hood. We are a very close family and have different time invested in the child. I did get over it.

"The kids are aware that Amanda is adopted. They must know that Georgia is the one who carried their mom. Her oldest child said to me, 'Now Grandma, you didn't carry mom in your tummy.' This pregnancy is a big deal with them as she is expecting their fourth child. They have asked me questions about adopting and I told them about the day we went to get her and then took her to each of the grandparents' homes so they could see her. It was exciting and if they ever wanted to consider adoption they should not shy away from it as it is really a neat experience. It is a different way that babies get into families. The only drawback is when they decide they want to find their birth family.

"I never have direct contact with Georgia. She is such a nice person and I can understand why it is important to know Amanda and her children.

"My two girls were not close growing up, but they are very close now. I really don't feel that I have lost anything as a result of these reunions except exclusive ownership of motherhood and grandmotherhood. I was just so naive when we adopted. Amanda is like me in the way she talks and uses her hands, but she is more outgoing. Anyone seeing us together would surely say we are mother and daughter. They would say the same thing if they saw her with Georgia. When you adopt you should be willing to accept all the birth relatives."

Ann and Elaine

Ann, the birth mother:

"I was nineteen when I got pregnant. We had just moved and my dad couldn't find work except as a bus driver for very low pay. It was like they were just starting their lives over. I felt very insecure – that they would end up raising the baby and I would have to get a job to support her. In talking with the lawyer, he said that the adoptive family was very nice and they were quite well off. It was so long ago and I was so young.

"After I placed her for adoption, I had some regrets. At first I wasn't sure I had done the right thing. As time went by, it didn't hurt as much. They say time heals. I would think about her every spring and wonder what she was doing. It was such a final thing and I thought I would never see her again. So it was very hard.

"When Craig and I got married our first baby had some serious problems and they had to induce labor when I was eight months along and we lost her. I thought this was punishment for giving up the other child. There was a lot of mental anxiety. That was my first bout with true depression. I didn't get to see our first baby and didn't get to hold Elaine before I gave her up so I lost two babies.

"However, it was not long before our next daughter was born. She was very healthy. It was like a miracle. Five years later another healthy girl was born to us. I was very protective of these two.

"Since you first contacted me, we have had some hard times. My husband became addicted to pain pills due to a wrist problem and this caused a personality change. I asked him to move out about seven months ago. I still love him very much and hope for a reconciliation. My mother and my brother both have died in the last year as a result of heart problems. When my mom got sick, my family moved in with Mom and Dad and we are still there. I think things will eventually work out and we will get back to normal if there is such a thing!

"I was so happy when you contacted me to tell me that Elaine wanted to meet me. I was shocked, excited, had lots of mixed feelings and wondered what she would be like. We exchanged letters first. She sounded quite spiritual and said she had no hard feelings. She had tried to put herself in my shoes. I thought a contact would be appealing. I could tell she had a warm heart. Our next contact was by phone – a four-hour conversation. Then we met at a restaurant. She is so outgoing and easy to talk with. We hit it off immediately. We just kept looking at each other and she would say how much her eyes were like mine. We compared notes – likes and dislikes. She is very sensitive and sentimental – that is Elaine all the way. I told my girls about Elaine about a week before I met with her. I let them read Elaine's letter to me. They were shocked – I could see it in their faces. Sherrie, the older one, started crying, was very emotional, but they were very happy for me. No more secrets. They both were very excited and Craig was happy for me also. He had known about it before we got married – I wanted to be totally honest with him. At that time everything was so secretive. Basically, you assumed that you would never see the child again.

"When Mom and Dad heard about Elaine wanting to make contact, they were so excited and happy. Mom was so emotional. She told Elaine that she was like a little angel when she saw her at the hospital through the window. She prayed every day that things would work out for her. Elaine became very attached to my mom and she just wanted to spend time with her. They bonded right away. She misses her a lot. My dad loves it when she comes over. Recently we all got together and went to dinner. We were celebrating Elaine's son's ninth birthday. Her adoptive parents were there, and her brother and sister-in-law, who adopted a little girl from Russia. They are like our extended family. Her parents always give me a hug when they see me. It seems it has come a complete circle and this is like a new beginning. Elaine is eleven years older than my daughter, Sherrie, so she is more like a sister to me. Her adoptive mother has told her that since she and her husband are older, she is glad that I will be here for her."

Shirley: Elaine, too, had some very difficult times soon after I was in touch with her. She had been with her boy friend for some time, thinking that it would result in a permanent commitment, but he kept stalling and about a year ago he left Elaine. She was devastated! They had enjoyed such a comfortable relationship so this was a total shock. He was a good cook and she had gained a lot of weight.

Elaine says:

"When, at the age of 6, my parents told me that I was adopted, I definitely felt different from others. I was a bit sad, but I was afraid to show that to my parents because they let me know I was special. I think that I was rather clingy with my mom for a while. I remember having tears in my eyes, but I didn't want them to know that I felt sad. I think I was afraid I was going to lose another mother. I tried to believe I was special, but deep down I was scared.

"They gave me a book, 'Why Was I Adopted?' It had illustrations. It was always a special book to me. It kinda helped lighten the load of knowing I was adopted. It combined wit and seriousness. They seemed comfortable talking about my adoption and seemed mostly concerned about my feelings. They wanted to tell me at a young age before anyone else told me as they knew that eventually it would come back to me.

"I have a brother, six years older, who is a birth child. Right after they told me I felt different from him, but I lost that feeling soon. I wondered if I am special, then what does it mean he is? But he is so special, too. I was sad that he came from our mom's tummy and I came from the tummy of another lady. Still, I would tell my friends I was special because I was adopted and they would tease me. As you get older and people find out you're adopted, they really think it is cool. I always wanted to be close to my brother. We did a lot of things together. He always took me trick-or-treating. We'd wrestle around, too. Now he's rather quiet, a lot like my dad. I wanted to be close to my dad, too – closer than he would allow. I know he loved me, but he is just not a very open person. I always felt that I loved him more than he loved me.

"All through my life I was asking questions about my background. For some reason, I felt they knew more than they were telling me. Then every year, they had a little bit more to tell me.

Maybe it was just that they told me as they remembered it. I wondered if there might be some secret things about my background. They always told me what they felt was true – kind of 'happily ever after' thing. They said that my birth parents were too young – just kids – and were not ready to raise a child. It was depicted as an act of love. But, you know, I was very special – it wasn't that I was given up, but I was lucky enough to be picked by them. When I was curious, I was cautious for fear of hurting their feelings. When I asked questions, my mom was very encouraging, but Dad was not as open.

"When I was 16, I became depressed and Mom suggested that maybe we should find my birth mom. I thought maybe sometime. Then when I turned eighteen, I became suicidal. She wanted to help, so later she found you (Shirley) and said that we really did need to do a search. I agreed for curiosity's sake. I also felt that I should find out my health history. I think that the depression was a result of my not taking my medicine and after I had my child, I had postpartum depression and from then on I knew I could not go without it. It is hard, it is actually a disease. Society doesn't accept it and so I have a hard time accepting it. I have been taking the medicine for nine years. From sixteen, it was on and off. I've seen different psychiatrists and found one that I really liked. He died two years ago. It was like someone else deserted me.

"I was hoping to find some answers when I met my birth mother, Ann, and possibly learn that depression runs in our family. But instead, that fact was denied. Possibly Ann felt that I was trying to point a finger. I have no desire to blame. I wanted to find out if this is a familial thing. It evidently doesn't run in her side of the family. There have been some suicides, but that is four generations back. My two half sisters have had to take anti-depressants. It may be from her husband's side of the family.

"I have never searched for my birth father and that is because I feel inadequate. That is really stupid, but I am very heavy now. I do have a pretty face, but I am almost a hundred pounds overweight. It is so embarrassing for me, since Ann is so petite. Her daughters are small, too.

"When I had my first contact with Ann, I was excited. I could not wait to see if her eyes were like mine and if we looked like each other. Then I wanted to know how it all happened and basically it was exactly like I had thought. I felt like I had known her all along. She was like a sister, a close sister and I could tell her anything. It was one of the things that I had fantasized about since my parents were so much older. They were forty when they adopted me. Everything flowed with Ann – we felt so comfortable with each other. Our relationship grows stronger every day. We have had a lot of comparisons. I would like to have a closer relationship with her daughters. The older one and I click, but she is so much younger than I am. Ann is so grateful to my parents for the way they raised me. My mom always says that I am her daughter and there is no thanking that has to be done. I think she has had some jealousy and hurt, but she seems to be more comfortable with the time that I spend with Ann now.

"I have met a lot of Ann's relatives. I was embarrassed because it was almost like I was a movie star. She showed me to everybody. It had always been a goal of mine to find my birth mom. I think the birth father's dad wanted her to have an abortion. The birth father had another girl friend. He was out of the picture. When she was depressed after the relinquishment, her mom told her that maybe they could do something to get me back. But there was nothing they could do."

Dana, the adoptive mother:
"My pediatrician told me that we should explain adoption to her when she was seven. We tried, but didn't get the right message across – she told the little boy across the street that she was an orphan. I told her that her real mother was a beautiful woman and the doctor said that she looked just like her. Then she never really asked any questions until she was a teenager. She had some friends who committed suicide and that was the beginning of her depression. She ran away a week later. It still is traumatic for her. The depression has lasted since then. She has been in and out of the hospital for different things. You would never believe what a challenge it has been for us. The split with her fiancé has not helped at all. She was in the hospital when her son had his first birthday – this was the remnant of her postpartum depression. She was three months pregnant when she married and divorced after two years.

"We were really anxious to find out why she was so prone to depression. That's why I contacted you (Shirley) to see if we could find the birth parents and find out if it ran in the family. I was very comfortable in initiating the search. When Ann was actually found, I felt a bit threatened. I am old enough that Ann could be one of my kids. Still I was happy because maybe now Elaine could get well. It was a bundle of mixed feelings. Then we really weren't able to learn if it did run in the family.

"When her son had his birthday, Grandma Ann came and it is just something that is there all the time. It's sometimes a little uncomfortable, but God puts us in a position where lots of people can love us and we cannot have too many people love us in different ways. Elaine never calls Ann Mother. That is her friend Ann. Her son has so many grandmas, he doesn't know what to do with all of them. He told me that he didn't like all these grandmas and that I am his favorite. So he is still my boy. The only contact I have with Ann and her family is at family affairs. We don't make contact on our own. She gives me a hug at the parties and thanks me for taking such good care of her daughter. I know she means well. Her mom used to call Elaine her little angel. Elaine still has a slight feeling of being abandoned. "I don't think I have lost anything as a result of this reunion. I'm glad I did the search and would do it again. God wants us to be loved by a lot of people. I do think it has helped Elaine mature. She has settled down quite a bit. A lot of the questions she had have been answered and she has mellowed out a bit. My brother who died a while ago had two adopted children and he didn't want me to tell them that we had found Elaine's birth mother... isn't that something?

"Elaine calls me every day. She tells me that she feels better after we have talked. She is also close to her father. He'd do anything for her. Her birth father is right here in town and yet she has not shown any interest in searching for him. Ann gave her a picture of him and they look so much alike. Elaine says that she doesn't want to disrupt his life. I think he has been married two or three times. She named her son after her dad. She adores him and he adores her."

Eric

"Being adopted made me feel special because my parents gave me lots of attention. They often read a book to me, 'The Chosen Child.' It was about welcoming a new baby into the family. I felt that they really did choose me. I don't recall ever having any feeling of animosity. They used the term biological mother or father when they talked about my birth parents. They approached the whole topic with confidence and I don't think they had any problem with it. I have a sister, twenty-one months younger, who was also adopted. We have a fantastic relationship. We get along quite well – at least we do now. We fought back and forth as we were growing up. Actually, she and her child live with us now. She was in the hospital after the birth just a month ago and she was unable to work the last three months of her pregnancy. She was on sick leave. So rather than her having to pay rent and other bills, we offered her the chance to stay here. She could then save money and prepare to be on her own. The father? He lives elsewhere. They are having problems. I try to help her but not interfere by doing things that won't be good for her in the long run.

"My adoptive parents didn't have any birth children, so they chose to adopt. I started asking questions when I was about five. One of my questions was, 'How much did I cost?' It was twelve hundred dollars. My sister ended up costing twice as much. But by that time there were new laws and it was more difficult to adopt. They told me that my birth mother gave me up so I could be placed with a family who could provide well for me and give me more stability. I felt that she thought more of me by giving me up than she would have if she had kept me. I have a birth sibling from the same mother and father. We have a good relationship and we are pretty much alike. It is amazing to me. I met her when I went to pick her up at her house and didn't realize that my birth mother was staying there. There are a lot of interesting quirks about it. I have a relationship with her and with my birth father, but no relationship with my birth mother.

"I know that my birth father had approached her when he decided to search for me and asked if she would like to take part in the process. He had waited until my birth sibling was older because he wanted me to know that I had a blood line sister, and wanted her to be of age. Later, my sister found me. It was all very interesting. That was about two and a half years ago. My sister told my mom that she had met me and explained to her that I have no ill feelings at all. I would like to tell her, 'Thank you!' I think she has seen a picture of me. Right now, for unknown reasons she has no interest in meeting me. It is frustrating because I don't have any negative feelings about it and would love to meet her and have whatever relationship possible. She may have a weird feeling and I might be able to heal that. She needn't have any sense of guilt because of me. I have been 100% happy with my life and it could have been the exact opposite. My adoptive parents are fantastic and I have somewhat of a relationship with my bio father. I have slightly backed away from it – not consciously, but it has grown distant. I owe him a phone call as I have not been in touch with him for a while. The longer it goes the harder it is to call. He has done his part in maintaining the relationship. He tees me off a bit, but it's nothing that's unbearable. Sometimes we don't click on the way we see things. I hold no grudges of any kind against him. Nor do I want to stay distant from him. Probably it was partly because I have been very busy. I have knowledge about half of my bio family, but no knowledge of the other half.

"I am three-fourths financially independent right now. I pay my rent, car payments and try to do as good as I can. I am getting some help from my parents. We do okay. My parents were as interested as I was when you (Shirley) located me for Hugh (birth father who did the search for Eric). I was really curious. I had always wondered what he looked like, what he was about, but at the same time I left it all up to him to find me if he wanted to. I had normal curiosity and think my parents did, too. They just waited for me to take the reins. They had always told me that they would be supportive if I ever wanted to search. In the transition of my girl friend becoming pregnant and my becoming a father, I felt that I understood a little more why they made the decision. We aren't married, but have been together for four and a half years. We see marriage in the eyes of God and not necessarily in the eyes of the law. Although there are common law marriage laws that apply.

"We absolutely never considered adoption when she got pregnant. It is wonderful being a father. He is the pride and joy of my life. He is two years, four months. He stays up unbelievable hours and does everything a two-year-old does. He is very hyper. My adoptive father says I am going to have an easy ride with him. He is nowhere near as active as I was as a kid. I was extremely hyperactive and had a lot of anger issues. Don't know what I was angry about – probably all due to what happened before I was born. I had Fetal Alcohol Syndrome when I was born. I took medications as a child – now I don't take any meds. I was considered to have ADHD (attention deficit hyperactivity disorder.) The FAS shows up in some of my behavior tendencies and size wise. I don't believe what doctors have told me throughout my life – medical or psychiatric. I have my own theories and am a big advocate for herbal meds, etc. I, like others, have had challenges. I had the notion that I was this totally unique guy in the world, really special, etc. Now I know that Hugh (birth father) and I are a lot alike. He showed me a picture of him at my age and we look identical. There was a lot of comfort in finding someone I looked like. When I was growing up, I always had a unique personality. Now to see a part of my history and my family is a real comfort for sure. Just to get some medical knowledge and learn what these people are like was great.

"We were living in real difficult circumstances in Missouri when Hugh came to meet me. It was a magical scenario. We got to know each other – very enjoyable. He took me by storm. He is very successful, articulate, and a great guy all the way around. I like him. He is an intimidating kind of fellow and that's part of my hesitation in calling him. We don't have the deep-hug type of connection, but we try to have a deep relationship. A lot of times I feel that he doesn't want to take part in it, and vice versa. Sometimes it is like we are being aesthetically nice to each other, but there is really no feeling of connection. There are little traits that I can relate to, but Hugh is Hugh and I am me and we travel different paths.

"We need to define our relationship. I recognized him immediately. He was good looking, healthy, and had an Arizona look. I haven't talked to him in over a month and that is by my choice in not calling him. I'm sure I'll be calling him pretty soon. He's met my folks and talked with them a few times. Don't know that they really want a deep relationship – probably not needed. I have met his mother, sister and brother as well as others. I really like them all. I'm very glad that I had this reunion. It's like some huge fairy tale – my biological father comes and finds me and then to find out I have a biological sister. He and my birth mother never really got together. When she conceived me, he didn't know about the adoption plan until she went to the agency. They didn't have a relationship and yet have two children together. She waited until the other child was nine before she called to let him know about her. This is the reality that is my life and it has always been extreme – either positive or negative. I prefer traveling around to the stability that I have now. My life moves so fast and I would like to just focus on my passions and creative interests. I feel that I am doing what is right and comfortable with my wife and I can abide the stability and taking care of my family. I traveled around for ten years on foot. We are going to stick around for a few years and see what we can do. We have some future goals."

Hugh, the birth father:

"I went back to Missouri to meet Eric right after you found him for me. We have had contact off and on for several years, but Eric has never been the aggressor. The last time I saw him was at a birthday party about four months ago. Eric and his girl friend moved back to the valley because she got pregnant. His adoptive parents had a home that they rented out. It was very run down. I'm a homebuilder and I made sure it was okay with his parents to fix it up. They were very good about the whole thing. I had the capability and the manpower to do it at a very fair price so, at my expense, I went ahead and gutted it and set it up in a manner that would be a nice place for him as his own. The baby was born and he is working as a waiter, probably still on drugs.

"I signed the adoption papers when he was born. I hadn't really known that she was pregnant. I was only nineteen. Actually, she told me she was going to have an abortion – then I got the phone call nine months later indicating that she'd had the child. She said that she wanted to place him for adoption and I had just a few hours to go to the hospital and sign the papers. I wanted to see him to see if he looked like me. I didn't know what my options were and I'm not sure I would have chosen any differently. I never regretted that he was placed for adoption, but I always wondered about him. He was on my mind a lot. As I got older my wondering about him got more frequent. I was in touch with the birth mother until about five years ago. She never had any interest in searching. She opposed my searching and didn't want to have anything to do with it so I made my own choice.

"Eric was twenty-five when we met. I first thought of doing a search when he was much younger, but I didn't think that was correct morally or legally. I got a lot of support from others with whom I had shared curiosity. When he was fifteen, I went to the agency and got non-identifying information about the family. At that time I also put updated information about me in the file so if he ever came looking. Then I waited until he was twenty-five before I initiated the search. When he was twenty-one, I tried to enroll the mother in the process because he has a full sister and I wanted to explain that to him. I also wanted him to know about her other children, who would be half-siblings. I have had one other child. I didn't help raise her because I didn't know she existed until she was twelve. She expressed curiosity about him so they now know each other. I wanted them to know that they had a biological sibling. They are now in communication but I don't know about their present relationship. My relationship with Eric is a bit strained now. He's not responsive to my communications and there is little attempt on his part to be involved. It had been good for the first few years. The last time we were together, everything seemed very good – hunky-dory. I have called several times and left messages and have stopped by on a number of occasions but there has been no response. I let him know I was always available if he ever wanted to pick it up again. I know he has to make his own choices. I have a separate college fund set up for him. I always leave presents on their birthdays.

"I am in touch with his parents periodically so I keep up on him that way. They have been very supportive of the relationship – right from the start. His adoptive sister is living with Eric and his family presently. It has been a while since I've been in touch with the adoptive parents. I contact them when I want to know that all is well with Eric whether or not he continued to have a relationship with me. At one point he was in trouble with the law – he was caught with some pot. They were afraid that he might lose the child. He did clean up his act. I was concerned, too – after all that is my grandson. I did set up some DNA tests to make sure that my daughter and he were full siblings. They were indeed 100% related. Eric is in my will. I am trying to do the right thing. The adoptive parents have sent me a card asking me not to give up on Eric. I haven't, I'm just trying to give him some space to grow.

"There is money for my daughter's college, too. I have told Eric's parents that I would support them 100% in anything he wanted to get into educationally, but I gave him a time line to motivate him. Nothing has been done yet. It has been a real disappointment. His parents know about all of my offers and they are very happy that I have a plan set up for the baby, too. I've set it up so they can contribute to it as well. They were afraid that Eric might take it to buy drugs.

"The first time I saw Eric, we hugged each other. I was looking forward to seeing him. He is a very smart kid. It was a rather crushing experience. He was living on the floor of an abandoned crack house or something. Total squalor. He had a commune type of mentality. It was awkward, but we went out to a few different places for the day. I still think his parents did the best they could. We all have our issues. The mother was well educated and they are still together as a family unit. I think they tried to do everything and provide all the right things for him. I think the environment was good. No one is to blame. If he'd just stay in touch with me, but I don't like always chasing him. For Christmas, I gave him one of my computers in hopes that he would use the E-mail. I got him an answering machine so he could keep in touch with people who are important in his life. But he has still pulled away for some reason. I had hoped that he would have some motivation for contact. I can't beat myself up for the choices he makes. I feel that I have done all I can do. I haven't given up, but would just like him to come full circle. Since his parents are such responsible people, I have comfort about the adoption decision. I don't think I'd have ever opted against it. I am forty-nine now – life goes by so quickly."

Claire, the adoptive mother:

"Although we talked about adoption very openly in our home from the beginning, I think Eric realized the whole process when he was about seven. Our daughter, Eric's younger adopted sister, never let on that she knew. Eric was always asking questions. He referred to his birth parents as his adoptive parents. He wanted to know when they were going to come to get him. He always thought he would open up the door one day and they would be standing there – as early as the age of four. Don't know if he was fearful or looking forward to it. He wanted to know if his father was a prince and if he owned an oil well. That came from the fact that he was part Syrian and he realized it was in the middle east and that is where the oil wells are. He wanted to know if they were rich. He was convinced that they were. It didn't occur to him that it would be incongruous that even though they were rich, they would give him up. He never asked anything that made me feel uncomfortable because his questions were so adult-like. They were very deep and made us smile. They were very thought provoking. It seemed the more open and comfortable we were, the more relaxed the kids were, too. Sometimes they would bring friends home and we would have to explain what adoption was to the friends.

"Eric was like the dream child until the fifth grade. He was in the gifted program from first grade and then the school system decided to put them in with the others. Everyone that they funneled back started to have behavior problems. They were not challenged. Eric didn't know what to do in a situation like that. First, he became the class clown. Then the class genius. One day he stood up in front of the class and announced that he was a slot machine and swallowed a whole handful of coins. He became a juvenile delinquent. He got into drug problems. He tried marijuana and his personality changed completely. At thirteen, he got to the point where his hormones went absolutely crazy and he actually attacked me and tried to strangle me. Oh, I had quite a few experiences like that, but I think it was primarily because he had ADHD (attention deficit hyperactive disorder). A lot of the acting out happened when his father was out of town, and I couldn't control him, typical of an ADHD child.

"We have a joke in our house and say, 'And we paid for this? Are we crazy?' We thought if we had been able to have children ourselves, this probably wouldn't have happened. It was and still is a challenge. Eric has a hard time holding a job. We practically pay for his total existence. If we didn't, he would likely be okay. He's a survivor. For seven years he hit the road and lived like a hippie. We told him that if he wanted to come back here he'd have to earn the money. Then his girl friend got pregnant – that puts a whole different light on it when there is a grandchild involved. They never considered placing the child for adoption. We all went to a counselor. He thinks Eric is bipolar. His ADHD was not diagnosed until he was sixteen and it is very difficult to get a teenager to take medicine that he doesn't want. He has never really accepted that he was ADHD. He's still not on medication. I have to admit that when someone comes to me and talks about adoption I say, 'Nuts!'

"Now we are having our challenges with our daughter. She just had a baby out-of-wedlock with an African-American man and they are living with Eric and his girl friend. He's not working. He's six years younger than she – twenty-five and nineteen. It's a bad situation. One would think we'd ask ourselves why we adopted, but we don't. We love our kids so much. After everything, we love them unconditionally. That is what makes it so hard. If we didn't care, it wouldn't hurt so much. My husband has a tremendous sense of responsibility. We took it on and probably feel more responsible because of the paper we signed. It's kind of like 'til death do you part. We have that feeling. I know some parents with birth children who have the same problems would say, 'Screw you.' I think we take on too much responsibility. I do think he really cares for his girl friend and his baby. He does provide food and up-keep – but he never finishes anything. He just can't seem to hold a job. Sometimes he sells drugs. That's his solution. So now we have grandchildren and we are supporting them, too. It's a nightmare.

"We gave the children all the information that we had been given. When you (Shirley) called here to try to contact him, I felt that our privacy had been invaded. It was uncomfortable, even though we had always wanted our kids to know. Now I think it has had a positive effect on Eric. I think it has helped him figure out who he is. We have an open relationship with Hugh. We like him a lot. He and my husband have worked together to fix up our house for Eric to live in. In fact, Hugh invested a lot of money in our house. He probably wanted to give Eric every advantage he could. He was too smart to give him cash. He calls us every now and then for an update on Eric. Hugh has a lot of expectations of Eric. He is a high achiever himself. My husband has high expectations, too, but Hugh expects him to be normal. We have a realistic awareness of his potential. Maybe we are indulging him too much. That has been my thought all along. I had thought that Hugh would be a good influence on him, but maybe we are all enabling him. With his ADHD, Eric just cannot live up to Hugh's expectations.

"Of course, Eric has not met his birth mother and he would like to. His full sister still lives with the mother who says she wants nothing to do with him. The sister didn't tell her mother when she had contact with Eric. If we ever had a wedding in our house it would be a miracle. We tell our kids that we bring new meaning to the word flexible. Our kids have given us a real challenge. I don't know if it is because they were adopted. It seems that they have always been doing things to see if we would still love them. They would do something and ask, 'Do you love me now?' What do we have to do – nail ourselves to a cross? I told Eric that we showed up in court more times than he did – ha ha.

"I have to admit I felt I had lost something as a result of Eric's reunion with Hugh. He wanted them to be with him at Christmas and other holidays and I wasn't used to that. I'm saying this because it was his father who found Eric. I don't know how I would feel if the mother had found him. Still, my husband thinks it is wonderful. He points out that Eric has another father and he could use some help. He thinks maybe Hugh can get through to Eric in places he can't. Eric didn't even call Hugh on this Father's Day. The first Father's Day after they met I felt sorry for Eric because he didn't know what to do. Hugh had offered to pay for school for Eric but I think the time limit just ran out. He wanted to go to culinary school, but decided he could not go to school and provide for his family. We told him we would take care of the bills for the two years he'd be in school, but he didn't go. I feel bad that he and Hugh are not communicating. When you see them together they have similar personality traits. They are always in motion – fun to see them together. I told Eric that Hugh still has a right to see his grandson. Eric really enjoyed the extended family, but the obligations that go along with it got too much for him (like funerals, etc.) Although I would like him to find his mother, I am still a little nervous about that. A lot of our needs were met in the adoption experience."

Laurie

This is the story of a birth mother. I was never able to contact the adoptee or the adoptive mother.

Laurie:

"When I was pregnant I made an adoption plan because my life at the time was upside down. I had a two-year-old, was separated from my husband and planning a divorce. Financially and emotionally it was just not an option for me to keep her. The baby was not my husband's. The birth father did not participate in the plan. The daughter I gave up, Leslie, searched for me. She was twenty-six at the time. When you (Shirley) first called I was kinda numb, not excited by any means, kinda complacent. My mother and I had talked about this. She had a co-worker who had a similar situation. We knew that a search would not be too difficult as Mom still had the same address and phone number. We felt she would be contacted by anyone who might be trying to get in touch with me. I told her to tell them that she didn't know where I am.

"I now have two other children besides the toddler, who is now thirty-one, a girl and a son, twenty-seven. He is the driving force behind the fact that I want no contact. He has no idea about a lot of the things in my life – about the pregnancy, the adoption and there were several other things. I was facing armed robbery charges. I wasn't raised that way. The person that I was during that short period of time is not the person I am now and that is not the way I live my life today. My son is an exceptional young man. He is working on his Master's degree. He has me on a pedestal and I don't want to diminish it in his eyes. My children don't know about the adopted child or the armed robbery charge. I never intend to tell them. I've never had any curiosity about the child I gave up because in my mind I was nothing more that a sur-

105

rogate for a childless couple. That's the way I've been able to survive all these years.

"At the time of the pregnancy, my mother was pushing for an abortion, but I could not kill another human being. The child does not ask to be conceived and it has every right to live. I gave her life and an adoptive couple the opportunity to raise a child. I don't resent her or the couple. I'm thrilled that I was able to bring the joy to someone else's life that I have been able to feel with my own children. It's not a regrettable thing. After her birth, it was time to go on to my next job in life. I had requested that I not hear the baby cry and not know the sex, but the papers I signed said Baby Girl on them. I had asked to be sedated completely. Then the nurse asked if I wanted to see her. Absolutely not.

"My one daughter would likely want to know her if she knew about her, but I know for a fact that my son would not want any contact. That is because of the type of relationship they have. She was a very delinquent child in her teen years and he holds a lot of resentment towards her for the things she did to him as a child and how her behavior affected our family in general. She put us through a lot of heartbreak. He would not be able to handle the thought of another child and would not feel that she is a part of the family. He has no tolerance for misdeeds.

"We lead a professional life. My husband works for a Fortune 500 company and my son is with the same company. He and his wife just had their first child. My daughter is not married at this time. In fact, I am raising one of her children – a twelve-year-old girl. She was born out-of-wedlock. She would like to have her back now but since I have had her since she was two, it would be detrimental to her. We provide the type of life my daughter wouldn't be able to. She has never before taken any responsibility for her. I've had some difficult times in my life and have met a lot of challenges.

"I did write a letter to the child I placed for adoption to tell her at that time of my life things were totally different and I was not who I am now. I hope she had a good happy, healthy life. It was okay to have contact through you (Shirley). I don't want or ever anticipate meeting with her. I hope the letter I wrote helps her understand how I feel. I surely wish her no harm. Otherwise I would not have gone through what I did. I have positive feelings for her but I don't think I could have a relationship with her. The updated health history is in the letter – she has the right to know it. I met my husband just three months after her birth. From the beginning, he knew my entire history. I did serve thirty days in jail and he came to see me every week. He is quite the man. I got the right one – long hard row to find him, but I found him."

Kathy

Kathy asked me (Shirley) to do a search for her birth mother. I located her quickly and she was excited, but she was still single, living with her parents and working in a department store. When the time came to actually sign a consent for the release of identifying information, she procrastinated for many months and finally decided she was not going to proceed with contact. I feel that her parents played a strong role in this decision. Kathy then asked me to do a search for her birth father. She has had a reunion with him and his present significant other.

Kathy, the adoptee:
"My first recollection about adoption was when a clerk in a store commented on how much I looked like my father. I knew that I had not been born to him and my mom so we looked at each other and chuckled. Once I realized that I didn't grow inside my adoptive mother, I thought Dad was my real father, but Mom was not my real mom. She didn't explain that I was adopted. I felt different from other kids because I'd often hear comments about their looking like one or another of their parents. I really didn't look particularly like anyone. My dad used to joke with me and told me that he'd picked me up at a grocery store. My parents have a birth son, who is ten years older than I. He's very different from me. He was out of the house when I was eight, so it was like being an only child. I graduated from college magna cum laude. I felt like I got more special treatment than he did. When I was placed I was a cute little baby and he was a preteen so the comparison was difficult, especially because he got into some typical teen problems. It had to be hard on him that I got all the attention. Mom had worked outside the home until I was placed with them. I talk with

my parents everyday. They have to know what is going on with my two children, whom they adore.

"I didn't ask a lot of questions as I was growing up. I felt it would hurt my mom's feelings. I do remember wondering what my birth mother looked like. I felt sure she would have brown hair and be beautiful, etc. I never wondered about my dad, wasn't curious about him. Mom and I would talk about it. We decided she was probably a dancer, could sew and all. In fifth grade, we had a big report to do on a country. We decided on Norway because my birth mother was from there. I likely had a lot of questions at that time. I thought the minute I turned eighteen I would do a search for her. When I got to that point in my life, I really didn't care. I was just too busy. It wasn't a priority. Ben (her birth father) told me my birth mother's name and I have found her address and phone number. I could probably call her but she doesn't know that. I was in Minnesota a while ago and could have driven by the house but I didn't.

"When I asked questions, Mom was supportive and understanding, but Dad wasn't. When Ben came to town, Dad didn't want to meet him, but Mom did. She would like to meet my birth mother, too. Dad wants nothing to do with either one. At twenty-three, I registered with ISRR, but didn't hear anything so I didn't think about it again. When I was twenty-nine, my daughter was in the hospital. They were asking for medical history – I felt helpless – they didn't know what was wrong with her. A few months later I contacted you. My mom was the catalyst. Dad was fine then, as long as it was for medical information, as long as they didn't interfere in our lives.

"Ben told me that at the time she got pregnant, my birth mother was very rebellious. She was dating him and a black guy. Her parents did not approve of either one. She comes from a very religious background. Her parents are now so old that she doesn't want to rock the boat. She may decide to get in touch when her parents die. Ben has had no contact with her. I think if I asked Ben to contact her, he would. I really think he knew she was pregnant. His significant other thinks he should call her and apologize. She and Ben have property in Mexico and stop to visit when they are en route. They stay with us and it is usually on short notice. They've just adopted a baby and are so excited.

"When I first met Ben, he came with his three daughters and his girlfriend. It was exciting. They all stayed with us. My husband and I are like two peas in a pod – very open. Ben calls me about every month or two. My parents have nothing to do with him. I always thought it was my mother, but now I find it's my dad. He always says, 'Well, maybe when they come out next time.' Whenever I got into trouble, he could not look me in the eye. It killed him to yell at me. If I did something terrible, he couldn't look at me while scolding me. There is no point in trying to debate with my dad because he is always right. He's so sweet and he loves me so much. He really wanted a daughter. It brings tears to my eyes because he looks at my daughter and calls her by my name.

"My parents were always there for me. My mom was not athletic, but my dad took me ice skating, hiking, swimming and hunting. They were really great parents. He has always been my advocate. He wanted me to live at home when I went to college and he didn't want me to move away after I graduated. I don't know if you ever wondered if you had done the right thing by placing a child with parents, but you never had to worry about my mom and dad because they were the best. They were there for anything I was involved in. They really didn't have a lot of money, but they gave me everything I ever needed. I never knew things were tight. Mom didn't go to college and Dad didn't finish, but they made sure that I went to college. They pressured me and I'll do the same with my two. I was always expected to do well. It was a matter of, 'You're going to go and you are going to get good grades.' They knew I could do it. I was outstanding student of the year in liberal arts and sciences in 1992. They knew my potential and I was expected to live up to it.

"I am close to one of Ben's daughters (my half sister) and I am so glad that he didn't raise me. I feel very sorry for those girls. I would probably have been raised by my grandparents somewhere in Minnesota. I am very thankful for where I'm at. Those girls had it very rough. They don't have a relationship with him. I have more of a relationship with him than his girls do. He portrayed himself as a great father, but there was once a restraining order against him. The oldest girl had to take care of her younger sisters."

Andy, the adoptive father:

"I was happy with just the three of us in the family, but my wife convinced me that we should adopt another child. I saw a friend with his daughter and thought that it would be nice to have a little girl, they are so cute. So we specified a girl when we adopted. In the beginning I thought that we should never tell her that she was adopted, but what I didn't like about it was that it was being dishonest, and she might find out later that we hadn't been truthful with her. We might run into an old neighbor who'd say they remembered when we adopted her so we told her she was adopted. She realized by the age of five that babies grew inside the mom, and that she didn't grow inside Renee. To me, adoption was like having your own child, but your wife did not have to go through the labor. We told her that her mother gave her up because she felt it was the best thing for her. You gave us a blanket that the birth mother wanted us to have. We gave it to her when she was five and explained that it had come from her birth mother. She kept the blanket over the years, until it wore out.

"She asked a few questions in her teens, but was not really serious about finding out until she was about to have her own children. There was a little discomfort but I was okay with it. When she decided to find her birth father, I was bothered by that. I felt no competition with the mother, but I wanted to hear nothing about him. I didn't meet him – no point in it. They have visited a few times, and she has seen his daughters and they have visited back there. If that's what she wants to do I guess it's okay. If I was in Kathy's shoes, I might be very interested in my parents, too.

"Through her contact with him, Kathy has found out a lot of information about her birth mother and that is good for her. So that satisfies her curiosity. It sounds as if her parents dominate her life. I think Kathy is satisfied with the situation. I don't think Kathy will make any further attempts to contact her.

"Kathy was a very easy child to raise. We just had the typical teenage problems like occasionally lying to me or her mother. All kids lie sometimes. We never had any serious problems with her because we kept her involved in things. She danced her whole life and was always on the pom line or the cheer line. At college she was a cheerleader for some time until after she got married. Her activities helped to keep her out of trouble.

"The reunion has not changed anything for us. I may change my mind and want to meet him some day. If Kathy would say that we were all having a big dinner, I might well go. She learned a lot from the daughters. The birth mother's parents seem to be the big factor in why they didn't get together.

111

"We were very pleased that you were able to match a child to us so well. We were thrilled to death to get her and when we went around to places, most people would say, 'Oh, she looks just like her dad.' We got a kick out of it. I always felt that if we'd had our own daughter, she would have been like Kathy. As I think back, I can't imagine her not being a part of our lives – and her daughter looks so much like her. We just gave her a doll that Kathy had when she was little and we have some of her costumes and outfits that we will be giving to her."

Renee, the adoptive mother:
"We always told Kathy that she was a chosen child. Adoption was not a familiar word around our home, until the later years. They had talked about it in school as there were some other kids who were adopted. We told her that the adoption plan was made for her because her birth mother could not take care of her. She felt that she would have a better life this way. She made a shawl for Kathy that I hung in my closet for years until I gave it to her as a gift from her birth mother. She has it hanging on the wall of her daughter's bedroom. I don't recall her ever having pumped us about anything. If the subject came up, we would tell her what we knew. She acted as if she couldn't care less.

"When she was pregnant the first time, she told us that she was going to do a search. Since she was going to be a mom, she wanted to know about the background. I thought it was good since I understood what the reasons were. Kathy has a picture of her birth mother. Ben gave it to her. You could write a book on those two. It is really strange that he kept it all those years. He must have cared about her. On the back it is dated 1969 and Kathy was born in 1970. The older girl made up an album of the three girls and the boy growing up and gave it to Kathy. She really likes those sisters, especially the oldest one. One of them said she thinks Kathy is one of the greatest ladies she has ever met and it has to be because of the way she was raised. She feels Kathy has all the right values and it goes back to her rearing. That was a nice compliment for us. I think I'm now game to meet them all. I think Ben is not what he tries to make people think he is. It is really good that he and the birth mother did not marry because they then would have raised Kathy and her life would have been very different. There has been more than one story of his relationship with the birth mother.

"I think this reunion has probably brought us closer together than we even were before. I think we're appreciated more. That's my own personal opinion. We were fortunate to be able to adopt Kathy. We really had no serious problems with her as she was growing up. She was the typical messy kid – how do you get a child to keep their room straight? She also occasionally lied to get out of things. She was never in with the smoking, drinking or drug crowd. Her dance and pom and cheer kept her busy. She now knows how hard it is to keep up with the kids and their clutter. She is a gourmet cook. Creates masterpiece cakes for the kids' birthdays. She was in a beauty pageant once. We are very proud of her."

Ben and Betty, the birth father and his girlfriend:
Betty first:
"Ben was very excited when he was contacted about Kathy. It was like a gift. It was a warm experience for him when he met her. It may have been a relief, too. It is kind of confusing to me as to whether he knew about his baby being placed for adoption. He tells me that he didn't know about it, but at the same time he mentioned to me about a year after I met him there was a possibility that the birth mother might have been pregnant but he didn't believe her. So there was a chance that she had a child as a result of that relationship. I questioned if he knew there might be someone out there and noted that it might surface some day. He was reluctant to accept it. When we got the letter we thought there was a possibility that this person, now an adult, would want to get medical information or something. Ben is quite a macho person and he has a hard time saying he is wrong. I'm not quite sure what the whole story is.

"The first contact was made by Kathy one evening and they talked for a very long time – it was a good night. He got off the phone very excited and anxious to learn what the next chapter would be. With the second call, we made plans to come to Phoenix. We came out with his two daughters. They stayed the weekend and we stayed longer. There is also a son, age eleven who did not come but is anxious to meet Kathy. He is by another wife.

"Kathy and her husband are both jewels. They are fun, not pretentious or self-righteous and very warm. We were touched that they would think that our visit was a special occasion. Kathy is very close to her family. Ben told his daughters right away. That was probably my doing. I felt they had a right to know and then what they wanted to do was their decision. The son was all set to go but at the last minute had to cancel. After the trip, Ben wrote a letter to her parents thanking them for everything they had done and said what a beautiful woman she had become."

Ben, the birth father:

"I was not really aware that a child of mine had been placed for adoption. I don't recall ever getting a letter from the agency. When you contacted me, I felt wonderful. I was elated. Yes, I did have a relationship with the birth mother but I never thought that there was going to be a baby from it. She was very, very introverted. I don't know how to explain the feeling, but I looked forward to meeting Kathy. After we met, I was sad because I felt that somehow I had failed her. She is very happy with the life she's had. She introduced me as her birth father, but has never called me Dad or Father, but Grandpa Ben. She sees her adoptive father as her dad. That's fine. You know, we all have to pay for our sins somehow.

"Our present relationship is fine. We talk regularly. I usually call her, but occasionally she calls me. She has a good relationship with Betty, too. It was a wonderful thing that you were able to put us together. I think a lot of Kathy and what she has been able to accomplish. Her husband is a great guy. It's like a fairy tale. It's come full circle now and we see that it doesn't need to be blood to raise somebody. It was the very best thing that could have happened to us and I hope when our newly adopted son is an adult that he, too, will be able to know his blood relatives. Hopefully we are doing something good by him.

"We have tried to have contact with Kathy's birth mother but she is a recluse, we think."

Pam, one of Ben's other daughters:

"I don't know how long Dad had known about Kathy but my mother heard about her before my two sisters and I did. My husband and I visited with Ben and Betty. We all started telling the story that my mom had received a letter from you (Shirley) trying to contact him. I haven't verified any of this with my mom, but you were finally able to get hold of him and told him about Kathy. He said he had been talking with her for about two weeks by this time. I was overwhelmed. I was the oldest and I've always taken care of my younger sisters in any way I could. I was thinking that she was the sister I was never there for. I wanted to know her immediately and to let her know that she was loved. I am so over protective and a worrier (started crying). I just wanted to know she was okay and the family who had adopted her loved her. I wanted to know that she was happy and healthy and that she's had a good life. Ben is my father, but I have never called him Dad because he was quite verbally, physically and emotionally abusive to all of us. My parents divorced when I was nine.

"He and Kathy were going to set up a time for him to visit and he wanted me and my sisters to go with him. We were astounded. More than anything else, we all wanted to meet her and know her. Ben paid for our plane tickets. We got to meet this awesome family that she and her husband have. The kids are just beautiful. Instantly some of those unknown fears melted away. She is so unbelievably beautiful. She loves those children and created a beautiful family for herself and those around her. I knew she had been raised well. I know that nurture vs. nature had given her those great qualities. She is a phenomenal woman.

"We have kept in touch with cards, occasional phone calls and E-mails. After the birth of my son I didn't want to pester her all the time. I sent her a birth announcement. She sent a card and said that she wished she had known that I was pregnant. We thought about how overwhelming it all had to be for her. Here is the life you have known and the parents and brother you have known and suddenly you learn here is your dad and here are all of your half siblings. We were not sure what she would want out of this whole thing. She looks so much like my middle sister. She came for my son's christening and stayed with us. It was a fun visit. She had such a wonderful wisdom to share about being a mom and all the little tricks of the trade that she had learned up to that point. It was wonderful to share that time with her. I haven't met her parents, but she talks a lot about them.

"I would like to see her more. Distance is the problem. She told me that a contact had been made with her birth mother and she didn't get the response she had hoped for. I guess it didn't make me curious, but sad for the mom to not be able to see this wonderful daughter she had. She just said she was not ready. Kathy was so excited and eager to meet her – I felt bad for her that she didn't. I don't really trust Ben, even though he's my father. I take him with a huge, huge grain of salt. I've seen how he has treated people other than just our family, the lying and manipulation. I just don't want Kathy to get hurt. That was my biggest fear. I wanted her to know he was capable of doing that. I wouldn't be able to forgive myself if she did get hurt and that's the protective part of me. I hope she is able to take him with a grain of salt, too. She has the ability to do it. The odd part for me is that I don't have the distance from him. He can come to my house any time. I just don't want to be open. My husband doesn't trust him and I don't want to expose my children. So it is important for me to tell Kathy what I know about Ben. He puts on the charm and then there is the other side of the coin that's so icky.

"I think what you do has to change people's lives. All I can say is that Kathy is amazing and I really love her. *(crying)* Thank you so much for a sister."

Alex

"When I was very young, I vaguely recall that when we would go shopping people would look at us because I had really blond hair and both Mom and Dad had dark hair and olive complexions, Mom would always say, 'Yeah, he's adopted.' She made it clear because people would comment about the difference in our looks. We really didn't talk about it a lot – more when I was little than when I got older. My sister was adopted, too. She did a search and her birth mother didn't want contact. That was an extremely painful and disappointing time for her.

"I thought about my birth background for many years and then I contacted you in 2001. I just wanted to find out what happened. Sometimes I felt rejected and there was some depression that set in when it really hit me that I was adopted. My parents didn't explain to me why I was given up because they didn't know. The impression was not clear as to whether she wanted to get rid of me or make a plan for me. I think all birth mothers want to make a better plan for the baby. They don't want to give them up. After thinking about it, I realized it was not what she wanted to do. I went to a financially sound, stable family and they love me very much. Still, I wanted to contact her to get the story from her. I felt a lot better after talking with her. I hope to meet with her someday, but right now, I'm not sure that I want to develop a relationship with her. I don't know when it might happen. I know she really wants to meet me. She sends me E-mails once in a while. She sounds like such a nice person. Maybe deep down I feel it is disrespectful because my parents are my parents. They don't seem to be bothered by it at all, but it feels that way to me. I want to show respect to them. I fear they might think they were not good enough, but they may just want me to get to know myself better.

"Jo, my birth mother, has told me the whole story of how it happened and it helped a lot – I know I wasn't just rejected. Before I did the search, a lot of my friends were asking me if I was interested in finding out. I wasn't until recently. One of my girl friends eventually talked me into it. She said that I needed to find out about my medical background. I learned that I have a half sister, nineteen, and we have exchanged pictures so I have pictures of Jo and my birth sister. I look a lot like Jo. She said I am built like my birth father. When he found she was pregnant, he took off. He wanted nothing to do with her. She still knows his name and she thinks she knows where he lives. I could do a search for him, too, if I decide to. The first time I talked with Jo, she had just lost her husband.

"I am still very close to my parents. They are easy to talk to. They encouraged me to do a search a long time ago. They have offered to buy me a ticket to go see Jo when I'm ready. I had Jo's number for about a month and just sat on it. The first contact, I was numb, it seemed awkward. Probably the next time we talk we will be arranging a meeting with each other. She came here once to visit her sister and she wanted to meet, but I wasn't ready. If she comes out again, I think I would be comfortable in meeting with her. I feel fairly relaxed about it now. I think the whole story made me feel better. She was not ready at that point in her life to raise a child on her own, so she wanted me to go to someone who was ready. My parents were very happy when I located her, but they have never had any involvement with her – never talked, etc. If I'd had a child out of wedlock in my early twenties, I think I would've considered adoption for that child, but now, no (he is 31). I would be willing to take the responsibility now.

"I haven't met any other birth relatives. I did talk with Jo's sister once. Jo called me when she was out. I would definitely want to meet my half sister and feel that she would be open to meeting me, too. I have gained closure about what happened as a result of this reunion, so I feel more comfortable."

Jo, Alex's birth mother:
"I know that Alex is doing fine and that he intends to get in touch with me when he is ready. As long as he is normal and I've seen pictures of him and he doesn't have six toes or something, then that is okay. He seems to be living a fairly stable life now.

"While I was going to summer school I got pregnant with Alex after I met his birth father. When I told him I was pregnant he didn't want anything to do with it, so he left, and that was very painful for me. I never saw him again. My mother had passed away so I talked with my sister who was always there for me. We weighed the pros and cons and I just decided that adoption was going to give him his only chance in life (not that it was going to tie me down). I thought it would be such a struggle for this young life to come into the world and have to learn to do without right away. I was twenty years old, and at about six and a half months along I made the adoption plan. I found the agency very helpful. They talked to me about whether I really thought this was the right decision.

"Alex was almost thirty when we made the contact with each other. When you called me, I was totally floored. I never thought it would happen – it was a very happy feeling. Wow! I couldn't believe it. I had always worried that he may have been stuck in a horrible family and had a horrible life. I didn't think that I would ever see him again so it was a shock to learn that he wanted contact with me. Before computers came out I had contacted ISRR, and I never heard anything back. To date I have not met Alex. We have exchanged some E-mails (last one over a year ago) and pictures. It was so fun to get them. I had lived my life with guilt feelings, wondering if he might have been placed with a dysfunctional family and it could have been worse than if I had kept him.

"It was very hard when people would say, 'How many children do you have?' Well, I have a daughter and then I had a son that I gave up for adoption. It is like having the hurt all over again. It was like a gift from God to know that he'd had a good life and had been given opportunities. From what he told me he really loves his parents and had a good home life. He said his parents were just wonderful people. He really admires them and feels very close to them. Maybe his fear of hurting their feelings has been part of the reason for his reluctance to have a face-to-face meeting. If I never meet him, I'm satisfied with what I know now. I know that my decision was a good one. If I had kept him all through his life in grade school and junior high he would have been the poor kid. It would have been sad – he likely would have been raised by baby sitters. But now he's had a good education. I knew it was important for him to have a father, especially a boy, he needed a father. It gave me a lot of comfort. It is just like a big hole in my heart has been mended.

"I've sent him pictures of me and sent him something for Christmas of 2002. It is nearly two years since I heard from him. I told him that I would not pressure him. I totally understand, but I want him to know how thankful I am that he gave me the opportunity to know that he is okay and to have the peace of mind it gives me. If and when he is ever ready, I'll be there. He looks like his father – blond hair, but my stockiness, my brother's height. I told him his father's name and where he was from. I didn't tell him my father is an alcoholic and I probably should have, so he would know it is in his background. My daughter has known about Alex since she was ten years old. She was excited and thought it was neat. I told her it was a mistake I made and had to deal with the consequences. I didn't give him up because I didn't want him, but I loved him enough to give him the opportunities that I could not provide for him. She is anxious to meet him, too. She and I are very close – she's been a real blessing in my life.

"Finally, my curiosity was satisfied and my prayers were answered. It was like a jaw dropper when I got your call. It took my breath away... it's something that you think about but try not to so you don't get your hopes up. The time right after I gave him up was one of the hardest times I have ever gone through. I can't tell you how many nights of tears there were, but in the daytime I would think of this: diapers, formula, what other things he would need, the poor kid. He would never have been able to join the soccer team because I wouldn't have been able to afford the uniform. It was so rewarding to hear about his life. You can't imagine what it was like. Oh thank you, thank you! I am so thankful that I made the right decision."

Rebecca, the adoptive mom:

"Carrying a child was never important to me so when we learned that there would be a problem in conceiving, we immediately decided to adopt. Caring for a child was important to both of us. I explained to our two adopted children early on that they had been in a mommy's tummy. My daughter asked if she was in my tummy and I told her no. We tried to help them understand that they were wanted and loved by their birth mother and us. I was very comfortable in talking with them (I think). I have always thought that the more people who love you, the better off you are. We tried to convey a feeling of love, not rejection, in the relinquishment. We told them they loved them, but couldn't take care of them in the way that they wanted them to be cared for. We gave them all the information we had, which was not a lot. It might've been easier if there had been open adoptions.

"Our daughter tried to find her birth mother herself. There was a man who was preying on young women who wanted to find their birth mothers. She ended up paying him three or four thousand dollars. He even told her that it was the wrong birth date and the wrong hospital and she still believed it and he connected her with a woman who was not even her mother. That made her feel awful. She couldn't come to peace with the fact that she was adopted. Her search resulted in her birth mother refusing contact. She was devastated. It has been a very big issue for her. She's had serious drug problems for several years.

"When Alex decided to search, we were surprised because he had always been very content. I had asked several times if he would want to search and offered to help him along the way. He said he didn't think he wanted to. So, of course, we figured it was a vote for us. He thought we were his parents and it was just fine with him. That's all he needed. I'm not sure, but I think it was one of his girl friends who encouraged him to search. I was very glad. I was so thankful that it went easy for him. I really don't see any difference in him since he made the connection. I don't know if he is glad he did it. He still hasn't met her in person. Is he afraid, or does he feel he would betray us? A lot of what Alex is, is because of his sister. He has seen the pain she has brought and he is determined not to do the same. I had thought by my encouraging and asking questions I had conveyed to him that it would be a good thing to do.

"I have never had any contact with his birth mother, but it never occurred to me. I guess that another person to love Alex would be good. I can see the adoptive mother and the birth mother becoming friends if they have things in common. I'm sure she is a very nice person. You know, I am second in line here."

Shirley: I assured her that she was not second in line as far as Alex was concerned.

Rebecca continues:

"Jo went through the loss of a baby – an experience that was different from mine. How would I go about removing his fear of meeting her? I might write a thank you to her for going through with the pregnancy and having a child that we had the privilege of raising and the satisfaction and fulfillment that he's brought into our lives. Would I need to ask Alex's permission? He is the doorkeeper and he may not want me to do it. But I will keep it in mind and try to follow up on it.

"I have a very close relationship with Alex. He didn't share a lot of the emotions accompanying his contact with Jo. It was like another event of the many events in his life. I'm not sure if he stuffed his feelings. As far as our relationship is concerned, it has not changed. I just wish he had gone farther with it. Maybe he will now. I had so much disappointment when my daughter was going through this thing. I had concern for her birth mother's welfare and her concern about this daughter coming into her life. It was so stressful it seemed she didn't want her in her life. I hope that somehow, sometime they can get together. Her parents had never known about her pregnancy and right then one of her parents was terminally ill.

"As Alex was growing up, he had some learning problems. He has other skills, but not the skills that get you through school. He is great at seeing relationships, and doing puzzles and other kinds of things that other people can't do. It isn't what you get rewards for. For the most part, he has been a very agreeable child. I never felt that I had to set limits for him. He could set his own limits. He knew when he should be in at night and who he should be with. His sister was an embarrassment to him all the way. He was good partly because of seeing her behavior, partly wanting to please us and partly because he knew it was right. He was always good at choosing his buddies. He had lots of friends and good social skills and people liked him because he was just an easy person to be around.

"We are all doing fine now and we just hope that our daughter will continue to get along. She's in a good relationship. She may have an idea of what she would like to be in the future. I hope she is not as difficult to live with now. I give her my best."

Gina

"Adoption was always a familiar word to me. My parents adopted me and my sister, who is three years older. They have no birth children. When my friends learned that I was adopted, they asked a lot of questions. They were almost more curious about my birth mother than I was. So that stimulated my curiosity. Although I've probably always been curious, I was more so in high school. That is likely when it started. My parents seemed very comfortable in talking about it as we got older and they encouraged us to consider a search if that was something we wanted to do.

"I was in my early twenties when I became curious about my birth background. Not really sure what triggered it, but I was trying to figure myself out, who am I? What do I want to do with my life? What is my health history? My nationality? The circumstances of my conception? And why I was placed for adoption? I was also curious about the circumstances of her life. I believe we were told her nationality, but I thought maybe the information was not correct. My sister's birth mother found her and she learned that the nationality information given to our parents was all wrong.

"Since I was curious about my conception, I think that I was really lucky – my birth parents were high school sweethearts. He was going to leave the country for about a year and this was their last night together. So she didn't learn that she was pregnant until after he left. When she told her parents, they decided that she should come to Arizona to have the baby. She stayed with a lawyer who had adopted children so she had the chance to see what potential there would be for a child in an adoptive home. Still it was hard for her to go through with it. It seemed that her parents had really made the decision about the baby's future. The birth father died so they were never able to get back together. They were really young, but they loved each other very much. I was lucky to be conceived in love. She told me that for years she cried to the man whom she eventually married about how guilty she felt and how worried she was. She struggled with it for a long time. But I know that her ultimate decision was made on the basis of love.

"When I decided to search, I had never heard of the CIP. I had tried a couple of other avenues first – Search Triad and ISRR. I felt that likely nothing would happen because if she wanted contact with me she would have registered with ISRR, too. I have a great relationship with her now, but Mom is my mom and Dad is my dad. Our first contact was when she called me and we talked for about two hours. We both had a lot of questions and then she came with her daughter to visit just a few months later. So I got to meet my half sister, too. We spent the weekend together and it was like getting together with an old friend. There were no awkward moments. We learned that we had a lot of things in common. We are both massage therapists, and we both enjoy the same things. We are a lot alike in other ways – the way we have decorated our homes and the way we dress, etc. It just felt so normal. She stayed with the lawyer who did the adoption – same house, neat for her and kind of a closure.

"We have had about four meetings. I have been to visit her and have met a lot of the extended family and she came out after the birth of my baby. I went for her daughter's wedding reception and I met more of the family and some of my birth father's family. We talk about once a month. My adoptive parents had a big dinner for her the last time she came. So their reaction to the reunion has been very positive. It was a very emotional moment when my mothers met. There were lots of hugs and thank-yous – to my parents for raising me and to her for letting them raise me. They were each so grateful to the other. Of course, I have thanked her for having me too.

"Now that I have a child I have a hard time imagining how anyone could be unselfish enough to give up a baby. I am close to both families, but I am closest to Mom and Dad because my history is with them. I love them all very much."

Shirley: The interview that I had with Gina's adoptive mother, Marcia, was very interesting. She told me that her other daughter had come to me for counseling about seven years before as she was pregnant out-of-wedlock. She decided to keep the baby and this very day was his seventh birthday. She told me that the daughter had later come to my office to let me know how things turned out (she was now happily married to a man who has adopted the child), but she missed me. I had just retired. She feels that she almost made the biggest mistake of her life by considering adoption.

Another note that Marcia added was that her sister had a son out-of-wedlock and it was that sister that I had contacted when I was searching for Gina. She took my number and had Gina call me. Marcia feels that her sister still mourns the loss of that child and that she should do a search for him. She always said that was such a difficult time in her life and she doesn't even want to talk about it. After all this, she may be open to doing a search. With my contacting Gina, she felt that it was all just mind-boggling. She doesn't feel that it is just a coincidence.

Marcia, Gina's adoptive mother:

"I wish that her birth mother, Liz, lived here instead of in another state. My children understood about their adoption at a very early age and knew that they did not come from my body, but it didn't seem to affect them at all. I was probably not comfortable inside because I never got over the fact that we could not have a baby. I was comfortable on the outside. But the minute you look at an adoptive child, you are hooked. Even today, at sixty-two, talking about it makes me cry.

"Neither of our girls had a desire to search until they were older. I suggested to Gina that she should do a search so she could get her medical information. Gina is not a go-getter and she likely would have never done the search, so it is good that Liz found her. When either of the girls asked, I gave them all the information that I had, which was next to nothing. With the first one, I was told some things that were not even true. She was very happy with herself and what she knew about herself. My husband and I were very happy when Gina was contacted by Liz. It would have been threatening if she had been only a small child, but at this age it was good because now she could get the information that she needed. We have met Liz. She has been here two times. You could tell that she had come from a very nice home. That gave us a lot of reassurance. They're in touch with each other fairly often and we are both very secure in our relationship with Gina. We get a lot of parental satisfaction from her. I must say that she did have some typical teenage problems and was late to mature. She is wonderful now, sometimes coming out with such a show of maturity that it amazes me. She is no longer on another planet. This reunion has benefitted all of us a great deal."

Liz would like to add:

"When I was pregnant with Gina, I kept going to the Student Health Services and telling them I thought I was pregnant and they said I was just under stress. Finally I went to a regular ob-gyn and learned that I was five months along. So there was no decision about continuing with the pregnancy as I would have never considered an abortion. Even though I had suspected it, it was still a shock. I had to go home over Thanksgiving to tell my parents. That was very hard. Back in those days it was still something that you were not supposed to talk about and it didn't happen in nice families. My father was a doctor and my mother worked at Planned Parenthood!

"The birth father and I were very much in love and that had been the first time I had ever been intimate with anyone. His father was also a doctor and our families had been friends for many years. He was going to Asia to do photography for nine to twelve months and I was going to school. We realized we would be spending a lot of time apart so this was our last hurrah. We were not just boyfriend/girlfriend but we were great friends. It was my first and real love. There was no way to contact him so he did not participate in the adoption plan. My father, who was very controlling, wanted no one to know. Being the dutiful daughter, I went along with what he said. I wouldn't think of going against his wishes. When the birth father came back, we got together to talk about his trip, but things were very strained. My father was there all the time. Dad treated him awful and he couldn't understand why. Ultimately our relationship ended.

"I decided to go back to school and met and started dating another old friend. I can't really say that I was in love with him but we had been good friends for a long time. I felt that he would be able to get me out of my family situation so I married him. I did see Gina's birth father once in a while but it was still very strained. He never knew about the baby. I was about six months pregnant when my mother called and told me that he had been driving up to Aspen, fell asleep at the wheel, ran head-on into a semi and was killed – just horrible.

"I didn't marry for love, but we had two children and were together for seventeen years. He became an alcoholic. We received counseling but divorced in 1990. Two years ago I married again.

"So why did I search? I had been talking about it a lot over the past five years. Both of my children had known from their early years that I'd had another baby. I had talked with them about a search. In my business I had run into a lot of people who were adopted and I've asked what would happen if their birth mother tried to find them. They said they would not like it and would rather do the search themselves. So I worried if I was doing the right thing and if I should even consider it. I turned fifty and my daughter said, 'You know it is time to do this.' She wanted to know her sister. So I decided to do it. It was time to put the past behind. Both of my parents had passed away and I would not have to face them.

"Some people cautioned me that she may not want to see me. They posed some questions for me to think about. Still, I wanted some kind of closure. If she wanted to see me, fine. If she didn't, it would still be some kind of closure. That is what I needed. When the adoption happened, I felt like I had an appendage cut off and I wanted to make some kind of reconciliation. It still felt like a big empty hole. It's difficult to go through life with it. For the first ten years after I gave her up, I'd wake up at night and just cry for hours. I never really regretted the decision as I knew at that point in my life I still had a lot of issues to resolve with my family. As I look back now, I think maybe I could have kept her, but then I felt placing her was the right thing to do. How would I be able to support me and the baby? It was so helpful to know that she could go into a loving adoptive family. I ached and grieved for years – even forever.

"Even now that I've found her there is still the ache of the years lost. When I started the search I just needed to know what happened to her. I think it worked out just as it was meant to. Now we have a very positive relationship. Not like mother-daughter because I am not trying to replace her mother. She is wonderful. Gina calls me Liz and introduces me to her friends as her birth mother. I have a wonderful relationship with her parents. They are so welcoming, warm and understanding. I don't think I could have picked more perfect people to raise her. I adore them.

"I talk with Gina about once a month and she keeps in touch with my daughter as well. She gets along well with my other daughter and my son who is a few years older than she is. When she met all of my extended family and some of the birth father's family, I would have expected her to be overwhelmed. She handled it beautifully. For her it was neat to sit at the table and see 'all these people who look like me.' I think she is the most wonderful daughter in the whole world. She looks more like me than my other children do. I think she got all of my genetic material. When people see us they are amazed. It's like looking at myself when I was younger. That gives me a lot of comfort. So nice to see how she is with her own daughter. We think the same way. It is funny to see that and know that she had been raised by other people.

"I have no doubt she was meant to be in this world. I now have so much comfort about my adoption decision. It is no coincidence that we found each other. A high level of healing has happened in my family and the birth father's family as a result of her presence in our lives. His father had gone into a deep depression after that horrible accident. Since he found that Gina is here, it has turned his whole life around. It is like part of his son is still here. This has been a great event in our lives.

"A friend of mine is in a group of medical wives and she told them about the reunion. They wanted to take me to lunch to hear the story and so here I was at this very fancy restaurant with all these friends of my mother who hadn't known of my pregnancy. They had so much insight about what was going on with my parents and how controlling my father was. They thought this was the most wonderful thing that could happen in my life and they all expressed how much they loved me. What a healing experience! It lent more closure that wouldn't have happened if I hadn't done the search.

"I don't have to hide anything anymore. Being a massage therapist, I work with psychotherapists and other health care professionals who know how to work with issues of trauma in the body, so I am very much aware of what happens when you hold secrets inside. People can get sick and over time it does terrible things to your body, so on a certain level it was killing me to hold that in all those years. Now I can be open and honest and untie all those knots. Seeing all the pictures of Gina in different stages of her life. I missed that, but her parents have been great about telling me funny little stories and bits and pieces about her. It was hard to know that I wasn't there to enjoy all those precious moments.

Now, having other children, I know how precious they can be. It has all been a most amazing experience."

Annette

Annette is the birth mother in this story. Her birth son is Randall. He is the one who did the search for Annette, but did not wish to be interviewed as part of this reunion story.

Annette says:

"I was only fifteen when Randall was born. I knew I couldn't take care of him. I didn't regret my decision to place him for adoption but there are moments of questioning because I never had another child. I think making big decisions in whatever road of life you choose, you always ask, 'What if?' When I was that young I thought I would grow up and have a family and the loss would not be overwhelming. But it turned out to be a very significant loss. When I was married, we never used birth control, but I just didn't conceive. He had a normal sperm count so the problem was likely with me. I was married four years, but it was a seven-year relationship and my last serious one.

"I decided I wouldn't go looking for my son. I didn't want to interrupt his life. Randall found me when he was thirty years old. When you (Shirley) first contacted me I was truly excited, astonished, hopeful and thrilled. We had long phone conversations first. We met about a week later. He came to my house and visited. It was wonderful – at least in the beginning. He seemed to say everything perfectly. You hope that your kid will grow up to be a good person, emotionally balanced. Initially, he met all my expectations. In reflection, I think it was an act – definitely. He contacted me in November three years ago, and at first it seemed really great. I was looking forward to developing a lasting relationship with him and making up for lost ground.

"I met his adoptive mother and father. They are very pleasant people. We went to their house and looked at a ton of pictures from his infancy onward. It was lovely. They were educated, responsible, dependable, emotionally mature and loving. He said he couldn't have asked for better parents, but he was still bitter about his life. He'd had every opportunity. He could've gone to college. Both his parents were college graduates. They encouraged him to go. He didn't have any interest in developing a career. He went into the Marines. He got very angry in the Marines and didn't stick with it. He started a family while very young. He had a child with his first wife, and two with his second wife. He had bad marriages. He had a violent temper and destroyed his marriages. He was quite messed up by then – having to pay child support to two separate households. I think he wanted his mother to fix it for him. I think the anger came from genetics. My father was a very angry man and destroyed the relationship with my mother. He was not an okay person. It is hard to know what came from his birth father's side, but it appeared that Randall inherited all of my bad traits and none of my good ones. I inherited my father's bad temper as well. I do believe it is far worse in men than in women. I have a feisty temper, but I am not impossible to live with. I don't get physically destructive and I confront people when they upset me.

"It seemed that Randall didn't want to apply himself for professional growth, but he certainly wanted to live high on the hog. I believe he gets an annual disbursement from his grandparents' estate. I think he was motivated to look me up because he was mad at his adoptive mother. She wouldn't give him money to bail him out of the financial trouble he was in. Once he bitched to me that they'd spent a lot of money on some remodeling and all the while they couldn't help him out with a little money. I pointed out to him that he was thirty and maybe they were hoping he could take care of himself. That angered him and he hung up on me. He didn't want to talk about his irresponsibility. I felt he was being immature, self-centered, ungrateful and mean. But he hung up before I could tell him. He did stay in touch – maybe to see if I was going to give him a generous Christmas gift. He never approached me directly for money, but I was getting a feel that he was going to try to see what I was made of. I let him know that things were very tight for me. I thought money would make a real crummy basis for our relationship. It wasn't like I had a lot to give him anyway. I would rather have a good relationship so if the need arose later it might be appropriate to do something for him, but I didn't want it to be the only reason he'd look me up – like if he was mad at his mother. I have only had one contact with his parents and that was while we were still on good terms. I gave him a modest gift at Christmas – a shirt and pair of pants.

"I noticed that right after the first of the year, after he got the family disbursement, he just disappeared. I received no calls and there was no attempt to move forward on anything. His major motivation for ever getting together became very clear. Things were tough for me. I was taking care of my mother who was dying of cancer. I had hoped he would take the time to get to know her before she died, but he didn't seem to have any interest. Even when she died he didn't show up, offering no emotional support for me. I am guessing at these motivations based on his behavior and the way he complained about his mom, he made me think she was really unfair to him. I haven't talked with him in well over a year. He did stop by on Mother's Day – I'm not sure why. It almost seemed like an afterthought. He had already spent the whole day with his parents.

"Sometime in the summer of 2002, we met and went to a movie together. He was behaving normally – didn't seem interested in dunning me for money and wasn't complaining about his mother. It was like he just wanted to touch base with me and that was pleasant. He asked me about his birth father. I gave him his name but didn't encourage him to try to find him. I didn't think it would be a good experience for either of them. I'm not sure if he ever did anything about it. The birth father didn't know about my pregnancy and didn't care.

"I don't have any continuing contact with the adoptive parents. I don't know where Randall is now (2003). The last time I talked with him he was living with his parents and having financial problems. I think he makes his own troubles.

"This has all been a terrible disappointment for me. I am really sad that he turned out that way, but then maybe it is the part he inherited from his father. I'm not that way. I take care of my responsibilities and I take care of people even when it is not a good thing. You can see the strong difference between genetics and environment. When you see this kid who looks so much like you, talks like you and tells you about his life – there are so many similarities.

"We both love Mexican food. It is like a craving for both of us. So with all the commonalities there was a bonding right away. We both thought that it was so great to get together. But there is a limit to the kind of relationship you can have with other people when your own life is messed up, and that is in spite of the fact that he was given every chance to have a good life.

"It's been over two years since I've seen him. I suppose it's okay that he looked me up. I wanted to know what had happened to him. It satisfied a lot of my curiosity. I was glad he has caring and loving adoptive parents. It gave me comfort about my adoption decision. I know he had a good childhood. So I feel sorry for his parents. Their other adopted son is very different from Randall, in physique and temperament. I probably wouldn't discourage people from searching for their birth parents although it didn't turn out well for me. By now he may be on the road to a better situation for himself. Maybe he is still growing up."

Faye, the adoptive mother:

"Randall always felt that his brother got more than his share of attention. Randall has had an abandonment issue since he was a teenager. That's why he wanted to meet Annette. He met her and that took care of it. At least, that is what my other son told me. He got out of it what he wanted. Sometimes he does wonderful things and I wonder, where did that come from? There is real good stuff in that kid.

"My husband's brother had adopted years before. We both loved kids and wanted kids, so it was a familiar concept for us and it was comfortable for us to talk about the fact of adoption. My other son, Ralph, has learning disabilities and was very slow in school. When he was about seven, he said he really wanted to see his birth mother and he wanted to know if she was black. Well, no, she wasn't. He then said that we had told him we didn't know her so how did we know that she wasn't black. I pointed out that he had blond hair and blue eyes and that children born to black women don't have that coloring. I asked him if it would matter to him if she was black. He didn't think so, he just wanted to know. I was comfortable with all of his questions, but not necessarily with Randall's. When Ralph first moved out of our house, right after high school, we found he had sent for papers to try to trace his adoption. Of course he wasn't old enough, but he never mentioned it to us. Still to this day he's not mentioned it."

Shirley: I finished a search for Ralph's birth mother and they have had contact.

Faye continues:

"When Randall told us he wanted to do a search, I told him I thought he needed to. That was right after he'd been hospitalized for a nervous breakdown. It was interesting because Annette had one about the same time in her life. She was hospitalized for depression. When he came out of the hospital, he was wonderful. He was a very decent person. He talked to us frequently. Once when we were up at our cabin he cried every night sometimes at two or three o'clock in the morning. When I asked him why he said, 'This is the hardest thing I have ever had to say to you, Mom. I want to trace.' That made me feel that he was very sensitive and really cared for me, but you'd not know it the way he's living his life. The only other time I've seen him that sensitive was when my husband's mother died. Randall was very close to her. She was a wonderful lady and he got the call about her stroke – neither of us were home. He went to the hospital and through him they contacted me. He handled it well, but as soon as I got there he came unglued. When she died, he was already married. In the middle of the night he and his wife came to our house and he got in bed with us. He needed comfort. He was scared to death and seemed afraid that he would lose us, too. I think he felt betrayed by his birth mother.

"Ralph said that he couldn't think of Randall as anything but invincible. He saw him as Superman, his hero, indestructible. I was actually relieved when Randall said that he was ready to do a search, scared, but relieved for him. I had some fears that I might be replaced. When I met her, I liked her. It was a big relief. For a while when he was seeing her maybe three to four times a week and I was seeing him every three weeks, there was some jealousy. He would say there is a lot of catching up to do. I did see that it was helping him. Why it stopped, I don't know. But we go for weeks not hearing from him.

"I have only met Annette once. We have no relationship now. We have talked on the phone several times. I like her. I admire her going on to school on her own and working. I was hoping that he would pick up on that a little bit, too. I felt she was very honest and forthright with me. Actually, when she came we were at a football game. Ralph got the baby book and pictures for them and left the two of them alone. They had never expressed an interest in their pictures before. I had them ready for them when they did. She answered all my questions and told me things I had not even thought of asking. That was very courageous of her. She told us the circumstances of her pregnancy. One sad thing she told Randall was that she never wanted to give him up, but her mother and the agency convinced her she should. If I had a daughter that age I don't know what I would do.

"Oh, the problems we've had with Randall. As a little kid, he was wonderful, a mother's dream. He was bright, handsome, everything that you would want a son to be. In first grade, he started to become very competitive and didn't like losing. Even when we played board games at home, he would throw the checkers or game pieces. We worked and worked with him. A teacher yelled at him across the room one day and I don't approve of that. (Note: She, Faye, was a schoolteacher.)

"He couldn't stand to lose. Major problems didn't show until junior high – then a lot of defiance and mouthiness. He never got into drugs. He only tried marijuana once--that is one thing I give him credit for, because he ran around with some kids who were into drugs. He's had a little too much alcohol a time or two but a lot of kids do that. I remember when he was getting ready to register for high school in his freshman or sophomore year. He said he was going out to shoot pink ball with someone and I asked if he had forgotten registration. He said he just wouldn't go. I told him that I believed he would. So he ran away, but you know where he went? Well, I don't know how he got there but he went over to his grandma's apartment – she was a widow at the time – and it was late at night and he didn't want to scare her. He spent most of the night in the bushes outside her window. She never knew it, thank God, or it would have scared her to death. We called Crisis and while we were on the phone, he returned to our house, but he would not come in. He was throwing his shoes at our door. The person we were talking to at Crisis was trying to give us directions on how to handle the situation, but he would not do as we asked. He has never liked authority.

"As far as the reunion goes, I think I have gained as a result. I was going to say that I felt a little closer to Randall, but at the moment, I can't say that. I gained more peace because of knowing about her background and knowing some of the problems that she and her father had that are showing up in Randall. So some of it is genetics and not the way he was raised. In all your education classes you learn about the environment that you set for the kids. Being an education major, I thought it would be the stronger influence. There are times we are very close, but closeness with Randall is kind of touch and go. When he is here it is just because he needs something or wants something. If he is deep down hurting or deep down needing, he comes to us. There is a bond, not a normal bond. We aren't as close as I had hoped. There have been disappointments and pleasures in the whole thing. I don't mean to be negative, but obviously, I am disappointed in what is happening in his life right now. He is still a good person. I talk with one of his ex-wives a lot and she says she will always love him even if he is married to someone else. He's been divorced twice."

Molly

"Being adopted made me feel a bit different, but I think I was indifferent to it. I didn't feel good or bad about it. I understood I had been born to someone else. It seemed okay talking about it, but when I started asking questions and tried to pursue it, there were not a lot of answers so the discussion shut down. I have an adopted sister, three years younger. There were no birth children in our family. I was in my mid-teens when I really became curious about my birth background. I was told my birth mother was married, but separated, had an affair and conceived me. She didn't want her husband to know and she didn't want me to grow up in an environment where the father would treat me differently. She felt that it was an act of love on her part to plan adoption for me, reassuring me that she loved me. I had some questions but didn't want to hurt their feelings, and was afraid they'd think I didn't love them. I believe Mom really didn't know a lot but gave me all the information she had.

"There were a couple of times I considered searching. First, at twenty, but my husband was afraid I might get hurt. I was out of my parents' home so I thought I could do it and not hurt their feelings. Then at twenty-seven, I decided I really wanted to do it. I didn't tell my parents until after I had talked with my birth mother for the first time. I told them I wanted to know my health history and get any other information I could. I also wanted to thank her for what she did. They didn't show a lot of emotion at the time. However, my sister told me that my father was really upset – couldn't understand why I'd want to bring up old wounds. When I personally talked to my mom and dad they told me they were happy for me. He was referring to old wounds of the birth mother, not theirs because of the infertility, I think. My father was upset at first, but they both have been supportive of me since I met my birth family.

"When I talked with you, you told me to register with ISRR and that was not productive. My first contact with Norma, my birth mother, was by phone and I was really nervous. I had fantasized about how the reunion would take place. I thought I would go and knock on her door on my birthday and say, 'Remember what happened twenty years ago today?' Then I would thank her for giving me a better life. All those fantasies were in the back of my mind. I was really nervous. My fantasies were not realistic, of course. Our first phone call was about an hour. Three months later I met her and her family. I was excited, but it was not the Oprah Winfrey show where everyone's crying. I was just indifferent, maybe a bit numb.

"She and her other daughter she'd given up for adoption met me at the airport. I have always felt close to that sister since we were both placed for adoption. I feel that we have known each other forever. We are true sisters. I talk with her twice a month. I have been to California to visit her and spent Christmas of 2002 with her family. My parents were fine with it – Christmas is not really a big thing at our house anymore. I talk with Norma about every two months, but I am closer to my sister. I don't see Norma as a mother image – Dorothy is my mother! (Adoptive mother).

"There has been no contact between my parents and Norma. There is no curiosity on either's part. That may change in the near future as I am marrying again in January and they will all be at the wedding. I don't remember how Mom and Dad reacted to the first meeting. I was in the process of a divorce and I think they were more worried about that.

"I have a Bachelor's degree in nursing and am applying to go back for my Master's. I was always one of those brainy kids, kind of a nerd. I think my mom is happy for me because she has seen how much I enjoy all my birth brothers and sisters and she sometimes makes things for me to take to my nieces and nephews. We've had three reunions now."

Norma tells her story:
"I have three daughters, counting Molly. I had a boy friend in high school and when I got pregnant his mom put him in the army and my dad kicked me out of the house. So I took a bus to Los Angeles to contact an adoption agency. That was my first child. It just broke my heart. I couldn't get together with the father. I con-

tacted the Provost Marshall in the army and the father denied paternity. Then I had six weeks to try to get her back even though I had no idea how I would be able to take care of her. I wanted her to have a good life where she would have brothers and sisters. They told me that she was placed in a home with two older brothers and that was a lie. She was the first child placed in her adoptive home. A sister was placed later. I had a letter and a picture of her that was turning yellow. I couldn't even look at it any more so I got rid of it. I wish I had kept it. She found me a few months before Molly found me.

"I got married and had three children – boy, girl, boy. My husband was a wonderful, kind, talented man. Suddenly he started being so weird and crazy and years later he was diagnosed as a paranoid schizophrenic, manic-depressive. It was very scary and difficult. I had to get the kids away. I moved to Arizona with my three children. That's when Molly came about. I really didn't want to have another baby. I just wanted to take care of the three that I had. When we went to court I was given full custody, but my husband tracked me down. I was so afraid of him. He stalked me while I was pregnant with Molly. I thought, 'Oh, I cannot have this sweet little baby around this crazy person.' I felt that I should give up my baby for adoption. As it turns out, it was a good choice for the baby. She had a good family life. So I placed my first and last child for adoption.

"The terrible part about it was that I was so heartbroken because I love my children dearly and would do anything in the world for them. Having, for the second time, to give the baby up for adoption did something to me. I kind of lost my memory and when I met Molly I thought that maybe my memory would come back. But I still do not remember any facts. I couldn't even remember the day she was born. Everything was just gone. My children were really latchkey children since they didn't have a father in their lives. Molly's birth father didn't participate in the plan.

"Molly was twenty-seven when she found me. When you (Shirley) contacted me I had just been reunited with my other daughter on Thanksgiving. We decided to have a reunion with all my kids. I can't tell you how happy I was when I spoke to that daughter on the phone and she told me that she'd had a good life so this just did something to me – I'd had a heavy heart and felt guilty and that made me so happy. Then came Molly. I had everything I ever wanted in life because I had heard that both of my children had good lives. They were well adjusted, smart and talented. I thought I could die happy now since all the brothers and sisters were going to meet each other. I felt good about the decisions I had made for them. It was my fault. I made horrible mistakes. Over the years you read about adopted children being abused and murdered. I couldn't have had better news than to know that they were alive and safe and happy. So the whole family spent four days together. The two daughters I had talked with each other before. They were anxious to meet each other.

"Now Molly loves me. I don't expect to be her mom, but now I know the brothers and sisters will always have each other. We have all developed a neat relationship. We all care for and love each other. All my children know that I stay out of their lives. They know that others will be there for them if they need them. They have spent some time comparing similarities. I have not met Molly's parents. They may not have been too happy about her need or desire to find out about her roots. Molly felt a little awkward at first and was afraid of hurting her parents' feelings. I don't think they want to meet me.

"My questions have been answered and to look at her and talk to her I know she had a good happy life and no horrible things have gone on. Both of them are better off because of my decisions and they know I loved them and cared for them. I feel that a big burden has been lifted. Unfortunately, I was not able to raise two of my children, but I feel so blessed – we now know that good things can come from a child being placed for adoption."

Dorothy, Molly's adoptive mother:
"We had been married for thirteen years and always wanted a child. I had thought of adoption, but wanted to wait until my husband suggested it. I had, for some time felt that we could love someone else's child. When we adopted our second girl, Molly seemed to understand the whole process. Both of them were very young when they realized they were born to someone else. One day one of Molly's friends asked her why her real mother had given her away. I waited for her answer and she responded, 'Well my real parents are right here. I don't know the mother who gave birth to me.' Molly never had any more questions. She was only in kindergarten and a very bright girl. We had explained everything when we went through the process the second time. We told her

that we would be seeing a judge. She had been watching 'Here Comes the Judge' so she was very excited about it and was anxious to see the judge pound his gavel. It took some time and Molly was very tired but turned around just in time to see him bang his gavel. She was so excited.

"Molly always wanted to show off her little sister to all of her friends. I was always afraid that she would just wake her up but the baby was a people person and adored her big sister. So right away she would wake up, smile for her friends and go back to sleep. One day I was walking by her room and Molly was standing at the side of the crib and looking down at her and just crying, tears streaming down her face. I went in to see what was wrong. When I asked, she said, 'We are not going to take her back, are we?' I assured her that we were keeping her because we all loved her.

"All I ever told Molly was a truthful answer to whatever she asked. She never knew she was from a family of brothers and sisters. I didn't want to tell her that. She learned of her brothers and sisters when she had the reunion. She never thought that her mother rejected her. If I had told her anything along that line it would have been that her mother wanted her to have a good family. She had few questions but started wondering about things that might run in the family, health wise. When she went into nursing she became more curious about it. I learned it was one of the reasons she went into nursing and the main reason she decided to search for her biological family. I gave her all the information the agency gave us but I didn't tell her she had siblings.

"She didn't tell me ahead of time that she was going to do a search. She waited and told us after she had found them. I really didn't feel bad about it because it has been good for her and made her very happy. It had a positive effect. If it had been a negative experience, I would have been upset about it. My husband and other daughter had warned her that she was opening up the birth family's life but also opening up her life as well. My other daughter did not want to search. Her situation was entirely different in that she was an only child at the time of her birth. I really wasn't surprised by Molly's curiosity since she had always been such a bright child.

"Apparently the whole family gets together once a year. I have a sister who lives fairly close. I called her to tell her about the whole thing so if Molly ever gets uncomfortable she could call her aunt to come to get her. I've told Norma to get in touch with us if she ever comes to the valley, but so far she hasn't. If she does come I would be happy to meet her but I won't feel badly if I don't. The reunion has not really changed things for us. I believe Molly still sees us as her parents and we have two lovely daughters who fill me with pride. They both have made a good adjustment in life. Molly came over on Father's Day and cooked a delicious dinner for us. She made some things that I don't cook myself and we enjoyed the day with her very much. I feel very lucky to have two wonderful daughters."

Emily

"I was seven when my mother explained all the details of adoption and how I had become their daughter. It was like okay, I'm happy, I love you and that is it. My parents had another child, a boy who was born to them six years earlier. Mom almost died having him and she could not have another child. There were different weird things that happened in my life. I had asked questions and mom told me as much as she could – that I was Hawaiian and Dutch. (She is Mexican and Dad is Irish.) She said I was from royalty – my mother was a Hawaiian princess. But I always wondered why my eyes shut when I smiled. She told me they are just almond-shaped and that's Hawaiian. One time a friend of my brother's came over and said to me, 'Chinese, Japanese, dirty knees, look at these.' I ran into the house crying because I was hurt. I had no idea I was Japanese. I knew I had those eyes, but my mom always said, 'Oh, no, you're not.' I never questioned her but I still wondered. I don't really know if she knew that I was part Japanese. I hate to think that my mom would lie to me. She now tells me that the adoption agency fudged a bit because, at the time, the war was still in the air and they didn't want to say I was part Japanese because they were afraid they wouldn't be able to place me. They told her I was a little bit Mexican, Hawaiian and Dutch. It was hard for me to find that my whole life was a lie. I don't have any Dutch or any Hawaiian. I know now that I am Polish and Japanese.

"People talked about others in their family whom they looked like and I never saw that in myself. I am definitely not like my family. I feel like a chicken with a bunch of ducks. I've always felt that way. I love my family, but as far as looking anything like them, there is no connection. It was so helpful when I got pictures of Betsy (her birth mother). One thing that was nice was that my daughter had Betsy's nose and mouth – full lips, and no one else in the family is like that. It's nice to have a connection to someone who is like you. My mom was so flattered if anyone said that I looked like her. Adoption was only talked about privately, but I don't think she was ashamed. She saw me as her daughter and it didn't matter that I was adopted. If someone asked, I would tell them I was adopted, but I didn't want to make her feel bad. I felt way different from my brother. I always felt he never got in trouble and I did.

"We really weren't treated differently, I just didn't agree with my parents in their discipline. They overlooked so many things with my brother so he just kept misbehaving. In high school he got involved in drugs, burned a field down, was stealing, all kinds of things. They'd always cover for him. I got in trouble, too. We just lived different ways. I loved school, he didn't. I loved athletics, he didn't. No common ground. I paid for the trouble I got into, but not like I should have. It was so minor compared to what he did. They were too lenient all the way around.

"I became more curious in my senior year and after high school. I wondered if Mom was blowing things up to make it sound good – like the nationality thing. She would tell people I was Mexican. I do have darker skin. Now if I mention to anyone that I have some Japanese, she gets really upset. She still wants to believe that I am like her. In her mind I am. I doubted her because she would never give me any paper work. She said she couldn't remember the hospital I was born in, but could remember the hospital for my brother. She denied having any adoption papers. I sent for my birth certificate – no hospital name. Maybe she was telling the truth, but it made me wonder. They told me that my birth mother gave me up because she was young, she loved me and was trying to do what was best for me.

"I never had any negative feelings about her (birth mother) until after I actually communicated with her and then I had bad feelings. It was painful, hurtful, that she didn't want to share identifying information.

"I told my parents that I was going to do a search and they were very supportive. They told me they wanted me to do what I felt I needed to do. But I didn't get around to it until I was thirty-one. I tried to do it on my own, but it got so complicated that I gave up. I called the agency and they referred me to the CIP. It was a matter of prayer that I picked you. It was scary to go through all the steps and I needed someone who would understand and care. My parents believed in God but I really had no spiritual upbringing. I am active in church now.

"The only contact Betsy and I have had was two letters from me with pictures and one from her with pictures. She didn't sign a consent so I could have her identifying information. I am hurt that it ended that way. I feel that a lot of information is being hidden from me and I keep questioning my parents. I now tell people that I am part Japanese and part some white guy. It is kind of an identity crisis. Betsy says she doesn't know about the background of the birth father. He was tall, blond, blue-eyed and Anglo. But how tall? There was so much more I wanted to ask her. It would have been so nice to hear her voice, to see her gestures.

"Maybe it's dumb. Other people know so much more about their background. They tell me that I am the lineage of my adoptive parents. I don't feel that kind of connection. I don't look like them and am nothing like them. I can see it in my daughter. She's like her paternal grandmother. They are similar in personality and traits. I adore my family and it was meant for me to be with my adoptive parents. They have had problems – my mom had a drinking problem and it has been rough for them. She was an alcoholic until I was in the sixth grade. She has battled depression. It was common for an ambulance to be at our house. If they hadn't had me I don't think they'd have made it. She's tried to commit suicide a few times. I'm glad I'm here for them. I love my parents a lot. They did their best. They had difficulties. My dad had a difficult childhood. They've always provided, they've always kept a roof over our heads and had love for us. I know that being her little girl, I was her rock. My brother would always side with Dad. My poor mom would be in pain – she needed me to give her a hug and tell her it was going to be okay and how much I loved her and I'd be there for her. Now my brother has his own problems. I take care of my parents. They don't make enough money. We supplement their income and make sure that everything is okay. I shudder to think if I had not been there for them, where would they be? They did finally get it all together and did all right. We never lived in one place longer than three years. They would decide that the grass was greener on the other side and then we'd move. We lived in tents, motels, apartments and trailers.

"I've seen people who were worse off. I began baby sitting when I was quite young and then got a real job and worked all the time so I had enough money to buy my own clothes and finally bought a car in my senior year of high school. My parents are really the most generous, kind people in the world. They would give you the shirt off their back. If they saw someone in need they would try to help out, even though they had little. My mom would have given me the world. There were so many things that she wanted me to have but couldn't give me. I knew that and it was enough just knowing what she wanted for me. Whenever they moved they'd give me the biggest room in the house."

Lily, the adoptive mother:

"Emily was five years old when I told her of her adoption. Some of the people we knew were aware that we had adopted her and we didn't want her to hear it from someone else. She was a bright little girl and she understood what I told her. I told her that maybe the other lady whom she came from had an accident when she was fourteen or fifteen and got pregnant. She said, 'No, no, Mama, she just didn't want me but you wanted me and it's okay because you're my mommy.' She thought that her birth mother didn't want her and I tried to straighten her out, but she has a mind of her own and always has. No matter what I said she would just say the lady didn't want her. It had to hurt. She told me that I was her mommy and that is all she wanted. She didn't ask any more questions. She was as happy as can be. I was comfortable in talking with her about it. That is the funny part. We are always comfortable in talking with each other. She's had like a sixth sense ever since she was a baby. She can feel things. Maybe her birth mother didn't want her. She gave her away and then she got married and had another child within a year. Emily showed me her letter and now that she doesn't even want to see her, she is really hurt, but she told me, 'At least I have you and Daddy, Mama.' Apparently she had an affair with a married man who was white, blond and blue-eyed, and she broke up with him. Betsy started dating a Mexican – I don't understand why she didn't find out she was pregnant until she broke up with the Mexican. She didn't know who the father was, but she thought it was the married man. Emily told me she is glad I told her about the adoption when she was young. If she was to find out when she was older or from someone else, she would've been upset.

"She started asking questions after she got married as she wanted to know more for her children's sake. She still would like to know who her biological father is. She says she doesn't want any thing from him. She just wants to know what to expect for her and her children. I felt it was normal when she started asking questions. I was expecting it. I was not hurt because we are friends as well as mother and daughter. Emily has brown hair and the most beautiful light brown eyes you ever saw. To me she is gorgeous. You can tell she has Oriental blood and a most beautiful smile. Her mother said she is Japanese. So Emily is half-Japanese and half-white. I was never threatened by her desire to search. Actually, I encouraged her. When you found her I felt good until she told me her birth mother didn't want to meet her. That really hurt. I haven't lost anything, but feel I have gained something since her birth mother didn't want to see her. I was mad at her birth mother for it. She is such a sweet girl. I feel I have gained more of her love. She knows I am here for her whenever she needs me and nobody else is. We never think of her as being adopted."

Betsy, the birth mother:

"When I found out I was pregnant, I went to New Jersey to stay with my father from whom I had been estranged for a very long time. I didn't want to tell my mother. After a month, I couldn't stand it any longer. My parents had been divorced for a long time and I thought I would have the baby over there. It didn't work out so I told my mother and she said I should come home. She was very good about it. I thought of keeping the baby – there was no consideration of an abortion. There was no way I could support her by myself. It all felt like a big drama. The cruel part was at the hospital. The day after I had her, they walked me down the hall, let me see the baby, walked me back to my bed and after that someone came in to have me sign papers. Very cut and dried, very indifferent, very cold. It was all like a fog, like it wasn't really happening to me. I can't remember if those were the papers for the release of the baby from the hospital or the adoption papers. It was a blur. I was crying. After I signed the papers, that was it. I don't recall their telling me to read them or asking if I understood them. I don't remember anything. I was totally emotionally distraught – a very strange feeling. There were times when I regretted my decision. On her birthday, I was sad and had some regrets, but still I knew it was better for the baby and me. Today there would be no question about keeping the baby, but then it was necessity. Back then it was just a horrible thing. What could I do? My mother had to work. I told the father of the baby about the pregnancy. There was no reaction except a brief concern and, 'What are you going to do?' He was pretty much uninvolved – not much of a relationship there. I said I was going to place her and that was pretty much it. It was all on my part to make the decision. You can tell when a person is not going to commit. I told him that was fine. He did not sign any papers. I have no contact with him now and have no idea where he is.

"When Emily wrote to me she did want to know the father and when I got the pictures of her, I knew who the father was. There had been more than one possibility. I'd been with three of four different guys on occasion so I really didn't know. When I saw her, I knew. That's how she got confused about the background of her father. I told her in my letter that when I saw the picture I was 100% sure who her father is. She wrote back and said she doesn't think it is fair that I don't tell. He was married at the time – it was a very bad situation – it was brief and I don't think it would be fair to exploit him by telling her who he is. I don't think it was the person that I had a better relationship with and with whom I thought I had a future. So I don't think it was the person that I wrote down originally when they ask all about the background. Just by looking, I know who it was. I don't know what his ethnicity is. He is Caucasian, has blond hair and blue eyes and has features similar to Emily. I remember him as a very nice person. I'm not going to say anything bad. It gave me some comfort to know who the father was.

"When you called, I was shocked, not too surprised that it had actually caught up with me and a little panicky at the same time. Can't say that I was happy. Both of my husbands knew about Emily. My first husband was a friend when I was pregnant with Emily. My present husband was glad you found me for Emily. At first I was going to sign the consent paper (for permission to share identifying information) and then I changed my mind. I can't tell you what was happening at the time. I have a million things going on in my life and it doesn't stop. The more I thought about it the more I decided to wait. I don't think the timing was right. I just wasn't comfortable with it. If it was just me and Emily alone in the world then I would want to talk and visit – yes, then I would want to do it. There are other people who would be involved and I don't think they are ready so I'm not ready. I am referring to my children. My son asked me who Shirley was. I told him that she is a woman that I have been talking with about a number of things."

Shirley: I was able to find her through her son.

Betsy continues:

"I hope Emily won't do a sibling search. I guess it would give her information about some blood relatives and she would see who she looks like and what they are like. I have given her my medical information and she has given me hers and right now that is good for me to know that she's doing well – and that she has a wonderful family. I always feel that sometime I will tell my kids when the timing is right. My sister, mother and husband know and at some point in time I will tell my kids but not right now. I don't know how they will react. I know them better than anyone else – I'm the only one who can judge. I wish I could just say, 'Hey, I'm going to pick up the phone now.' But I just can't do it yet. I guess I'd be calling you (Shirley).

"The search satisfied a lot of my curiosity – the information in the letter she sent about how she grew up, who adopted her and the kind of life she had. She talked about it in a very positive way. I had wondered if she lived on a back street somewhere, whether she'd had the opportunity to go to school, whether she had grown up in a foster home, what kind of life style she had, that kind of thing. There were times when I got on the Internet and tried to search, but of course, I came up with a blank. That letter and her pictures made me happy and satisfied me that her life has been good. I sent her pictures, too. (All forwarded through Shirley.) So it's given me comfort about my adoption decision. There are times when I think, 'How can I tell the kids, how would it be to meet and what exactly would I say?' So the letter and the pictures were the best for me. If I had found that she grew up in a foster home, I would have had a guilt thing going on for a million years. The answers made it all right for me so I can die in peace. I have two other children and a stepson. My husband has relatives who live in Utah who are very good Mormons. His sister-in-law is into genealogy so I get a little cramp in my neck whenever she talks about going deeply into the family background. Emily has three daughters. I sent pictures of my other children to her. I think this has been a good conversation, maybe I needed to talk about it."

Sydney

"When I was in grade school, my mom used to lie down with me sometimes and it was then that I would ask a lot of questions, about all kinds of things. I knew I was adopted and the only way it made me feel different was like I had a bigger family – two moms and two dads. It was kind of like a stepfamily. Lots of my friends had stepparents so it was like I had stepparents, too. My stepparents were my birth parents, because the parents that I grew up with were my real parents. I did know that I grew inside the step mom and I would not be able to meet her until I was older. My mom seemed a little nervous when she talked about it. Then there was a case where a girl went to court because her parents wanted her back. That made my mom very nervous. I think she worries a lot. I have a brother who was adopted and is three years younger. Since I found my birth family, he has opened up a bit and is starting to want to know more about his gene pool, too. It's been good for both of us.

"I first wondered if Jeanine (birth mother) thought about me all the time. Did she remember my birthday, etc.? It progressed as I got older. I wondered about any health problems in the family so I would know what could happen to me in the future. The main thing, though, was if I looked like her. I do look quite a bit like her except our noses are different. I wanted to know if I had any brothers and sisters. I had a close friend who looked quite a bit like me and I always wondered if she could be my sister or if that person could be my aunt or another – my grandma. I was always walking around looking to see if there was anyone who looked like me. Adoptees do a lot of imagining. It was difficult for Jeanine to tell me why she gave me up. She didn't really want to get into the details. She was in a bad relationship with her boyfriend. He wanted a boy, but really didn't want a baby at all. They chose adoption – she was against the abortion thing, which is good or I wouldn't be here now. She gave me life. I think it was very hard for her and I know that she loved me. She was only seventeen and I'm now twenty-one and I know I'm not ready to parent.

"My adoptive parents were understanding of my curiosity. There was some discouragement, but a lot of encouragement as well. They couldn't provide all the answers I wanted. I knew at fifteen I would do a search when I was old enough. I had been a difficult teenager for them. Sometimes I felt that they loved me too much. All my friends were going to sleepovers and I wasn't allowed to go when I was thirteen. They were very overprotective. When I asked them why they told me that they couldn't have any more kids and they didn't want anything to happen to me. They wanted children to fulfill their dream.

"I tried to do the search on my own – went on the Internet, but I didn't even have a name. We contacted ISRR, but that produced nothing so we contacted you (Shirley). Now I have had a reunion with Jeanine. I found that my grandma (her mom) lived about two miles away from us so I talked with her first. She offered to fly with me to the state where Jeanine lives. She showed me some pictures of her, but it didn't help much. I talked with Jeanine before we left and learned that I have a younger sister and two brothers. When we got to the airport I looked for anyone with blond hair. I heard someone yell, 'There they are!' I turned around and it was my two little half brothers running over to us. Jeanine ran over too and I went to her and we had a big long hug, which was great. I cried and she was holding back tears.

"I look a lot like my sister and I have a picture of her that she let me keep. She has a smaller button nose, and blue eyes. I had always wanted a sister. I had pretended that a girl at school was my twin and we were called the Doublemint twins – long blond hair. It is awesome to have contact with people who look like me – people who have the same blood and the same gene pool, same everything almost – it is awesome – a very special feeling. The hole inside me is filled. It is wonderful. I spent a week with them and felt quite at home. I felt so accepted by everybody. My little brother always says he loves me and that makes me feel so good.

"I've been working long hours and I didn't get a chance to call her on Mother's Day. That upset me. I called my adoptive mom, though, but I didn't get to see her either. I haven't talked a lot with Jeanine lately – we are both so busy, but she always welcomes my calls when I have time. My mother has talked with my grandma a lot.

"Later Jeanine came here so I got to see her again. My folks were okay about the reunion, but when I told my mom that I really like it over there, she was very upset that I might move there. But I wouldn't do that – just a fleeting thought. My mom was happy that I found Jeanine. I know she was a little jealous. I guess that was natural. I don't feel closer to either of them. I would like to be closer to Jeanine, but sometimes I feel if I talk with her a lot that my mom would get jealous. I sure don't want to hurt her feelings. Otherwise I would call her once a week if I had the time. Right now I feel that it's excellent to be adopted. I wouldn't have picked a different life."

Jeanine, Sydney's birth mother:
"We placed Sydney for adoption because her father didn't want children and we really couldn't afford it. I don't remember if we were married at the time, but we did marry ultimately. I never regretted it because I felt that I was giving a child to someone who couldn't have children and it was like God's gift to them. The father didn't sign papers because I wasn't sure he was the father so I felt that I should do it on my own.

"Sydney was nineteen when we met. I was shocked when you (Shirley) called me – very shocked! My husband and I had talked a lot about it because he is the father of four children who were placed for adoption. His former wife placed them and he has just recently been in contact with them. It has really been a whirlwind for us. I wish you had done his adoption, too because his was a different scenario. It was not a comfortable one. He really wanted his kids. They have just recently been put back together and his girls keep in close touch with him. When you called me, I had very mixed feelings. I was scared, happy, nervous, and excited. My emotions were just going crazy. I actually met Sydney about six months after you called. When she got off the plane, she ran to me and I ran to her and I picked her up and swung her around and hugged her. It was a little awkward at first because I knew about problems her parents had with her and so it was a little wild because I had a daughter just a year younger who was a total terror all the time she was growing up. They were like two peas in a pod, but it ended up being okay. We contact each other every now and then. We had a good time with Sydney and our children when we went there to visit. Now his girls contact Sydney occasionally and they get together. It's like they are related even though they're not. I've talked with her adoptive mother occasionally, but not for a while. Sydney told me she was having jealousy issues. That bothers me. I'm certainly not trying to take her place. But I would like to be a part of Sydney's life now. I guess her feelings are very normal. She just wants to get to know me. I pointed out that getting to know me was like getting to know herself. I do occasionally feel that I am in a mothering position with Sydney. She is a part of me and I want to be there for her in her happy moments and in her sad moments – that is, if she wants me to be there for her. I gave birth to her but Audrey is her mother and does the mothering. I don't want to take anything away from Audrey.

"Besides my daughter, I have two boys, fifteen and thirteen. My children have always known that I placed a child for adoption. They thought it was neat. I always had a picture of the baby – they'd ask about her and wonder if they could ever meet her. They have known about my husband's girls as well and we thought it would be so nice if we could all get together some time. I told them I thought Sydney would get in touch with me. It just came a little sooner than I expected. When I got off the phone with you that was the first thing I told everybody – 'You are going to meet your other sister.' They said, 'Oh, cool!!!' They were very happy. Sydney and my daughter talked fairly often, but they can't now – my daughter's in jail. She was on probation for check fraud and she violated her probation – she didn't do her community work. It has been hard but I think it's going to help her grow up. I think my two daughters meeting each other has had a positive effect on both of them. They have changed a lot. I feel somewhat responsible for Sydney's change of behavior – not just because of me, but I think she knew it was time to grow up and prove to everyone that she could do it. Maybe meeting me just kinda helped that along. It was helpful to her to know I didn't reject her. That changed her own feelings about herself. Now she has more self-confidence.

"I've had a lot of curiosity through the years and the reunion has satisfied it. She looks more like me than my other daughter. I'm glad I made the decision that I did. My mother was sad when I made it – she cried and had second thoughts. This reunion meant a lot to her. She and my husband had encouraged me to do a search, but I thought I had to wait until she was twenty-one."

Audrey, the adoptive mother:

"We adopted two children, Sydney, and Brent, three years later. They grew up being familiar with the word adoption. I'm not sure when they realized they were born to someone else. That probably came over a period of time because they heard it over and over. We explained that the adoption plan was one made with love and concern for them to grow up and be the very best person they could be. We always told them that if they had a desire to search we would help them. Perhaps I was a little curious myself – Sydney presented such a challenge for us during her teen years – but Sydney was the one who actually started us on it. One morning she wanted to know who her birth mother was and where she was. Since we've met them, there is not a doubt in our minds that they had her best interests at heart when they planned adoption for her. When she actually wanted to go ahead with the search, I did feel some discomfort and had mixed feelings. I had some fear about possibly losing her and that was pretty scary. Still, I think I always knew this day would come. Had I been adopted, I would surely want to know. I was trying to put myself in her shoes and I would have done a search. It certainly did not seem out of the ordinary or uncharacteristic to want to know. Brent showed some curiosity as Sydney's search progressed. I was more vocal about helping than my husband. I knew when Sydney expressed curiosity that I'd be willing to be involved if she wanted my help. Sydney began asking specific questions: Where does she live? Do I have any brothers and sisters? Perhaps my curiosity was heightened by these questions. I admit that I was more curious than their dad.

"The information we got from the agency was typed up and we made a copy for Sydney. She wanted to take it to school to show her friends who knew she was adopted. We were not happy about that and told her she couldn't do it. Not that it was something to be ashamed of, but we just didn't think it was the right time. But she did it anyway. As an adoptive parent, when the search wheels are actually rolling, you wonder if she will forget who you are, will she want to have anything to do with us? Will this other woman overshadow everything we've done? Then I said to myself – the eighteen years we've put into her cannot be wiped out – and that gave me some peace.

"The first time Sydney talked with Jeanine, I felt that they should have privacy and they'd want me out of the room. Instead, she wanted me right there by her side and if I went into another room, she'd follow me. That gave me some reassurance that she was still my daughter. But it didn't erase all my fears. Jeanine lived in another state – I worried that she would want to move there and have a brand new family. When Jeanine was found, I was relieved that she was open to contact – then I knew Sydney wouldn't be hurt. I think I even cried – I was so relieved.

"We've met Jeanine. She is very nice and sweet, but she doesn't initiate contact with Sydney. All contacts are made by Sydney, and only seldom at that. The times we have seen her have been initiated by us. She told us that if Sydney had not done a search, she would have done one when Sydney was twenty-one. If Jeanine came to town, Sydney would want to see her. Apparently their curiosity has been satisfied and there isn't the motivation there was before. Further, this reunion has not had any effect on Sydney's relationship with me. When something comes up that she needs to talk about, I am the first person she calls. I feel that her closest relationship is still with me. Sydney's been a very difficult person and we've had our challenges. She realizes that we are her parents. Yes, Jeanine gave birth to her, but in the event of a catastrophe or dire need, we are the ones she calls. She is still our daughter and we are still her parents. Now, she doesn't seem to need more contact with Jeanine."

Shirley: At the time of my last contact with this family I was told that they had just learned of Sydney's out-of-wedlock pregnancy.

Justin

"My sister and I were adopted and that meant we were special. I am so grateful that the fact of adoption was handled in a very open and positive manner in our home. When some friends found out they would act surprised and it seemed like negative energy, but I was able to talk about it freely, so it made it all okay. I never felt it was anything other than a positive experience. I am so close to my adopted sister and miss her dearly when I don't see her. Our adoptive parents have no birth children.

"I guess I was about eight when I started asking questions: Tell me about my parents, What do you know? Who do I look like? Nationality? They associated the relinquishment with love, although they couldn't give me the specific reasons – they hadn't been told. They were always very accepting of my curiosity. But I hesitated because I had to make a decision about how I would tell my mom when I contacted you to do the search. I felt that she would be sad, like it would hurt her. I don't think my questions were ever threatening to her. I don't know, maybe they were. I don't want to ask questions if the response might be highly emotional. Still I was afraid she might possibly think I was looking for another mother. Like she might say, 'Wasn't I good enough? Why do you need to find her?' She was very emotional about the death of my father.

"When I finally did tell her, she smiled, but her eyes welled up with tears and she said she knew this day would come. But she was okay with it! She explained that it was fine and wondered if she'd get to meet my birth mother, too. It turned into a very positive experience after all. It was such an incredible relief.

"Although my birth mother died a few years ago (before I had a chance to meet her), I am still in touch with some members of my birth family. I learned of the CIP program through the Internet. With the search we learned that my birth mother had passed away, but you were able to put me in touch with her stepfather, the man who raised her from the age of eight, and his present wife, Joan. We've had countless phone conversations, but have met only once for about ten or eleven hours. I felt good that I could have contact with someone who had known her so well. The meeting was a bit tense to begin with because I was still having trouble comprehending just how he was related to her. I wanted to see some resemblance to a family member, but he wasn't a blood relative of my birth mother.

"He told me amazing things about her – her likes and dislikes, her love of cooking, her admiration of beauty and modeling. I did see pictures of her and a video. She looks a lot like me – extreme similarity – the eyes, the chin, the dimples, the same cleft, the same crooked smile. The picture of her at sixteen resembles me at sixteen. It was the most incredible feeling of joy I think I've ever experienced. Even though I couldn't speak to her or hold her it was the connection I needed to make. For a while our contact was pretty strong, but after a time our busy lives took over again. Other than that, everything is still the same. Joan E-mails me every week. Joan had spent a lot of time with her, too. Her stepfather and Joan knew she had placed a baby for adoption. She spoke of me often. She had talked about wanting to search for me, but didn't know how and didn't think I would want anything to do with her. "The day I spent with them was the biggest delight. I couldn't have asked for more – amazing! Thinking about it and going back there just fills me with so much love and I needed to feel it today. I felt a bit down before we had this talk today. But my ups and downs are not from that. I learned that I had a half sister born to my birth mother later. I wanted to know more about my birth grandma. I'd been so close to my adoptive grandma. Grandmas are special! I was thinking of the whole family unit. I always thought or dreamed that I might have a brother or sister.

"I first suspected that I might be gay at around the age of nine – it was confirmed in later years. To me people are just human beings and that is essentially where I go with everything. It was really a relief when Mom finally realized I was gay because then I could come out of the closet. But then the distance came. That was a big disappointment for about four or five years. It took her a long time before she would cross the threshold of our door. She'd come over but wouldn't enter.

"I've always wanted a child. I still have about ten years left to play with. I will likely stop thinking about it when I'm in my forties. I do think it's in the realm of reality – not necessarily through adoption, but not through the consummation of marriage, either. I would not get married, but I would use my sperm and a woman's egg. If I couldn't I would most certainly adopt."

Ronnie, step-grandfather of Justin:

"Ilene's mother and I dated some time before we married. Ilene (birth mother) was eighteen when she left home and she just wandered around. This was in the early '70s and she got in with the hippie group where she met and married her husband. She later divorced him and somewhere along the line got pregnant. She was doing drugs at the time and when she was four or five months along we learned about it. She was in Phoenix but they moved around so much it was hard to keep track of her. She lived around with different friends. She finally came home and stayed with us until she had the baby. She chose adoption – she was definitely not ready for the responsibility of caring for a baby. We told her she could keep the baby and stay with us if she would stop using drugs. We would then support her, but I was not going to have a baby left here at the house and have her running some place else to keep the drugs going and continuing the hippie lifestyle. She was still using drugs when she came home. We were very concerned that the baby would be affected. As far as we knew she stayed away from anything really heavy during the pregnancy. She still went out with her friends. I imagine they still drank or whatever. Since I've met Justin, I don't think he was affected. He is a very nice boy. I feared that she had taken about everything you could dream of that was going around the streets then. She was really heavy into the hippie lifestyle.

"Ilene was a cheerful, beautiful little girl. She had a lot of good friends other than the ones in the drug culture. She was a happy girl. From twelve to eighteen she only gave us the normal teenage problems. She would sometimes tell us that she would be staying at the home of a friend and that friend would tell her parents that she was going to stay with us, then the two of them would take off to somewhere else and we didn't know where they were. She wasn't into school functions – football games, basketball games, etc. She was a good cook and enjoyed that. Her mother taught her well. She liked the kind of music they played back then. She dearly loved animals – especially stray ones. If they were hurt she would doctor them.

"I have told all of this to Justin and answered all his questions about her and her mother. Ilene's other child, Natalie, completely cut off ties with me after Ilene died. I haven't heard from her since. Her father was not married to Ilene. There seems to be a lot of ties between Justin and Ilene. He really likes animals, enjoys cooking and is good-looking. Ilene had a very good heart. She was always giving to other people. She tried very hard at the end to quit everything and she did very well at it. After she had Natalie, she was down to just a bit of drinking, but she was living with an alcoholic so it was difficult. But by then it was really too late. Natalie was thirteen when Ilene died, so she was thirteen years younger than Justin. Ilene had some kind of a lung problem following a bout of pneumonia. Unfortunately, Justin contacted me just six months after Ilene died. I was married to her mother for twenty-seven years. She was my first wife and she'd been married before. I tried to contact Natalie after I heard from Justin, but she had moved. I even went to the address, but no one was there. I thought it would be great for them to know each other. I'm not sure if I ever told her that she had a brother running around out there somewhere. I used to say to Joan that one of these days we ought to try to find him – see whatever happened to him – see what kind of a boy he turned out to be. She wondered if he would ever do a search.

"Justin came over with his mother and they chatted with my wife. I had just missed them when I got home. We are not in touch by phone but he said he would plan to visit again soon. My wife keeps in touch by E-mail. His adoptive mother is a lovely lady and they are welcome here any time."

Virginia, Justin's adoptive mother:
"We adopted Justin and then Hayley, about two and a half years later. We read books about adoption to them so they'd understand how they came to be in our family. I think they felt they had been chosen. You placed children that fit so well with us. Justin was like his dad's side of the family and Hayley is something like me – the complexion and stuff, but she had blonder hair. Justin had a bit harder time understanding why his birth mother gave him up 'cause she was just one year younger than I was. I told him that she could have aborted the pregnancy, but she didn't. It was just not possible for her to take care of him. Hay-

ley's parents were very, very young so it was easier for her to understand. That has to be difficult for a child. Stan (my husband) died in 1989 – fifteen years ago – with a heart attack in the middle of the night. The children were sixteen and eighteen. They took it very hard.

"The kids never asked many questions until Justin one day wanted to know how old his mother was. I told him that I would give him all the information that the agency had given me. But there was something I couldn't tell him (this is hard). She wasn't sure who the father was (crying). There were two possibilities. Justin was so hyperactive as a child and I always remembered you told me that she had smoked marijuana but supposedly stopped when she got pregnant. When he was born they weren't sure if he was addicted or not. There were things I couldn't tell him. I didn't want to hurt him. He learned it from his step grandfather. That man is Justin's only connection to his biological family. Oh, he does have a half sister, but when Ilene died the father took the child. Not Justin's father, but another man she had married at one point.

"Justin was always more inquisitive than Hayley and he is still hyperactive. He has finally gone to the doctor because he had anxiety attacks. I told him that I thought he needed something to calm him down. He didn't tell me he was going to do a search. Everyone knew but me. I asked him why he felt he couldn't tell me. He was afraid he'd hurt my feelings – he was protecting me. He had come home for a birthday the year he found out all the information. The day he flew in he was late because he was in Phoenix, seeing you (Shirley) and others (cousins) then drove down to Tucson for the party. He didn't tell me he had seen you, just said he had stopped by in different places. The next day, I was getting ready in the bathroom putting on my makeup (my kids always talked to me when I was doing this). I told him to come sit on the counter and talk with me. Then I learned there was more than one reason that he came home for his birthday – he had been searching for his biological parents. I thought, 'Well, this is to be expected.' It didn't upset me. He said, 'Oh, Mom, I am so glad that I was with you and Dad. I think I would have been dead by now if I hadn't. They are all dead.' I started to cry because he looked so lost – he seemed to have been searching for such a long time. I was sad for him. We were very emotional about it. I was sorry he didn't get to meet her. He told me about all the drugs and stuff and said that his dad and I had saved his life. He was angry at her. I told him not to be too harsh because she did do two good things. She had you and your half sister. He couldn't understand how she could do drugs. It just blew his mind. That's probably why she died as young as she did. It was very sad for him. His story only got sadder. He was afraid that when we went to see her stepfather there would be a house full of druggies, even though they sounded okay on the phone.

"I took him past the step father's house before we went to the airport so we could see what it looked like. It turned out to be a nice little neighborhood. So he decided to call on them. His step grandfather wasn't there but his wife was and encouraged him to come in. We didn't see any pictures then, but he said that his grandmother and grandfather were a true love story. Then she said (and this was a real heartbreaking thing for me) that his mother's death was really a needless death. She wouldn't go to the doctor to get help. She had liver problems because of all the drinking and just didn't want to go to a doctor. She had a potter's funeral. This was a pretty nice house and car and I was devastated by it.

"Justin first felt that Ilene let him down, not knowing who his father was. Then some time later he went back and they gave him pictures. They felt that he really didn't look like anybody. His mother had died just a year before we made the connection.

"I am glad Justin had this reunion. I have always told my kids that the more people who love you, the better off you are. These people seemed to genuinely care about Justin. He suggested that we have them to dinner sometime. I said it would be fine – for him to just let me know the date and we'll arrange it. When I learned that he was gay, I was worried that people wouldn't take the time to find out what a good person he is. He's a wonderful person. He has a heart of gold. You know how mothers are. Stan, his father, never knew he was gay. He would have had a hard time accepting it. The man I am dating has accepted it very well. I didn't tell him until he met Justin because I didn't want him to judge Justin before meeting him. I don't want anyone to hurt my kids.

"I don't think parents of adopted kids should ever be upset if they want to reunite. It is very natural. It's up to each individual person to decide what they want to do. Things have changed a lot since we adopted. I wouldn't have wanted an open adoption. I wanted to raise my children without any interference – I can honestly say that. I fear it would have caused some confusion. I don't know anyone who has had an open adoption, but I think that if

three or four people are trying to parent a child it may be difficult."

Marty

This reunion has a rather different twist – it didn't turn out as most reunions do.

Marty tells her story:

"It was probably around the time I started school that I realized I was adopted although I likely didn't understand all the implications of it. It made me feel different, but my parents told me that since I was adopted it made me very special. I was not familiar with the term birth mother or birth father – we never talked about my adoption. I have a brother who is also adopted. There were no birth children in the family. Nevertheless, I've always been curious about my birth background. My adoptive parents never explained the reasons why I was placed for adoption – if they did it was when I was very young – I don't remember what they told me. I never shared my curiosity with them.

"I was twenty-eight when I decided I would search. When I told my parents, their reaction was horrible. My mom was terrified that I'd leave the family. My dad understood that I needed to know where I came from. I was treated by my mom as the bad daughter for about a year.

"As you can see, a search was a definite no-no in this house. I'm not sure if it meant that I might be disinherited or what, but I surely felt I had done the wrong thing once I did have contact with my birth mother, Lillian."

Shirley: After a fairly long involved search, I was finally able to contact Lillian through her sister, who later was furious at me as she felt that I had scammed her into giving me Lillian's address and phone number by telling her that I had worked with her several years earlier. This was not a lie. I had worked with her as a counselor at the agency through which she placed her baby girl. She felt that I hurt Lillian seriously.

Lillian's point of view:

"I had absolutely nothing to give a child at the time of the relinquishment and felt it best for her if I made it possible for her to be placed in a financially stable home with two parents. My family was practically destitute and I was going to school trying to get my degree. I would have had to quit school and get a job to support her. It was a very difficult decision. Also, at that time, there weren't many girls who kept their babies, so social stigma was a factor. There weren't the government programs to help as there are now. I did and didn't regret my decision – I never had another child. When I married, my husband had two children by his previous marriage and he wasn't anxious to have more children. We discussed it and decided not to. His children were four and six. His wife had custody, but when they were with us, it was like they were mine, too.

"The birth father didn't participate in the adoption plan. I didn't name him. It had been a pretty short relationship. Marty was about 28 when you contacted me. Do you remember that I hung up on you when you called? I talked it over with my husband and we decided to contact an attorney who called you the next day. You explained to him all about the CIP and he said I would call you back after thinking more about it – probably in about a week. I called the next day. I was really scared when you first contacted me because I had never told anyone. My husband didn't know. I had kept it a deep dark secret. When I hung up on you, he knew something was wrong – then I came out with everything and we decided we should get an attorney's advice.

"Once I got her identifying information, I called her first. It went very well. I think we talked for at least a couple of hours. My husband's children now know all about it and their reaction has been absolutely positive. Marty and I talked a lot – several phone calls – at one point every single night for a couple of hours for several weeks. We gave each other our life histories. Right after Memorial Day I was to have some surgery done. She knew about it and asked that my husband let her know how it went. He did call her and she really cut him off – thirty-second conversation. She wasn't very positive and wanted to get off the phone fast. She said they had company (maybe her parents.) She hadn't told them about the search. Once she did decide to tell them, her mother said, 'I don't want to hear any more about it,' and walked out of the room. That was at the beginning. It was after that when she sent me an E-mail and said she couldn't contact me any more. She had to take a break, things had just gone too fast for her. We had discussed the possibility of my coming to Phoenix that summer but she said it would have to be done while her parents were on vacation so they would know nothing about it. It seemed like she wanted me to come in the back door to keep it from them. Perhaps they are dependent on her parents – financially or some other way. I think her parents are quite well off. The counselor had told me that her father was very influential, at least in Arizona. I don't know that her father was as opposed to it as her mother. Maybe because it was her birth mother, not father, whom she had contacted.

"Marty's parents had a file on the adoption in their home office and she sneaked the file out and found the name of the agency. She went through it and found what she wanted to know. It makes me concerned about the type of relationship they have. Maybe after they both pass, she will get in touch with me again.

"My husband and stepchildren have taken this very well. He has been totally understanding and supportive. I couldn't have asked for more. We are very committed to each other. The stepchildren were very concerned when the contact was cut off – they only bring it up with their father – they don't want to hurt my feelings. The contact I have had has satisfied some of my curiosity, but it is now so frustrating. She sent me a picture by E-mail and when it arrived, our mouths flew open because she looked just like me. I showed it to a friend and she said, 'Oh, my gosh, that is you when you were younger.' In spite of all this, I still feel that my adoption decision was right because I needed to give her what she needed in life. There was so much they could give her that I could not. It was the right thing to do.

"She always called me by my name, not Mom. Another thing that scared her was that I told some very close friends about her and her daughter and they said that I had a granddaughter. I told her what they said and she E-mailed me and said, 'You are not her grandmother.' I think that scared the daylights out of her. That's why I'd have had to visit when her parents were out of town.

That's when she cut things off and said she would contact me when she was ready. I did tell her that genetically her daughter is my granddaughter and she is my daughter. But would I ever replace her mother and daughter's grandmother? NO. She is Marty's mother and Marty's daughter is her granddaughter. It is so hard to talk on the phone or E-mail and really get the feel of what is being said.

"I think Marty misunderstood what I was trying to get out of this. I think she thought I was going to come back and reclaim them and ask them to give up everything they have. She just got so scared. I remember reading a story about a girl who had found her birth mother and had met her grandmother, too and the adoptive grandmother had said, 'Well, you can never have too many grandmothers.' That was such a neat way for her to handle it – very open. I wish Marty's mother could be the same way. Another friend of mine had adopted two children and she made scrapbooks of pictures of them so that if they ever did go back and look up their birth parents, she would give them the scrapbooks so they would know what they looked like at each stage of life. I'm a little jealous of that. I think I have a right to be jealous and also a right to be angry with her adoptive mother. I think her father was more open to it but he didn't want to cross his wife.

"It was ironic that in my own mind I had named her Marty and when you told me that her name was Marty and she had a brother named Michael, I was shocked because I had always thought that if I had a girl I would name her Marty and name a boy Michael."

Shirley: In learning about how the fact of adoption was handled in this particular case, I knew adoption was never talked about in this home. Still, Marty knew she was adopted. An infertility problem had required the couple to adopt. Perhaps the adoptive mother never resolved her feelings about her infertility. For any adoptive parent who is infertile the pain is never resolved completely. They have questions like: What would a child of mine have looked like? What would his/her personality be like? How would they have been different from my adopted children? Because of that they may become very possessive.

Amy

"In first grade we started a family tree project and that brought up the whole issue of who I was related to so I started asking my mom questions and she explained about adoption even though I had heard the word before. However, I think I was too young to understand or care at the time. I did realize that I'd been born to some other woman – it made me feel different. Whenever it was brought up, I was really uncomfortable. I was an only child. My friend's mother was pregnant with her little sister and I wondered why I didn't have any siblings, why my mom couldn't have children. I wasn't like my friend. Not having siblings made me feel different. It was kind of sad – I was a bit angry and I felt awkward around that friend after that. I was the unlucky one, I thought. I was jealous of her.

"Later I came up with a lot of questions: Who was my birth mother? How old was she? Had they ever met her? Had she picked them out? And all the details of the whole adoption process. They only knew what the agency had told them. She was a teenager. I had negative feelings toward her and when I was in high school I blamed a lot of the feelings I was having on her. Why did she do this to me? I formulated a story that she got pregnant with me – my birth father just left her and she was forced to make this decision. It was kinda all his fault, and then her fault for not being stronger. She could have done something to keep me. She must not have loved me, but of course this was not true. It was just easier for me to believe. I felt very rejected. That's what made me want to do the search. I did want to find the truth. Obviously, you don't give up a child because you can't take care of her. You want to give her a better life. Otherwise she could have chosen abortion which is the easy way out. But she carried me to term and went through the whole thing so I knew she loved me.

"All through high school I knew I wanted to search and was able to talk about my curiosity with my parents. I didn't think it would hurt their feelings. They might have some fears that when I found her I would want to live with her, but there was no need for that because I know who my real mom is and she is the one who raised me. I just wanted to know whose hands I had, whose nose I had. My mom said that if she were in my situation, she would want to know, too. They said that my birth mother was young and didn't have anyone to help her and wanted to get somewhere in life.

"After she was found, I actually received a card from her for my eighteenth birthday. At the time of our first contact, I was very nervous. I had come to Arizona after we had been writing each other for a while, and we had talked on the phone and exchanged pictures and E-mails. My cousin drove me past her house and there was a little green car in the driveway. We'd made arrangements to meet at my grandma's house and we were all there when I saw a little green car come around the corner and I knew it was her when she drove up.

"Now we have more like a sister relationship, not a mother-daughter, more than friends. We are on the same mental level. We look alike – same jaw. She told me my birth father's name. They were in love. It was not a one-night stand – they'd dated for years – just not ready for the responsibility. They broke up after my birth. Now we talk every couple of weeks, mostly on weekends when she is not working and we E-mail occasionally. She has no other children. She had a hysterectomy. She totally got along with my parents. We had a big family affair recently and she sat at the table with the whole family. My grandma loved her.

"I haven't married yet and I'm pregnant now. When I first realized it I was scared to death and adoption crossed my mind over abortion because I don't believe in that. I'd pick adoption over that any day, but I've definitely decided to keep the baby. We (the birth father and I) will be living here with my parents for about a year and then we will get a place of our own. Don't know yet about marriage. Need to get a few things straightened out first, but it would be just a ceremony at the clerk's office when we do. He will work and save and I will take care of the baby."

Linda, Amy's birth mother comments:
"I had been in some truancy trouble with the courts in my earlier years and was sent to a wonderful counselor for help. When I

realized I was pregnant, I felt that I needed her help again. I decided on adoption because she really thought it was the best thing. She felt that if I gave up the baby I would really be able to move on with my life. In the beginning, it was not my decision, but I went along with it because previously when I had followed her advice, things had worked out well, or who knows where I'd have ended up. I owe everything to her. She was a great influence on my life. She was more than a counselor, she was a great friend as well. She was more of a mother to me than my own mother was.

"In the early years, I don't think that I ever regretted my decision, but later I sometimes wondered what would have happened if I had kept her. I do know I would never have been ready at that time in my life. I don't know how I'd have made it. My mother said we'd have just taken care of her and worked and done what we could, but who knows. My mother and I didn't get along well at that time, so I relied a lot on my counselor. The birth father didn't participate in the plan. He knew about the pregnancy, but I kept my distance – I didn't want him to interfere – I knew it was my decision – it was the best plan for everyone.

"Amy was almost twenty when she contacted me. Now she is going to have a baby and I am going to be a grandmother. I will get to see the baby as we are very active in each other's lives. Initially, I didn't think this would have such an impact on my life. I thought we would meet once and that would probably be it. I was invited to her grandparents' anniversary party. I was very comfortable in meeting all the relatives. I sat next to Amy's father and got to know him and it was a wonderful experience. He introduced me to everyone as Amy's birth mother. Everything was out in the open. I think they all thought I had given these people a gift.

"When you (Shirley) first contacted me I was very surprised and knew that you had gone to great lengths to find me. I was happy that she wanted to find me. I also knew that I'd welcome her with open arms. I know of some rare cases where the mother doesn't want to be found. Like in the movie where the daughter knocks on the door and says, 'Hi, I'm your daughter,' and the mother says, 'No, you aren't' and shuts the door. I knew that was not going to happen to me. I knew I would be as much a part of her life as she would want me to be. We have a very straightforward relationship. I have nothing to hide in my life so there is no problem in answering any of her questions.

"I made the first call and talked with her mother, Suzanne. That was a bit uncomfortable for me. It is easier for me to talk with Amy, probably because she is related to me. Our personalities are quite a bit alike. I feel like it is an interview when I talk with Suzanne – she asks a lot of questions. I need to try harder to develop a meaningful relationship with her. I really enjoy talking with her grandmother. When I first saw Amy, she was sitting on the stoop of her grandmother's house and I thought, 'Oh my, she looks just like me, but has her father's eyes'. She has black hair and ocean blue eyes. They are beautiful. A lot of the features in her face remind me of when I was a little girl. I never had any other children. My mom has met Amy and they've E-mailed a bit, but they don't really have a relationship.

"The reunion has meant so much to me. She is no longer just out there. It has put some closure on it. I know she is very grateful that I made the decision to go through with the pregnancy – that I gave her to a very nice family. She went to every prom and wore beautiful gowns, she was a cheerleader, in band, and has been given every opportunity. They are sending her to college and have bought her a car. I can't say that they gave her more than I would have, because who knows what I could have done. But they did give her a dream life, a life that every child deserves – comfort and love and opportunity. I don't think she ever wanted for anything. It has given me a lot of comfort about my adoption decision. I gave her both a mother and a father and most doctors will tell you that you really need both. She calls me Linda and sometimes Mom in her E-mails, but she doesn't want to show any disrespect to her mother. I'm okay with her calling me Linda. I sometimes sign off my E-mails with Mom, but now I am writing Grammy.

"Regarding her pregnancy, oh, I don't think I am in a position to judge. I think she needs to do what is best for her. When it comes to her financial security, she should be married, so that if, God forbid, anything should happen to him, there would be life insurance and all so she and the baby are taken care of in the event of his absence. I think those kinds of things are important. I think a marriage is good for your financial future, but I don't think she should just jump into anything.

"Since I have never married, it has given me a lot of confidence and put me in a position to be a little bit too independent – not let anyone in, not let anyone be a part of this little world I've built for myself."

Suzanne, Amy's adoptive mother:

"We tried for eight years to have a baby and I was thirty two when we adopted Amy. She is our only child. Most of her curiosity came when she saw other pregnant women. I told her that she was in a stomach just like that. I didn't tell her that we picked her out because I don't think we did. We were probably picked for her. In third or fourth grade they did a family tree project and I don't think they were very careful in how they presented it because I know that she was feeling different. Also, a lot of people told her that she didn't look like her mom. She looks more like my husband. She wondered if she should tell them she is adopted. It doesn't really matter – it is none of their business. If it's someone you know well and you really want them to know, then tell them. She told one girl in her ballet class that she was adopted and the girl asked me how much we paid for her. Amy just looked at her and at me like "what are you talking about?" I told her that we don't pay for children. She was about ten when she seemed to understand the whole process. She seemed to kind of resent her birth mom. She'd asked why she gave her up. I told her she was in high school and didn't have any help from home. I'm sure she loved her and she wanted a picture of her when she was born. Amy wrote a poem about it in high school and it didn't put her in a very good light, but I think it was to get rid of some of her anger. That's why I wanted her to find Linda and did the search. I wanted her to know that this person cared about her.

"I think Amy now feels better about herself. Linda is an important part of her life, although she's not her mom. When she got a picture of Linda, she said, 'Oh, that's why I look like this or that.' She got to know herself better. Their walk is a bit the same. They found more commonalities when they met.

"When she was in junior high we learned that she had attention deficit disorder. Unfortunately, we didn't really get her on medication until high school. I have friends who have adopted kids and some of them want to know about their birth parents and some don't so I guess there are all kinds. It seems normal for an adoptee to be curious about their background. Although I do think Amy is a lot like us because we raised her. But then medical history is very important, too.

"When Amy asked questions I told her when she was eighteen I would try to get a search started to find her so she could meet her. It didn't come up again until after she graduated and then she asked me if I would do the search. She had heard about the CIP (probably on the Internet) and we got the directory, saw your familiar name, since you were the one who placed her with us in the first place, and I called you to get the search started. I did have some concern that she might be hurt if her birth mother did not want to be contacted. You know, as a mother you are always protective of your children – always thinking two steps ahead. I did feel it was the right thing to do to make her feel complete. As it turned out, Linda never had another child so it was good for her to know about this one. She thanked me for taking care of Amy. She was very nice.

"On the day we were going to meet at my parents' home, Linda called to say that she would be a bit late and she was a little sick to her stomach. I think she was nervous. Amy was nervous, too. My parents were pacing and I started to play the piano just to relieve the tension. Then she showed up and my parents left us alone for a while. There were lots of hugs and we took a lot of pictures. Still, all three of us were nervous. We just didn't know what to expect. We had a nice conversation and then Linda wanted to take Amy to dinner to meet her mother and stepfather. We thought it a bit strange that she only invited Amy, but Amy was okay with it. After all, they had been in touch by E-mail and phone for over a year. We took Linda to dinner the next night and she met the rest of my family. She brought a scrapbook of her baby pictures and we could see how much she looked like Amy at the same age. Amy was excited about the whole thing.

"They are like friends or relatives because they look like each other. I think of Linda more like Amy's sister, but not in a motherly way. At the big family dinner – my parents' sixtieth anniversary – one cousin asked Linda if she was related to my husband – similar coloring. She said, 'No,' but my husband said, 'We are kinda related.' I think she had a good time. This has been a good reunion because if your child is happy and complete then you are happy and complete."

Heidi

I did a search for Heidi's son and he was willing to be in touch with her, but to date has not been willing to meet her in person.

Heidi:

"When I talk with Dean's adoptive mother she tells me that he really loves getting my letters. It puts a smile on his face, but if it were up to him, he'd probably discontinue any contact. That's because he enjoys being alone. His mother feels it would be a positive thing if I was in his life. There are few people whom he trusts. He is obese and autistic. She says it is because of the medication he's on. I made an adoption plan as abortion was not an option for me and I was not financially prepared to take care of him. I was only seventeen when he was born. I wasn't spiritually or emotionally mature enough to raise a child. I wanted more for him. We were very poor and I wanted him to have a mother and a father and a better education. I never regretted my decision. The birth father also participated in the plan. I'm still in touch with him as he calls me on my birthday and Christmas. We married after we had Dean and were married for eleven years. I didn't want another child, but he wanted to have a son to name after him (junior) and I didn't feel right about it. After we'd been married about eight years, we decided to try to have a child, but it just never happened.

"Dean was twenty-one when we made contact. I had thought of doing a search for many years. Actually I had wanted to know how he was doing from when he was eight years old. I sent a letter to the agency to see if they could send it to the family. They said they sent it and did not receive it back, but there was no response. When I talked with Dean's mom she told me that they did receive the letter. They just didn't reply. I said that I would love to hear

how he is doing and I wouldn't try to contact him or try to interfere. Maybe they could send me a picture. They were likely having
a difficult time adjusting to the death of his father at the age of
five. She was raising the children by herself. When I told others I
wanted to do a search, they encouraged me. The agency told me
about the CIP. I initiated the search right away.

"Two years have passed now. He's sent me an E-mail telling
me that he wanted us to correspond. He wanted me to write letters, not by E-mail, but he has replied to me by E-mail. I don't
think his writing skills are all that great and he is uncomfortable
about it. He has a job working as a dishwasher. His mom tells me
that he's really thrilled with my letters. I'm in touch with her periodically. I just talked with her about a month ago. She E-mailed
me to tell me about his situation and from the sound of it he knew
nothing about our contact. I didn't want to do anything behind his
back. I wrote him a letter asking him if it was okay for me and his
mom to be in contact so we could get to know each other, too. He
told her to tell me that it was okay. She called me and I confirmed
it again.

"She told me a little bit about his growing up and she
expressed her concern that I may not love him unconditionally
and would reject him because of his weight and stuff. It really
upset me that she would even think something like that. That was
another concern of mine, E-mailing her back because I was afraid
it might sound negative since I was so upset. I don't know what
would even give her that idea. I had certainly not refused to see
him or anything. She said that some people had rejected him
because of his weight. She also told me that he was kind of turned
off by one of my letters because I spoke about church and the fact
that I am active. I don't know if these are her thoughts or his. I
don't really know what he is thinking. Maybe she thought I was a
little too religious for him and I wouldn't accept him because he
wasn't. I told her I didn't know why he would even get that
impression. Now I'm feeling that I might not live up to his expectations. He won't accept me for the way I am? It's very confusing.

"I send letters or E-mails about every two months because I
don't want to make him feel too pressured. I don't receive anything from him for long periods of time. She has sent me some
pictures of him by E-mail. They are about two years old and he is
pretty overweight. I'm not sure if the medication she mentioned is
the medication for his autism. He has diabetes now and is going
through a class to try to control it.

"Knowing what I know today, I'd do the search again. It didn't turn out the way I thought and hoped it would. I wish we were having more conversation so we could get to know each other better. I had encouraged him to call me and he did, but I was not at home. He left a brief message to say that his grandma was not doing well and he didn't know when he would be able to call me back. I haven't heard from him since. That was the only time he has called me.

"His birth father was also interested in searching for him and wanted to meet him. He knows I have done a search and is aware of the outcome. My biggest concern is that I'm not going to be able to be myself with him. I don't know what is coming from him and what is coming from her. Obviously, he is overly sensitive. I'm going to have to walk on eggshells. I'm not able to have direct contact with him and it puts me in a very uncomfortable position. I don't even know what to say. What if I ask him the wrong question and he isn't happy with it? He's in touch with a lot of people and she can't control everything anybody says to him, so maybe I should just be myself. I want to be totally honest in letting him know that church is an important part of my life. I was just talking about myself and things I was involved in. He has to accept me just as I have to accept him. I know the first E he sent back was not written by him. I sent him a card after he tried to call me. I said it was really nice to hear his voice and told him that I saved the message. It's still on the answering machine. I hoped I could talk with him soon. It's been some time since he left the message. Maybe he's trying to muster the courage, which is very understandable, and I'm being very patient. That's extremely hard to do. He has to have a poor self image – due to his overweight."

Dean, Heidi's birth son:

"I can't remember when the word adoption was not familiar to me and my sister. It just seemed like the normal thing to be since that was all that I knew and my parents never had any children born to them. Although I never became particularly curious about my birth background, I occasionally thought of looking for her, but never put any effort into it. I would be able to find out what she looked like, but I never thought of any questions that I might ask her. Whenever it did come up, my parents encouraged me to do it, probably more than I wanted to, or at a time that I was not particularly interested. My mom would bring it up occasionally, but I never got into it.

"When you first contacted me I was pleased and somewhat excited at the idea of meeting her. I still plan to meet her someday. I have no idea when. I'm not particularly looking forward to it, but still open to it. I've written to her about three or four times and she has written to me about seven to eight times. I'm always happy to hear from her. Whenever she writes, I think I will write back, but something comes up and I don't do it. I did receive a Christmas card from her and I'm still planning to send her a card. I keep busy doing other things. I have a couple of pictures of her from one of her letters. It was interesting to see what she looked like. I only see a little bit of a resemblance. I don't have a picture of my birth father. Heidi and my mom talk once in a while. I think my mom is happy about the reunion. I think she wants me to meet her, and I plan to. I don't think I'm being pushed, but she is more excited to have a reunion than I am. I'm glad Heidi did the search for me. I may have never gotten around to it. Now we know who and where she is and how to contact her."

Adele, the adoptive mother:
"We wanted to share our love and our lives with children and we couldn't have any so we adopted two – a girl and then a boy two and a half years later. The only time the fact that they were adopted became an issue was one time with my daughter's closest friend. I mentioned that she was adopted and later found that my daughter hadn't already told her. The reason that she hadn't told her was because she believed that people treat you different if they know you are adopted. So then she quit telling people she was adopted and just kept it to herself. I don't know if Dean had any reservations about telling people. I asked him and he said that he told people if they asked. I wondered why anyone would ask and he said, 'Well, if it ever comes up.'

"I had no reservations in talking to them about adoption. I had a sister who already had adopted a six-year-old child. I don't know when my children realized they had grown inside someone else. We really didn't discuss it in those terms. They knew what having a baby was all about because my sisters were having babies all the time and they knew that I didn't give birth to the two of them. We never looked at it from the other side except that we knew what the wishes of the birth parents were – they wanted them to be part of a larger family, they wanted them to be Catholic. They knew all the information we had about the birth parents. Dean knew that they were very young. We didn't really talk about their feelings about the child in terms of love or betrayal. It was just what their mother decided. She definitely didn't want to have an abortion. I think both of them are very grateful that their birth mothers decided to go ahead and give birth. You don't want to say someone loved them and then gave them away. If someone loved them, they gave them away only because they wanted something better for them.

"It was openly discussed, maybe riding in the car, to and from school or whatever, so they never seemed to have a need to ask a lot of questions. Or when my sisters were pregnant, I would tell them I didn't carry them like that. Then they'd say, 'Oh, yeah, Mom, I knew that.' They had her height and weight and hair color. They never said they would like to meet her or anything.

"I haven't met Heidi – only contact has been by phone. At first Dean seemed very excited about it, but it waned very quickly. That has to do with his personality. I have tried to push him for quite some time. I asked him, 'Why don't you call her and get together with her?' Last Christmas, we visited my brother-in-law who lives quite close to Heidi and I suggested that he stop by to wish her, 'Merry Christmas.' His response? 'Oh, Mom you've got to be kidding.' I think it would be good for him. She seems like a remarkable person and everything she has written and said has been extremely loving and wonderful. I think it would be positive for him to have another person in his life who loves him. Can't have too many of those. But being a loner he stays away from everyone. He knows his birth father has children so he has half brothers and sisters and his father wants to see him as well.

"I don't know what truly is inside of Dean. I don't know if he is afraid of what might happen. I don't know what holds him back. He needs more people in his life. He talks about Heidi every now and then. One time when we were Christmas shopping he said, 'Well, maybe I could get this for my birth mother for Christmas.' I told him that would be nice. But then there was no follow through. She is likely waiting for his permission for them to get together. The only way they will get together is if she pushes it a little or at least says, 'How would you like to get together on Saturday?' Give him an option to say yes or no. Then he'd have a hard time saying no. I think he might do it if she set a time and place. I think it would be wonderful but I have reached the point where I can't do any more about it. He needs to do it himself. They have to work it out.

"I think there would be a positive effect knowing that someone is looking for you and wants to meet you. I certainly have seen no negative effects. Maybe he's afraid. He's just not predictable. It would be so nice for him to meet his birth mother, birth father and siblings."

Katy's Letter

This is a letter written by Katy, the adoptee, shortly after she had been put in touch with her birth mother.

"Dear Darlene,

"Honestly, it feels strange to address you as 'Darlene', because I really feel comfortable calling you 'Mom', but not knowing your comfort level with it, I refrain.

"Thank you so much for your willingness to have contact with me. I'm sure it has been a difficult process for you. The whole decision to search for you was not taken lightly. Of course I've wondered about you my entire life, but it was actually six years ago that I took the first steps to find you. I really didn't know anything about you until that time. I went to Family Service Agency and received non-identifying information, which was actually a lot to me, after knowing nothing for twenty-eight years. My adoptive parents have been supportive all along, for which I am truly grateful. It was neat to learn more about you and yet sad to hear of how difficult the entire situation must have been for you. After some time had passed, I pursued two avenues of doing a search – on my own or using a confidential intermediary. But I believe God shut the doors at that time. Meantime, He has done work in my heart, and He moved on my heart recently to try again. From that point, I truly have been trusting in whatever God wanted to happen. I chose CIP because I respected your privacy and wanted to give you the option to say, 'No'. I feel so bad for stirring up so many feelings and reminding you of such a difficult time in your life. I honestly didn't know if you would even be alive. I just didn't want to come to the end of my life realizing I never tried. Not knowing you has been like a missing puzzle piece.

"The one thing I've been wanting to tell you my whole life is, 'Thank you! Thank you for choosing to give me life! Thank you for doing the selfless and hard thing! Thank you for giving me a wonderful life!' I totally believe this was God's plan for me. He turned a not-so-wonderful situation into a blessing!

"Next, I thought I'd share with you a condensed biography of my life. I was never ashamed, but even proud to say I was adopted. My adoptive parents told me at a young age and always made me feel it was a special thing. I learned later that my adoptive mom had a few miscarriages and was unable to bear children. They adopted a boy first, and then me, one-and-a-half years later. I have had a life filled with love in a stable family (my parents have been married forty-three years). I am truly grateful. We've had our difficult times, as all families do, but my parents and I are close and we enjoy spending time together. My brother, on the other hand, has been rather estranged for the last two years. We are at a loss to know why, but we love him and hope one day he'll turn around."

Shirley: She then went on to tell the story of her life, including her accomplishments, her likes, dislikes and interests. She finishes with....

"To sum it all up, I'm so thankful for my life and thankful to you for making that life possible through your unselfishness. It truly was the right decision. My hope and prayer is that our contact will be a positive thing in your life and bring healing and resolution to this part of your past. Regarding the future, I want to continue to let you lead this in whatever direction you feel comfortable. So, until you let me know otherwise, I'll let you initiate further contact.

"With a thankful heart,

"From your daughter with love,

"Katy"

Ryan

"Being born to someone else was the reason that being adopted made me feel different. I didn't look like anyone in the family, even my cousins, and I had different likes and dislikes than they did. So now it is a big relief to know some people I do look like. I knew my sisters had been born to my adoptive mom and knew that I had not been. I still felt like a definite part of the family, accepted and loved as if I had been born into the family. References to birth parents and/or biological parents were always made in a loving manner.

"I became curious about my birth background at the age of nine or ten. I felt that my mom was very open about it. I believe I knew as much as she did. I wasn't hesitant about asking questions and they were answered right away if she had the answers. I don't think they knew the exact reason why I was placed for adoption, but they talked about it in such a way that it sounded like an act of love, not rejection.

"When I was nineteen, I tried doing a search, but it didn't go anywhere. I went to the agency and got as much information as they could give me and also joined Adoption Triad, but never contacted ISRR. That was before the Internet and I was on my own and had no money so I gave up. It was frustrating. About the time my birth parents started searching for me, I was putting information together about who to contact so I could start looking again. I hadn't heard of the CIP.

"When I did have my first in-person contact with Donna and Ralph, my birth parents, I was so excited and happy. It was so great to see people who looked like me. I do look very much like Ralph and my brother. However, we'd had a telephone conversation before that. That conversation lasted about two hours. Donna was crying. When they came here they brought my sister and brother with them so I got to meet everybody. Now we have a very close relationship, talk a couple of times a week. They call me and

I call them and I talk with my brother and sister about every two weeks. Donna and Lydia (adoptive mom) like each other and talk every so often, but they are more like acquaintances than close friends. Lydia was all for the reunion. She came from California when they came here so she could meet them.

"If I had ever found myself in Donna's and Ralph's predicament, I think I would have considered placing the baby for adoption, too. Right now, I still feel much closer to my adoptive mom. My adoptive father died when I was only four. She married about eight years later so she was a single mother for some time. Adoption worked out okay for me."

Donna, the birth mother:

"I made an adoption plan because Ralph was not ready to get married at the time. He didn't think that pregnancy was a good reason to get married and I thought that made a marriage rather shaky. I was nineteen and he was twenty-three. Frankly, raising a child without him never crossed my mind nor did abortion. That was my choice. I never asked anyone else we just talked it out ourselves. My mother didn't offer any advice, but she did ask if I had thought about abortion and I was appalled. My father, at the time, was over in Vietnam, so I didn't even get to talk with him. He was probably the comforting parent for me. I had begged my mother not to tell Dad and she insisted that he had to know so I wrote him a letter and told him. He wrote a very loving and accepting letter back to me that made it all okay.

"I did regret my decision when Ralph and I decided to get married. I asked myself, 'What have I done?' And Ralph felt very guilty, but I didn't find that out until we found Ryan. So many feelings surfaced and were resolved almost instantaneously. Ralph had participated fully in the adoption plan by providing family health information and signing papers for the adoption.

"At the time of the reunion, Ryan was thirty four. I probably thought about a search from the day I got married. I occasionally mentioned it to Ralph, but he was not interested in the beginning. As the years went by, he changed. I told our children (ages eighteen and sixteen) and they were excited about it. Then Ralph said, 'If that's what you want to do.'

"At first the children were really shocked, but they were happy that they had a brother. It was because of them that I became determined to do a search so they could know their brother if they wanted to. I guess what kept stopping me was my own fear of rejection and anger. It was so comforting when I found he was accepting and happy. He seemed to know that it was a sacrifice for me and my motivation was love. I still suffer guilt for having given him away. His response to that is if I hadn't placed him for adoption, he wouldn't have the life he has today with the wife and children he cherishes so. To watch him, his wife and children is an absolute joy. He is completely wrapped up in all of them.

"He didn't have the easiest life growing up and nurturing parenting was not always available (there were some tragedies in the adoptive family's life). Even his adoptive mother states that she gets such joy in seeing him interact with his wife and children. A friend of the family says she was close to him and has seen the joy that has come to him with his reunion and felt it was so fun to see him just meld with his birth family. Everyone has been supportive all along except for my sister who has two adopted children. She didn't encourage me to proceed with a search. She told me that would be her worst nightmare to have her children's birth mother come knocking on her door. She feels it would devastate her. But since Ryan and I have been reunited, it's been tremendously healing for her, too. They have some serious problems with their daughter and she now acknowledges that the separation from the birth mother could have had a negative effect on her. My sister's had a challenge in trying to bond with her.

"Presently, I am in touch with Ryan as often as I am with my other children who live some distance from me. We are very close and have a wonderful relationship and we both can verbalize our loving feelings for each other. I honestly don't feel any different toward him than I do toward the two that I raised.

"My father is dead and my mother is in the early stages of Alzheimer's, but she has really been tuned in to this. she has always encouraged (pushed) me to search. She will probably meet Ryan soon. Ryan and his wife have recently met Ralph's father and stepmother so he has met his grandfather. The search was so helpful in satisfying my curiosity. I met his mom and I know he had a secure and happy childhood. I have gained some comfort, but I have both kinds of feelings, knowing that the road was pretty rough at times. Perhaps Lydia loved him in a different way than I would have loved him. His life was not exactly the life that I had hoped for him when I made the adoption decision. I was so comforted when I was in the maternity home in talking about adoption. Ryan's two adoptive sisters are wonderful women and have beautiful families. So you know Lydia had to have been a great mother, especially when she had to parent alone part of the time. There had to be some great parenting, and nurturing love. It shows throughout the whole family.

"Ryan looks so much like my two other children. You can hardly tell Ryan from my other son. His mannerisms are so much like ours we tilt our heads, hold our hands and stand in the same way. I feel that I have fulfilled my obligation to him and I have done right by him. I'd encourage any one to do a search. I'd really push them to do it.

"One thing that gave me so much comfort was the way Lydia handled telling Ryan about his adoption. She said she knew we felt we had to do it, but he'd been conceived in love and the adoption plan had been made on the basis of the birth parents' love for him. He never felt we had just gotten rid of him with no positive feelings at all."

Lydia, the adoptive mother:
"Although we had two daughters, I had four miscarriages and we wanted a large family. We looked into adoption and were fortunate enough to adopt Ryan. Then we had two daughters and we adopted another daughter, so we did get our big family after all. We talked to them about adoption. We wanted them to understand there were other people who loved them. We knew of a family who hadn't told their adopted son that he was adopted until he was an adult and it caused some serious problems in the family. We wanted to be very open about adoption with our children.

"The death of Ryan's father came about the time that he had realized the loss of his birth parents, so it was a very sad time for him. I tried to reassure him of their love for him and their thoughtfulness in making an adoption plan. That was comforting. There was a definite reason why they couldn't keep him, but they loved him so much they wanted us to have him. They wanted to make a secure plan for him.

"At eleven, Ryan expressed curiosity about his back ground. I'd always told him that when he was ready, I'd help him try to find them. We always wanted to thank them and we always prayed for them on his birthday, and at Christmas time. We told him they loved him. As a single parent, it was very important to me to help him become a whole person and to become a man by having the kind of relationships I felt he needed more than just me. Our family was huge and there were always uncles and older male cousins and other people around all the time. They were all a part of his life. Of course, it was never the same with his father gone, but they were strong male influences. When he talked of a search, I had to constrain my own curiosity and be sure I didn't impose on him my desire to find them. I wanted the search to be at his instigation.

"His curiosity would surface from time to time. He was a rebellious teenager with long hair and an earring. With his first two search attempts he thought they didn't respond because they might not be pleased with what they found. He had some feelings of inadequacy at the time. I explained to him about the possible outcomes – it could be grand and glorious or it could be that they'd be people he wouldn't want to know. He accepted the possibility it wouldn't have a fairy tale ending. He wanted so much to see someone he looked like. When we first saw a picture of Ralph, he was shocked and so was I. He said, 'I just saw myself twenty years from now.' He called me right after he heard that Donna had been looking for him. I'd heard about the CIP. I told him I was expecting a bonus at work and would give it to him so he could look for them. He called me to say they had found him. I was thrilled for him, but I was also apprehensive about the possible effect on his life. I wanted to make sure no one would hurt my baby.

"Now I have met the birth parents and I feel that a new branch has been grafted onto the family tree. They are wonderful people. Of course the love for Ryan is the primary bond. We've done a lot of story telling to each other. I had a little episode of, 'don't call her Mom.' Then I thought I was being a little selfish so I told him to call her whatever he was comfortable with. He does call Ralph's father, 'Grandfather' and that's fine.

"I feel we have both gained a lot from this reunion. There have been times when we've had problems in our relationship, but it's just as strong as my relationship with my daughters. I always felt that the more love you give away, the more you have. I so appreciated being included in the first weekend we spent together. It was Father's Day and Ryan's sons gave Ralph a Father's Day card. There were tears in their eyes and it was such a special moment. We have so much to share with each other. We each have so much appreciation for the other – her gift of Ryan to me and my gift to her of raising him with love and concern. Ryan named one of his boys after his adoptive father. If he decided to add their name with a hyphen, I would be very accepting of that. I feel that the reunion has been such a wonderful blessing for all of us."

Julia

This is the story of Julia who was placed for adoption at the age of three. She elected to not be interviewed for this book. However, both her birth mother and adoptive mother were interviewed.

Sandra, Julia's birth mother:
"I talked to Julia about being interviewed, but she said she wasn't ready to talk. I agreed with her – it takes time to get ready to talk about it. It means letting all of your feelings out. We've met on four occasions since we first made contact. We E-mail each other frequently. It used to be every day but now just a couple of times a week. I initiate the contacts more often than she does, but she is very receptive. I haven't had any contact with Jenny, the adoptive mother – I don't feel that Julia is ready for it. She'll let me know when she is and I respect her for that.

"I really didn't make an adoption plan for Julia. To be honest with you, I didn't know that was what I was doing. There were marital problems and I thought we were coming to the agency for family counseling. My husband was the one who made the plan. I wasn't aware that I was giving up all my rights to and responsibilities for Julia when I signed the papers. I didn't realize that was what had happened until four days later when my husband didn't bring her back after his time with her."

Shirley: It was routine to make sure that the signee understood the implications of the papers they were signing. I, Shirley, recall that after he signed the papers, he went into the parking lot and slammed his fist onto his car. They hadn't come in together.

Sandra continues:

"I definitely regretted it. We even went to court to try to get her back, but it was too late, the adoption had been finalized."

Shirley: It took from 9 – 12 months for an adoption to become final.

Sandra continues:

"It was extremely difficult then and has been through all the years. She was three years old and a gorgeous child. Evidently we both had participated in the plan in that we both signed papers. I have remained in touch with him in the event she ever wanted to find me as it would be easier under that name than the married name I have now. I wanted to make myself accessible.

"I did the search when Julia was twenty-nine. I have another girl, who is twenty-five and she's met Julia. I first thought of doing a search back in 1990 when she was twenty-one. Everyone supported me in the plan – all the grandparents – my folks and his. His parents went to court with me to try to get her back. They knew nothing about the adoption plan either, so he deceived everybody. Julia has no desire to meet him. I made other attempts to find Julia through a lawyer before I contacted the CIP. He was not able to find her. I also registered with ISRR but Julia had not registered. She still has a lot of questions about the whole thing. She has not wanted me to communicate with her adoptive mother as I think she was afraid that I would find out about some of the things she had done in life. You know, teenage years and stuff like that. I don't tell her I love her because I don't really love her. She's an adult and I don't know her as an adult. I know her as a three-year-old. It is hard for her to accept that I could love her as an adult and carry that through all these years. There's no question that I love her, but she doesn't understand as she has never had a child. I don't know about her relationship with her adoptive parents. I just don't talk with her about it.

"My daughter is aware that I placed Julia for adoption. She has always known from when she was a little girl because I didn't want her to be shocked by it later in life. My daughter and Julia speak on the phone and they have met twice. They send letters and cards back and forth and get along quite well. That gives me some satisfaction. The search surely relieved a lot of the discomfort that I had. One of the feelings was that when some big disaster would happen like the 911 event, or others, I'd always wonder if perhaps she had been one of the victims – then I'd never get to meet her. I didn't know where she was, what she was doing, what her family was doing – was she in the building, was she not in the building?, etc. We had only been in touch for two months prior to 9/11 and so we both felt an urgency to meet. I flew to her city so we could.

"I suppose the reunion has given me some comfort that the adoption plan was okay. She was in a good home, was given good care and had an education. She graduated from college and has a degree in marketing. She plans to marry next year. Our contacts eased off some from the very beginning and we are now in touch depending on what is going on in our lives. It is difficult because I don't want to smother her. You do have to cut the apron strings, but I never got to do it with Julia as they were severed by someone else. I'm learning to take my time. She is my flesh and bone. I do know she's safe and has a good head on her shoulders. I can live with that. I know I can't go back and change anything that happened. I work with some local adoption groups and have gained a new point of view from members of the triad. I have had a lot of experience with adoptive parents, birth parents and adoptees.

"Again, Julia is just not ready. She had considered a search before I found her because she knew some day she would meet me. She does things in her own time. She will come around. I just don't want to be pushy – I don't want to lose anything that I already have. I did a lot of reading before I did my search. I knew that was the only way to go. I had to be prepared. She hasn't done any reading or checked any articles. I've sent several, but I don't know if she's read any of them. I know the anticipation of this interview made me nervous, but it wasn't difficult to do."

Jenny, Julia's adoptive mother:

"My first husband and I adopted Julia. When she came into care with the agency, she had a cotton ball up her nose which had become infected and created a very bad odor. She had to be anesthetized to have it removed. We had a son, age six, who was born to us. We were hoping to adopt an infant – we wanted more children and weren't able to have more. You called and suggested that we meet her and then decide if we wanted to go ahead with the adoption. And we did! She was a beautiful little girl. Ultimately it surfaced – she had been sexually molested. Her paternal grandfather had urged the parents to place her for adoption as he felt that she was not getting good care in her home and the parents were neglecting her. We had applied to adopt several times and then moved before that could be accomplished. Because of our son's age, it worked out okay because there was less difference in their ages. She turned three the day after we got her.

"I don't really think she realized what adoption was until she was about thirteen. She felt different from other children. She didn't talk to us, but I could tell from her behavior. I didn't learn a lot about it until the last few years. When Julia wanted to contact her birth mother she told me she wanted to ask her why she threw her away. That revealed a feeling in her that she never talked about with me. I tried to talk with her about adoption and wanted to take her to the library to help her find her mom. She always refused. They had a group meeting there every Wednesday night. I don't know if she felt too vulnerable. Around that time she ran away a couple of times. She had very low self-esteem. She was hanging around with kids of whom we did not approve. It was a very difficult time for her. At first, we were really angry with her. I finally realized that this was about her, not about me. So I tried to work with her to resolve it. I always thought it would be interesting to talk with some of her friends at school – no chance. Maybe I'll get a chance at her wedding next May in Maine. She has been with this guy for some time and he treats her very well but we aren't crazy about him.

"Since the wedding is in Maine, it is going to be difficult for a lot of people to get there, but Sandra is definitely planning to attend. Initially Julia was not going to invite her because she told Julia that she really didn't know she was giving her up. I told her I didn't think that was possible so Julia had harbored some angry feelings toward her for a while. The only time she talked about her other mother was when we were driving and she'd point out a house and say that was where her mother lived or she had lived. I'm not sure if she actually recognized an apartment or other living areas. She was around five when we explained that she had been born to another woman. She may have been older. She never asked why she gave her up. I remember telling her that her mother loved her enough that she let her come to live with us. Sandra's parents did not want the paternal grandparents to have her. The parents were both trying to get on with their lives and she was not getting enough attention from them. I think Julia does understand that they were not hoodwinked into giving her up. She was very angry at Sandra. I've encouraged her just to move on. She told me that as far as she is concerned I am her mom. I encouraged her to include Sandra and her sister in her life. I think her feelings for Sandra are guarded and it will likely take a long time to forgive her. Julia is pretty open about things.

"At first she was really angry even though Sandra brought her a gift for every year they were separated. She tried to make it meaningful things. Maybe a peace offering. I reminded Julia that Sandra was only eighteen years old – how many are ready for marriage and raising a child at that age? And Julia was born immediately. I think in time it will be better. She needs time to sort everything out. I think I figured out why she was acting out. I believe I called you during that time to see if you knew where her mother was. I prayed that Sandra would have a desire to meet with her and have some contact. It seemed to be the piece of the puzzle that was missing for her and she needed to know it. I'd told her everything I knew. Sandra hasn't encouraged her to know her father's family at all. Apparently, Sandra carries a grudge. I also told Julia that she had been sexually abused. I told her that she may not remember, but we had to have her treated so I told her I felt she needed to know. When I heard you were seeking Julia for Sandra, I was glad that she wanted to give medical information and I hoped she was going to give more than that. It was upsetting for Julia at first, but I think it has been settling for her. She may not think that but I think it has been good for her. Sandra and I have exchanged E-mails and I will meet her at the wedding. She was very worried about whether Julia would accept her so I tried to encourage her as well. I haven't heard anything since she met Julia. She may have thought I was trying to boycott the situation in making it negative. Perhaps her own guilt feelings made her feel that way. I was never a negative influence in that situation. I have a very positive relationship with Julia and I think she can only gain from this. I think there was a missing part of her life – until it gets fixed it will be hard for her to move on.

"I am really glad that we had the opportunity to adopt and have her in our lives. We went through some difficult times especially with stepchildren living in the house (present husband's). At times I felt like a really bad mom. But I kept telling myself to hang in there, I was doing fine."

Trevor

The story of Trevor began before he was born with the following letter written by his birth mother, Christine. It was given to the adoptive parents the day Trevor was placed.

Christine:
"To my dear son or daughter,

"This is not going to be easy for me to say. Please keep an open mind.

"When I got pregnant with you I was only sixteen years old. I was not married and didn't wish to marry the father. I felt that you shouldn't marry just because you get pregnant, because usually the marriage doesn't work out.

"It wasn't the easiest decision to make. I knew one thing for sure, I couldn't abort you. It was my mistake, not yours. Especially since you had no voice to speak. I just couldn't end someone's life like that. That's why I had to make a decision whether to keep you or not.

"It was the matter of what is best for you and what is best for me. I didn't want you brought up without a father or a mother who couldn't give you all the things in life. Sure love is one big thing you would have had enough of. But there is just a lot more I had to think about.

"I was young – just a kid who'd have been raising another kid. I was not yet ready for the mother role in my life at that time. I knew deep down in my heart I would not be a good mother. I had too much growing up to do first.

"That's why I put you up for adoption. It was a lot better for you. I only wanted what was best for you. Think of yourself as God's gift. You were given to two beautiful people who could not have their own children – people who were just thrilled about a chance to have a baby. It just so happens it was you. They were people who could give you all the things in life you need and want that I would have wanted you to have.

"You and the parents you have are very special people. Remember you are God's gift. You are number one and always will be.

"Just please remember I loved you enough to give you a chance at life, a good life. I just hope and pray that you can understand what I have shared with you.

"Lovingly yours,

Christine"

Trevor, the adoptee:

"I have always loved my parents, so feeling different because I was adopted didn't matter to me. They gave me her letter when I was older. It is a very touching letter that made it clear that she loved me. When I met my birth mom, her whole family was so gung-ho about it and very excited because they knew I was going to have a better life because of what she did – and it was true. My parents were happy, too. A lot of my birth family relatives live here and we get together with them on Thanksgiving, Christmas and other special occasions. It's nice because we live quite a ways away from my parents' families. It is kind of like getting to know myself better because I can see some of them in me. They are really close to me in their personalities and actions. Kinda cool.

"I have one adopted sister, three years older. I get along great with her, but when we were growing up we fought all the time. I have half siblings I've not met yet, and look forward to meeting them. My birth mother told me that I am the oldest and I always wanted to be. I became curious at about ten years and then it was off and on until I was a teenager – then I really became curious. I wondered what she looked like, what she was doing, where she was. I never asked why she gave me up, but felt it had to be for a good reason, and I have been much better off. Actually, I'm the only one in my birth family who graduated from high school. They've had a rough life.

"I was twenty when my adoptive mom started the search. She tried a couple of other things before she heard of the CIP. I understand that we were both registered with the registry, but they never put us in touch with each other. I have had several visits with my birth mom. When I first saw her, I thought, 'Wow, that's my mom!' I didn't cry or anything. I just stood there calm and gave her a hug. She was bawling and I started asking her questions. It was kind of a weird feeling. It took me about a year to get over it – thinking she was my mom. What do I say? What do I call her? I call her 'Mom' now. I call Frances (adoptive mom), 'Mom', too. I feel closest to my real mom – er, the mom who raised me. Christine and I talk by phone about every three months. My two moms are in touch all the time. My parents are very happy about the reunion. They took me right in and made me feel like a part of the family. My parents think I am lucky because some adoptees' parents want nothing to do with them. We are so close to them. They are like our Arizona family. I'd encourage anyone to search for their parents and even if they don't want a relationship, they can at least get a picture to see what they look like and also get their medical history. I have a picture of Christine right here by my phone."

Frances, the adoptive mother:
"We went through a lot to facilitate a pregnancy, and then decided to adopt. It took a year before we adopted our daughter. Soon after her adoption was final, we applied for Trevor as we knew we didn't want to have an only child. Adoption was familiar to us. My maternal aunt had a baby out-of-wedlock and she went up to a farm in Illinois that was owned by my father's brother, and he and his wife adopted the baby. So my cousin Paul is my birth cousin and I didn't know it until a couple of years ago. I'd thought he was just adopted into the family when he really was a part of the family all the time. So when we told them we were going to adopt, they were happy, happy.

"We were very open with the children about the fact that they were adopted and once they understood they sometimes used it against us: I know my birth mother would not make me do this, etc. I still made them clean their room any way. I never felt threatened that anyone would come after them and take them away. Even though it was disappointing that we couldn't have a baby, I never felt cheated. But I did wonder what they'd have looked like if they had been born to us. I've had a lot of pleasure seeing the resemblances between Trevor and his birth relatives. It tickles me pink to see all these people who look just like him. He gets a lot of pleasure out of it, too. It's like he's getting to know himself. It has really been a positive experience for him. My daughter hasn't done a search and I want her to. Because of the letter Christine wrote, I just knew he was going to be welcomed. If I want a good cry, I get the letter out and read it. Until the time I gave him that letter, at fifteen, he had thought there was a married couple out there who had him and couldn't afford to keep him.

"Trevor was teased in school because he had attention deficit disorder so we put him in a private school. Christine may have used drugs while she was pregnant. It was likely because of that her parents kicked her out of the house and she moved in with the birth father. They had her come back home when she got pregnant. After meeting the birth family I see a lot of ADD in his family – lots of drug use by his father, uncles, etc. If David had been kept, he would have turned out like them. When he started showing signs of ADD, we took him to psychologists, occupational therapists, child development pediatricians, child advocates, all to help him make a good adjustment in school. That poor kid had so many professionals interfering in his life. It was hard for me to cope with an ADD child. When we finally got educated about it, we were able to help him along and he graduated from high school. Thank goodness. That's helped him get jobs. He's doing telemarketing. It will take him a while to figure out where he is going to fit in. He has shown no interest in college. When he wants something nothing stops him from getting it. Both of our children are very bright. I think Trevor has a very positive self-image – I think we have helped with it.

"I guess I brought up the thought of a search first, but once he heard about it he kept asking me if I had called that lady (Shirley) yet. Both birth mothers had put a note in the file that the agency could release their names once the child was nineteen, but when we called the agency, they said they no longer could do that – one should use the CIP. I just never pursued it until I talked with someone who had done it and was very pleased. I hope my daughter will pursue it if only to get medical information. I'd love to see some people who look like her. It's probably selfish on my part because it would meet some of my own needs.

"At the moment Trevor and I met Christine, I just started crying – so did she. She had a big sign at the airport, 'Welcome Trevor Smith.' She was with her mother and sister and sister's baby. I couldn't take my eyes off her. We spent several days there and she and Trevor spent a lot of time together. They took him to church with them. They were all so gracious and pleasant. She and I have a very positive relationship now.

"We are really all part of a big family because we are so close to Christine's relatives who live here. Trevor knows none of his father's relatives – we are considering doing a search for him. I think this reunion has been a win-win situation for everyone involved."

Christine, the birth mother:

"When I realized I was pregnant, abortion was definitely out of the picture and the birth father decided that he didn't want me or the baby any more. I was not living in my parents' home at the time, but my mom and I made amends. I told her I was pregnant and that I wouldn't move back in because I didn't want to put a burden on her. It worked out that I was able to pay for everything myself. I paid all the hospital bills, took care of myself really well, got a job and cleared the way for my responsibility of being a mom. I considered keeping him but prayed about it to make sure of what was best for him and me. My mom told me that she wanted me to make the decision myself, but she in no way would be able to help me with raising or taking care of the baby. It would be my total responsibility. I knew it was God's will because the birth didn't hurt like the births of my other two. It was absolutely pain free. I went home the next day. I didn't see the baby. I knew I would have a chance to meet him if I was obedient to God and did the right thing for the baby and not think I could do it all by myself – that would be when the time was right.

"After it had all been done, I never regretted it because I knew it was what I was supposed to do. It was really hard. When the birth father and I went to sign the papers, he asked me out and I said that we had just put our kid up for adoption so I couldn't see how he could ask me out. I smacked him in the face and walked out. At first I told them that I didn't want him involved because he didn't want us. He was twenty-three and I was sixteen. They insisted that he sign the papers, too. I didn't want him to have anything to do with the decision making. He would have stayed with me if I'd had an abortion, but I wasn't going to do that. I told him I could just stick him in jail, but I wouldn't have done that either. He was old enough to be responsible so I was very mad. Later, his sister said he regretted that he didn't have the baby.

"Trevor is really blessed with some great parents. I got to celebrate his twenty-first and twenty-second birthdays with him. I am so glad they have a close relationship with my relatives who live near them. He calls both me and Frances, 'Mom.' When you called I just knew it was about him. My dad thought it was about some unpaid bills when he called to give me your number. I told him that I had no unpaid bills, so he encouraged me to get back in touch with you. I knew that God one day would let me meet him again and it was only a few weeks later. The adoptive mother has relatives who live near here and they were coming for a reunion. I knew as soon as I saw him who he was because he looked exactly like my other son and he had a lot of characteristics like my family. He really doesn't look at all like his birth father's side of the family. Frances and her sister had put a scrapbook together for me of pictures of Trevor from the time he was an infant. It was great! When he was younger he looked a bit like his birth father. Regarding me, he said that he just wanted to meet me and see what I looked like. That satisfied his curiosity and he was ready to move on. In that way he was like me. I think they want to meet his birth father and I've given them the information but they haven't pursued it yet. I have a sister who lives in the same city where their family reunion was so I went to stay with her and got to see Trevor every day, which was really nice. We really had a bit of a bond starting. Frances had a lot of questions and we started to bond. Trevor was an ADD child and they wanted to make sure there were no drugs involved during the pregnancy. They have taken care of him so well. They spent lots of money on his teeth and had all the resources to pretty much give him whatever he wanted or needed.

"Frances and I really hit it off – she is so sweet and loving. She's sent me a Christmas box the last two Christmases. His dad is loving, too. Trevor is lucky. All I would change is the role that church and spirituality play in their lives. I would like him to be baptized. That's very important to me. God chose the perfect time for me to meet him. He was blessing me because I had come back to the right way of life. I am not of religion, but of spirituality – Pentecostal church. Frances is active in the Catholic Church, but not Trevor or his father.

"My other two children learned about the child I gave up in their mid teens. They then started asking about him. I don't have them with me because they were raised by their dad. I was married and divorced and I gave him custody of them – so I have lost three children. I have been married to my present husband three and a half years, but cannot have any more kids. My last pregnancy was very hard on me and I had my tubes tied. Then just before turning twenty-two, I had a hysterectomy. I don't ever see those kids. They have nothing to do with me. I write to them and I paid child support until they were eighteen. Their dad discourages contact. My son would like to meet Trevor someday, but not my daughter.

"Now you can see why this reunion meant so much to me. It satisfied all my curiosity. I was absolutely thrilled. The rest is just a bonus now. He was raised well and had the best of everything. I am comfortable with the decision I made and I am comfortable with God. We don't have a lot of contact with them, but they do plan to move to a nearby city where her family lives, so we then can have a lot more contact. They are such tremendous people. He recently had a girl friend who had aborted a baby and he thanked me again for giving him life. If I had been living my old ways, God would not have been good enough to give me Frances and her husband to raise Trevor. I would not have wanted them to meet me in the condition I was in. I have only been living a spiritual life for seven and a half years and I can't imagine going back to the way I used to be. I was into drugs and alcohol. I went into the Alcoholics Anonymous Program at the age of fifteen. So I've ended up with none of the three babies in my life."

Rachel

Rachel's adoptive mother had died, so I interviewed her adoptive father. Although there had been a reunion with her birth mother, I was unable to contact her so she could be interviewed.

Rachel:

"When I was in kindergarten, one of my classmates told me her mother said when she was pregnant she felt like there was a little butterfly in her belly. So I went home and asked my mom if she felt like there was a little butterfly in her belly. She told me about adoption and how I got into this family. I felt rather special because Mom told me that I was chosen. Then we adopted my brother and that kind of put things in perspective. He is three years younger than I am. Our parents did have one birth child years later and that was a surprise. She looks exactly like my mom. The resemblance is uncanny. I was eleven when Mom died and Dad pretty much raised us after that. He did marry two years later, but the marriage didn't work so they divorced but have remained very close friends. In fact, they are on a cruise together right now. I like her. We talk fairly often and share meals occasionally. I really felt no different from my sister, the birth child. They never favored her. They were always very fair.

"I've always been very curious about my birth background. I actually tried to locate my birth mother about five years ago, but I never got anywhere because all the records were closed. I was reluctant to ask my parents about my birth background because I was afraid it would hurt their feelings if I brought it up. I wondered where my birth mother was and what she was like. I don't remember when Dad learned that I had done a search. It may have come up in a conversation, but I really didn't place a lot of emphasis on it. When he did find out he was very understanding about it. He had been asked to talk to the Confidential Intermediary group and he enjoyed it a lot. I was about nineteen when I decided to search. I went online and tried to search on my own. I contacted a friend of my mother's – another adoptive mom – and she told me Mom had told her that if I ever wanted to contact my birth mother or father that she would support me wholeheartedly. That gave me so much comfort to know my mom was open to my searching and accepting of my curiosity. I felt I was hurting her looking for another mother. I called some of the hospitals around town and they referred me to the CIP because they have access to closed records. I called the agency and they referred me to you (Shirley), the person who had placed me with Mom and Dad.

"I was very excited when I met Evelyn, my birth mother. Our first contact was by phone and we talked for a couple of hours at least. About six months later she flew in to Phoenix to meet some of her relatives. She, her sister and I got together. I felt strange because it was like seeing a familiar face – we share so many features. When you are in an adoptive family you don't share a lot of features so it is strange to all of a sudden see someone who looks like you. There were no common characteristics with my adoptive family. My eyes are very much like Evelyn's. There were similar mannerisms that you don't really notice, hand gestures and other little things. It was really neat to get to meet her. I found it very easy to talk with her. We haven't really been in touch since she came to visit. She doesn't have a phone. She left her job and moved to Alabama. I have also met her other daughter and some relatives on my father's side, but I haven't met my birth father. From what I've heard, he is not a very nice man and I have no interest in meeting him. When Dad learned that I had done a search, he was very interested. He wanted to know what she was like. He didn't have a lot of questions, though. I'm still very close to him. The reunion has not affected that.

"Now that I have a child it's hard for me to imagine how a woman could find the strength to give up a child for adoption. From the moment they put my son on my chest, it was crazy affection. I don't know how she could have done it. It had to take a lot of strength. I've never had any question that she loved me. We don't keep in touch because it is really hard to keep track of her. The other daughter, my older sister, and I are so much alike. We have the same favorite color, same favorite potato chips and other things. It seemed strange having so many things in common since I had never met her before."

201

Chuck, the adoptive father:

"At a very early age before her mother died we explained to Rachel that she had grown inside another woman. We always conveyed the idea that the reason for the placement was because she was loved so much. It was presented as a good thing and her mother cared for her. Rachel was about twenty before she really started asking questions. We'd had comments along the way that the kids looked like us and people were really surprised when they learned they were adopted. I think you (Shirley) were asked questions before I was, when she got in touch with you about the search. She told me that it really didn't matter to her because we were her parents and that's all she really needed to know. Still I was nervous about it. Maybe we weren't getting along so well at that time. I was scared that I might have to give half of her up to someone else. I was jealous and apprehensive about what was going on. I might have been angry at myself because I hadn't given her the opportunity to talk to me about it first. I have always told them if they ever wanted to search for their birth parents, just let me know and I would be glad to help. I may have said this when something came up on television. I said it just to be a nice guy and I meant it, but I'm not sure if I ever thought they would do it. You say it to give them a comfort level.

"It was a real shock to me when she told me she was going to do a search. Oh, gosh! I think she talked with our friend who is an adoptive mother first. I think it was a female thing. I think my son would come to me first. That's the way I chose to look at it. We never shared the information that we got from the agency. She never asked for it. Maybe it was when she was thinking of starting a family that she got curious about medical information and that is when she first thought about a search. She did say she looks a lot like a sister she has. I think the health thing was important to her. I think she was pregnant before she got married. One day she said she had something to tell me, 'I'm not only married, but you are going to be a grandpa.' I was a grandpa six or seven months later. My son is also married. He has no desire to search. I learned that Rachel had found Evelyn (birth mother). I was taken aback about what the next steps would be – a little scared and apprehensive about what was going to happen. She had talked with her on the phone and they were making arrangements for a meeting in Phoenix or somewhere in the Midwest. Not sure if that ever happened. It was all hot and heavy for a few weeks or months and then it was all dropped. She did have pictures of her. I think Rachel just didn't have the interest to rush back to see her. Once everything came to the surface and she knew it, I don't know if she dropped the ball or if they did. She had met a sister or half brother or somebody here in Phoenix. She did tell me that it really was not something she wanted to pursue. I don't want to put them down, but she told me after she met them, that they weren't really what she hoped they would be. She said they are like friends now. She knows she is connected to them blood-wise. She made light of the whole thing. She didn't show any feelings to me, but she may have wanted to protect my feelings. Knowing Rachel, she would be scared about what I might think. To my knowledge, she has no relationship with them now. It has been a year and she says she doesn't talk to them.

"Our relationship right now is wonderful, great, really good. It feels good to be a grandpa and I am so happy for her because she is so happy with that little boy. We talk almost daily. Yesterday, I got two calls – one at home and one on my cell phone because she wanted to tell me that he finally used the potty. Grandpa had to hear that. She is very happy in her life. I want her to do whatever makes her happy – not necessarily what I would choose. No, I would like to see her in a nice house and see her car cleaned out once in a while. She owns her house. She visits me about once a week and I get to see the baby a lot. She is a good mom just like my wife was. That gives me a lot of satisfaction.

"I think I have gained even more security as a father as a result of this reunion. If Rachel ever thought she didn't have it good, she now knows how good she had it. They had a good emotional upbringing and security most of the time. They had to put up with me and I have to give them credit for it. I'm not the easiest person to be around and they had no choice. Since my wife died, I had to exercise more control. I was a single parent for one and a half years, then I married, and divorced after one year, but we are still very close. We probably shouldn't have divorced, but there were differences with the kids. She had a son, four, at the time. He was a brat and my kids were brats in her eyes and when you start pitting kids against each other, it's a mess. We weren't levelheaded about it. The kids were fine doing what kids do. They did know there was a strange woman in the house and, as a mother, it was hard to beat my first wife. When she died, it brought a closeness among the four of us and that was never going to go away with the two adoptees and the birth daughter that we had. Actually, it would have been better for the kids if I had stayed married to my second wife."

Carolyn

I was never able to contact Carolyn, the adoptee, or her adoptive parents, but I did have the opportunity to talk with both of her birth parents who have had a reunion with her. Andrew, the birth father, did the search on his own.

Yvonne, the birth mother:

"When I was pregnant, I knew I was not ready to take on the responsibility of parenthood. I wanted my child to have an intact family. She definitely deserved one. There were really no options other than adoption. I never regretted the plan. Initially, Andrew, the birth father, was not in favor of it but he realized my heart was set on it and it was the right thing to do. I told him that I was the one who was carrying the child so it should be my decision. He came on board after that. The last time I spoke with him was two years ago – one year after we met Carolyn. We worked on searching for her together, but he did most of the work. He found someone who was able to contact her. This person didn't live very far from her and Andrew asked if she would mind contacting Carolyn and asking her if this is something she is willing to do. I had many times thought of doing a search before then. I wanted to wait until she was twenty-one – until I thought she was old enough to emotionally handle the prospect of meeting me. We filled out the papers, but never followed through with the CIP. Andrew was able to get the information we needed.

"When I told people what we were planning to do, I got both types of reactions: Don't you think you should wait for her to contact you – she will then be really ready, are you sure about this? Others thought it was a wonderful idea and encouraged me to go ahead. I'd put in my name with ISRR while she was still young, thinking that it would be there if she was interested in contacting me and that would make it easy for her. I was also in touch with Search Triad, but the possibilities were so stymied because of the limited amount of information. Finally, I agreed with what Andrew was doing because we were not going to be contacting her directly. There was going to be a third party involved to ask her if she wanted contact with her birth mother and father. I was prepared in case she wasn't interested.

"The last time I talked with Andrew, he was very unkind and hurtful to the point that I had to leave work because I was so upset. I think it was because she made it very clear that she preferred my company over his. She was very blunt. She told me she really didn't want to have contact with him. She had already tried to tell him that. He wasn't understanding it. So his feelings are hurt. He's not going to take his feelings out on her, but the person who is involved in that emotional triangle is me. I recognize and understand it but I truly don't need this in my life and I have asked him not to contact me again. Further, Carolyn and I have a rather nonexistent relationship at this time – by her choice, I think. The last time I saw her, a year after we first met, she told me that she plans to go to New York. She is a very talented girl and is hoping for a career on Broadway. She can sing and dance well. I had always been interested in that but never pursued it. She said she would like to see me again before she left for New York, but we were never able to come up with a convenient date. Shortly after we met, I received a Mother's Day card from her and it was the only one I ever got. I think her mother had some influence on how she handled it, more than her father. He was more open to the idea. She told me her mother was having difficulty accepting the fact that she wanted to have contact with me.

"Our very first contact was by phone. What a feeling! Andrew had called me – he had spoken with her and I knew about what time she was going to call. My heart was pounding and I was trying to be calm. I didn't want her to be overwhelmed by my reaction, or frightened by it. I was overwhelmed. Then meeting her was beyond anything I could have ever imagined. She was in college and was doing a performance of West Side Story. She wanted me to come to see her perform. I said, 'Absolutely. I will be there.' Andrew went on a different night. My relationship with her is completely separate. I wanted that evening to be just between her and me. My husband and son didn't come with me. I could never explain the sense of pride I had in watching her up there knowing that she came from me, knowing that she was flesh of my flesh. It was so amazing. She has such tremendous talent and she was doing something I had always dreamed of doing when I was her age. It was just bizarre watching someone I knew I didn't raise, but was connected to biologically and seeing her doing what it was that I always wanted to do.

"I haven't met her adoptive parents. She told me some day her mom would like to meet me. There is so much I would like to learn, but I leave it up to them because I don't want to put any stress or strain on the relationship. I'd love to meet her mother. Three years ago when I last spoke to Carolyn, there was no discussion about future contact. I told her that if she wanted to write or E-mail me I would love to keep in contact. I left many options open. I wrote her after I received the Mother's Day card and encouraged her to call, but nothing. I have to assume that she is just living her life – that's what I tell myself to make me feel better. It's very difficult.

"Again, I wonder if she is safe and happy – all the same questions I had before. Any woman who's ever had a child, birthed a child, could understand it and where it comes from. It will never go away. Even on my deathbed, I will still be thinking of her. That's one thing she doesn't have with her mom – a biological connection. I don't have a phone number if I wanted to get in touch with her tomorrow. I do have her New York address of three years ago. I would feel uncomfortable trying to pursue her at this point. I don't want to complicate things for her. I want the relationship that she has with me to be a source of joy for her. I know that she is very busy. I told her that she knows where I am and I would let her know if it changed. She said she would want to know. She did say that one day she would like to meet my son since he is her half brother.

"We are a lot alike. The way we laugh is similar. She and I have always loved Barbie. We have the same sense of humor. I think every birth mother wonders if she would recognize the child she gave up. Would we get along? So finding the similarities is really cool. I would not trade the little time I have had with her for anything in the world. It was the most amazing sense of relief that I could touch her and hold her and know she was real and safe. All the worries were allayed. When I hugged her for the first time, I didn't want to let her go. I told myself this was my baby and the last time I held her in my arms was when she was three days old. When we went on a tour of the campus, she held my hand all the time.

"My son has known about Carolyn for a long time. I didn't want it to come as a surprise. He's had a lot of curiosity about her. He wants so much to meet her. He is lonely as an only child and would love to have a sister. My contact with her satisfied my curiosity, but now I am concerned all over again. At least, I know my adoption decision was the right one. I am a very touchy-feely person and when we were at the restaurant she wanted me sitting right next to her. She was huggy, so she is like me in that way too.

"She told everyone she was going to meet her birth mother. I was standing outside her dressing room after her last performance and the whole hall was jam-packed with people. I thought there could not be that many cast members, but then I realized they were all gathered around to see this meeting take place. I knew her the minute I saw her as we had exchanged pictures. I felt my knees buckle and then we were embracing. We both were crying and I looked around and there wasn't a dry eye in the hall. There were grandfathers and teenagers there who were crying, too. A very emotional time. I hadn't thought it would be that public, but it was just so amazing because it was wonderful for me and they were all so happy for both of us. I told the director that the last time I had seen her was when she was three days old – he then started to cry. I felt so supported. Through the years I had moments of feeling so alone when I was wondering what was going on and wishing I could let her know that I love her. It was mass love. Everyone standing around and celebrating our connecting after twenty-one years of being apart. Whenever I tell people, they get teary-eyed."

Andrew, the birth father:
"It was about the time that Carolyn turned eighteen that I thought I might be able to find her. I met with her birth mother and talked about it. We decided to hire a private investigator. It cost $500 and it didn't pan out. He didn't do a thing for us so I started to do the search on my own. I went to the agency to get non-identifying information. I started doing some first name and birth date searches. I checked a lot of databases and put together a list of all the girls named Carolyn with her birth date. I got a list of twelve, but only three were viable. I thought one might be her, but I didn't do anything about it, and looked for other ways. When she was twenty-one, I checked that database again and got the

social-security number. One was an Arizona number. That gave me about 95% credibility. Then I looked for her parents, assuming they were still living in Arizona. I checked to see if they had divorced. I heard from the agency that the adoptive mother was a little tense about the adoption issue. I looked into probate and there was a case that listed all family members: Carolyn, her parents and her adopted brother. I had obtained his first name from the agency. I could've tracked him down but I had no desire to do it.

"Back to the beginning: We thought that Yvonne might be pregnant. She had a positive pregnancy test done at Planned Parenthood, but then her period came so she went on a trip to Europe with her parents and got morning sickness over there. She told me right away. She was not happy about it. We had only been dating a short time – about six months. I didn't make an adoption plan. I was forced to sign adoption papers by Yvonne and the agency. She threatened to take me to court if I didn't sign the papers. I was told that I would have to pay court costs. They wanted my rights taken away and I would have to pay lawyer fees. I was a freshman in college, paying my own way, working full time and I couldn't take the hit. Yvonne also told me that if I didn't she would leave me. I loved her dearly and do to this day, but I just didn't trust her. My wife knows this. Yvonne told me that we could have more children later. She said we were too young to raise a baby and refused to marry me. It is a different kind of love because I hold some ill feelings – I felt betrayed. I am now happily married.

"I am not in touch with Yvonne – she said she didn't want to talk to me again. I didn't like the adoption plan. I wanted to keep my daughter. I was finding ways with my family that I could raise her. Both my mom and sister promised to help me. I was the youngest in my family by eight years. Carolyn was twenty-one when I found her, but I didn't have contact with her. I told everyone that I wanted to search for her – parents, sister, brother, wife, two stepdaughters. I never kept Carolyn a secret. I was proud of her. Others were pretty indifferent to it, but my wife was quite supportive. I have no other children. Carolyn is the only one who is my birth child. My stepchildren are quite self-centered and have shown little interest in meeting her. My first face-to-face meeting came after I met another adoptee who thought I might be her birth father. It so happened that adoptee told me she liked me better than her own birth father. Carolyn was in Colorado and my friend was in a town near to her. I gave her contact information for Carolyn so she'd have the option of contacting me. She did. Carolyn said she was not interested in direct contact with me, but then, because she was caught by surprise, turned around and said she would like to think about it for awhile.

"I gave all my contact information to Yvonne. She didn't do anything right away. Then one day out of the blue I got a phone call from her. It was an exceptional shock. There was an eclipse of the moon and we were both out on our porches watching it. It was magical. (He started crying.) I actually had a counselor tell me that I had a problem because I was infatuated with a girl with whom I'd had no contact for some time. That counselor needs some education about adoption, so I fired her. Anyway, when Yvonne called, we hit it off and it was great – a long conversation. We had so much to talk about – to catch up on twenty-one years. Ultimately, Carolyn invited me, my wife and Yvonne to come to see her. She was in a play and it was going to play three nights. Yvonne was going on Friday night, we were going on Saturday night and her adoptive parents were coming on Sunday night. We went to her play and it was awesome. That was the first time I had seen her. I realized that she had inherited the best of both me and Yvonne. Due to Yvonne, she could carry a tune and due to me, she could really belt it out. We never met her parents. Her mother was against it. You may recall that they accused you (Shirley) of giving me information that made it possible for me to find my daughter. That's not even close to what happened. I don't recall who gave me the information in 1999. (Shirley retired from the agency in 1998.) When her mother learned that I had found Carolyn, she chastised Carolyn and forbade her to meet me.

"The night she was in the play, she came out and was hugging me and introducing me as her dad or father. I thought that was a little strange since she said that her parents had threatened her. But her response to that was, 'So what? I am twenty one years old and I can do what I want.' She was willing to risk her mother's wrath by calling me Dad. We had breakfast with her on Saturday. She said she could not be with me at all that day – her parents were coming in. But she wanted to have breakfast with us on Sunday before we left. She said she would give us a call. Well, we never got that call. We went to breakfast on our own. When we got back there was a very upset message on the phone from Carolyn, saying that she couldn't contact me now. Things were not going well and she would contact me in a week or two. We never heard from her again.

"I tried several times to reach her, but couldn't. On the Fourth of July she was involved in another play. I sent her a letter that I would like to come see the play, and told her that if she didn't want me to come to let me know. I told her that if I didn't hear from her, I would assume that it was okay. We showed up. I got a written message at intermission to stay away from her out of respect for her and her mother. It also said that she would talk to me soon about my, so far, disrespectful ways. It was Carolyn's writing. I've had one other letter, finally, that spelled things out: 'I have not returned your calls because you have been too forceful and now you have threatened me. When you found me, I didn't get a choice in that I thought there was a possibility of a relationship, but what you wanted and what I wanted was different. You can't just pop into my life and expect to have a relationship. I already have a life.' I have no idea how we threatened her. It was bewildering to me and my wife. I didn't want to be her parent, but like a doting uncle. I wrote back to tell her that I was available if she needed information about her birth background. She always says she is going to call me. Never does. I am sure all hell broke loose when her friends were told that they were not her real parents, but her adoptive parents.

"I could track her down any time I wanted. I purposely have not changed my cell phone number and we live in the same house to keep the door open for her to contact me. But nobody ever tries to contact the birth father. It is usually the birth mother who does the search. Something I read said that the perception of birth fathers is horrible. They get the girl pregnant and run away.

"My search satisfied a bit of my curiosity, but I still have this burning hole inside of me. I feel like a major piece of me is missing. I'm not satisfied with the way things turned out. I have her address right now. She has moved several times. Her parents are divorced and the place they were living in was quitclaimed to her mother. Carolyn went to New York and had her resume in for some of the productions there. You can find out a lot on the Internet. Some people might call it stalking, but I am not stalking. I just want to know what is happening. She and I share something – we are both bipolar. This is all the more reason she should know everything about the medical background. Maybe she will never have children, most actresses don't. She is now back in Colorado. This should make an interesting story for a book – one with an uncertain ending."

The Bluhms

Beverly and her husband had decided to place their expected fourth child for adoption as they were having a real challenge with their youngest child. She was not developing as her brother and sister had. The doctors said she would always be like an infant. They felt she was severely mentally retarded. The Bluhms elected to keep her at home rather than institutionalizing her, and therefore felt they would not be able to handle another infant, too. Although they often wondered about that child, they never had any regrets about their adoption decision. They hoped that there had been a nice family for him and that he was growing up happy and healthy. Beverly's husband died in 1986 of a heart attack.

Beverly when told David was looking for her:

"I was scared and pleased and I was wondering why and what that was all about. Mostly I was curious about what had happened to him and what his life was like. All kinds of thoughts were going through me. He was 32 at the time. He made the first call to me, but had a hard time getting up the nerve to make the call. His wife, Joan, had to dial the number for him. She did get on the phone and told me that he was interested in meeting me. I was interested in meeting him, too. We decided to meet that very day at a mall that was in easy access for both of us. I had a lot of weird thoughts as my head had been going on about bad times, too. I thought maybe he was angry and he was just going to scream and holler at me and just tell me what an awful life he'd had and what an awful person I was for doing what I'd done. I was scared and I thought, "Well, if I am in a public place it is not so likely to happen. So I thought the mall would be a safe place. I also thought that maybe he would want to kill me.

"He had his wife and kids with him so I decided that he was not going to do anything crazy. I took my husband with me (note: second husband). My husband spotted him right off and told me that my son was right there and that he looked exactly like me. The meeting went real well. The children seemed to have an idea of what was going on as apparently David and Joan had told them of his adoption. I'm not sure if they realized that I was his birth mother. We talked for about two hours.

"We are still in touch with each other, but not as much as we were in the beginning. That first year we visited each other at least every other week. We talked it over about telling our families and he ended up telling his dad and his mother about me. There is also a stepmother, but this was before his adoptive mother died on that fateful day, 9/11/01. I have met his father, stepmother and his sister, Megan. His dad said he was glad David had met me. We visited in each other's homes the first year and even in his sister's home.

"I ended up telling my children because I wanted them to meet him and him to meet them. They had not known anything about it. They were real good about it. They were like, 'Oh boy, another brother.' In fact, my son Bart made a joke about it afterwards. A few days after he had arrived home for Christmas, he was telling some people what he got for Christmas and he named a couple of things and then said, 'A brother!' They all couldn't wait to meet David and it happened within a month of our first meeting. They keep in touch with him, too.

"Meeting him really satisfied my curiosity. It was so nice to hear about his growing up and that he had a happy childhood. He has grown into a nice young man. I was able to fill him in on all his medical history on both sides of the family. These were things important for him to know.

"He doesn't call me Mom, but Beverly. Still I get gifts from him and the children that say, 'Mom' on the card. It has certainly been a good reunion. The only negative thing is that our visits have slacked off and we don't see each other nearly as often as we used to. In fact they have almost dropped out of our lives right now and we have been curious as to why. I would like to continue frequent contacts. When we call, we usually talk to Joan and she says that they are just so busy with so many things. Joan has recently had a hysterectomy, too. My daughter, also named Megan, and her husband and children got quite close to David and his family. They feel this loss, too.

"Joan said she felt the reunion had brought a kind of peace to David and had changed him in ways for the good. I was glad to hear that. I think she was the instigator for the search and she did a lot of work in starting the whole process. She is a nice lady. I like her a lot."

Shirley: David knew that he was adopted from an early age. He didn't feel different from others, even though his adoptive parents had a daughter after he was placed. He felt that his mom and dad would go out of their way to make sure that he felt an integral part of the family, and was equal to her. David never really asked any questions about his birth family and was never told the reason they placed him for adoption. However he started to have some medical problems so he decided to do a search to get some medical history.

David talks about the reunion:
"I was a little anxious in the beginning, wasn't really scared or anything. It was kind of different for the first little while. Now we talk and correspond every once in a while, but usually around the holidays. My dad and stepmother met Beverly when we had an Easter get-together at our house. They got along very well. That was not too long after my dad had remarried. I feel closer to my dad than I do to Beverly. He and my mom had divorced before my mom died of lung problems.

"I also met my full brother and two sisters. That was different. I look like them. My brother is a quadriplegic as a result of an accident several years ago. He has a place of his own and one of my sisters and someone else take care of him and his apartment. Knowing what I know now, I would definitely do the search again – oh, definitely!"

Joan, his wife, says:
"I knew he was adopted from the time I met his family. They were pastors of the church I attended. After we got married, I remember little things about what he said that led me to believe

that he would like to know about his birth family even though he said he would never want to find them. I think he didn't want to hurt anyone's feelings. Also there were times at work when others would talk about whom they got their traits from and he would think that he didn't know from whom he got his traits. I would talk to him about it and sometimes he thought he might like to, but then when he had some medical problems we wondered what might be handed down to our children. We knew he had stomach problems and abnormal liver function so we were afraid there might be some underlying things that we didn't know about. We did find out that a lot of men in his family had heart problems.

"I have seen a big change in David since the search and I am not the only one. I think he is more open and confident. We are really glad we did it, regardless of the outcome, or whether we stay close or not. There is one thing that has been confusing to us. They told the kids that she went back east to have the baby and she just came home and told them that he had died. Her children were a little older. We have been in contact for three years now and she still has never told her mother about David nor has she told the mother of his biological father.

"Her children have told her that she really needed to tell Grandma. She didn't want to tell anyone about it. When she first met David, she felt that he wanted her to tell her other children, his siblings. David took her off the hook and told her that if she didn't want to tell them, he would accept that. He was glad when she told them and he got to meet them. He does look a lot like his siblings. He looks as much like them as they look like each other. We have only seen the dad in pictures, and David looks more like his mom. There may be some questions that will never be answered.

"During the first year we had a lot of contact. Shortly after that I had a hysterectomy so we kept in touch by E-mail and going to visit once a month. Now we are really busy and so are they. We have another family living with us right now, too. We haven't seen them since Christmas. That seems to be okay with David. I think what he wanted to accomplish he accomplished and we weren't kidding ourselves that we would meet these strangers and there would be some magical bond or anything. They are good friends, but can you replace thirty-three years? No, but you can become good friends and acquaintances together and have a good time. They certainly are good friends of ours – no magical bond. Maybe some people find that but it depends on the makeup of the people.

215

David is not like that anyway. He is kind of a closed person, but he is very close to his dad. They see each other daily as they work at the same place. I think David got the job for him. My family says David is different. He is far more outgoing and confident.

"My mother found this thing in a magazine about buying a book for $1000 to teach you how to do your own search. It was so big I knew I couldn't go through it. It is sitting in my closet like new. Then in a theater we saw a promotion for the Confidential Intermediary Program so we got in touch with you. I think the best thing David has gotten out of this is meeting his siblings. One time we went to Oregon and stayed with his sister there. We wondered about his brother in a wheel chair. I would love to go to clean his apartment and visit with him, but it is so hard for us to get down there. I never had a brother and so it's like, hey, I have a brother now. The whole thing has been really special for us and we try to keep it special for them. David got a lot of pleasure out of the fact that he has both a biological and an adoptive sister named Megan. The biological sister was shocked to find David since they had been told that he died, and to all of a sudden learn he hadn't died and she had another brother."

Shelley

Valerie, the birth mother:

"From way back I have always wondered where she was and how she was doing. But each time I considered doing a search, I worried that it would not be the right time and wondered what she might be going through at that particular age. I waited until it felt right and contacted you. Why did I need to do it? There has been a missing piece since the day she was born, a knot that needed untying and a space that needed to be filled. Especially after 9/11. There had been times when I regretted my decision. I never wanted to make that decision, but I didn't have any options. I was 20. The birth father participated in the plan and signed papers, too. I am not in touch with him at the present time, but I do know where he lives. I don't know if he ever had any regrets. He's married, has a family, and has never told his family about it.

"I finally made contact with Shelley when she was 32. It really didn't matter if others encouraged me or not, because by that time I had decided to do the search and there was no talking me out of it. My mother said she didn't like it but she understood. She felt that I would be opening myself up to more hurt and felt it would be best to let it be. She knew it would bring back a lot of old memories. It did. But now I have met Shelley and I am delighted with her and happy to get to know her. I am much happier since I found her. Everyone in my family sees a difference in me. It is such a relief to have all my questions answered. I had made a point of seeing that it would not be difficult for her to find me if she ever attempted to. I still live in the same home that I lived in when she was born – my parents' home. I still have the same phone number!

"She had told me that she never would have done a search. I believe she was afraid. Her brother had searched – his birth mother had recently been released from a psychiatric hospital and ended up not wanting a reunion.

217

"Before I learned about the CIP, I had signed up for every possible avenue I could think of. As a matter of fact, after our reunion, her mother got on the Internet and went into the Search Triad web site and said to Shelley, 'There you are, Shelley, there is Valerie looking for you.' I had asked for the paper work twice before, went over the list and each time would put it away. It just has to feel right and you have to be ready 'cause you don't know what you will encounter. She could have rejected me. She could have said she didn't want to have anything to do with me. Once I contacted the CIP, I started the search right away.

"Today Shelley and I have become friends. She warms my heart. I can't imagine not having her in my life now. Her birthday was February 14 and I was trying to think of something that would be appropriate for her. I have a charm bracelet with a lot of little mementos on it and she commented on it so I got one for her. I had some meaningful charms put on it – a heart, a covered walk, a picture of her little dog, a birthday cake. I had them spaced out around the circle of the bracelet. She put them all together so she could look at them all at the same time. So that made me happy.

"She visited here four times last year. I haven't visited her yet. I've met many members of her family. Her mother and I are on friendly terms. She is very pleasant.

"I also have a son and another daughter. They both know her and love her. I told them about her after they were adults. They were very shocked. They could not believe it. They didn't know what to say or how to react. They both see that I am much happier now. My son is in the service. I think he would like to be closer so he could get to know her better. They had no questions at first, but when they had time to think about it, they wanted to know who she was and where she was. They thought it was great when I told them I was going to do a search. They wanted to meet their other sister. The reunion has answered all their questions as well as mine. Even though she was raised in a very loving home and family, if I had to do it all over again, I would not give her up. Knowing what I know now, my older brother and his wife would have stood by me and helped me but my parents would have nothing to do with it. No one in my family knew about my pregnancy. It was a secret until years later. I was sent to a maternity home for the last few months of my pregnancy. Extended family members thought I was in Colorado.

"Do I regret my decision? Ohhhhh – both of our lives would have been totally different. As far as the adoption is concerned, it was a good thing, but I don't believe in the idea of living with people who are not your mommy and daddy. It must have been very difficult to live with people who were not part of her. She had a very good adoption. For that I am grateful. As she put it, 'We can't go back, Valerie, but we can sure enjoy from here forward.' If there had been any possible way for me to take care of her, I wouldn't have given her up. It was certainly the most difficult thing I ever did. I'm just glad that I can know her now. Several years ago, I may have done a search for Shelley. My other daughter had a serious illness at the age of two and a half and may have needed a bone transplant. I thought if she did, I would then do a search for Shelley since they are half sisters."

Shelley relates:

"I don't know if I ever thought of doing a search, but I did think of trying to find the answers – who gave birth to me, the circumstances of my adoption, but not necessarily the actual person. I never really thought of actual contact as some adoptees do. I asked a lot of questions as I was growing up. I had two older brothers who were also adopted, so, being the third adopted child, it was just an everyday reality. I knew I hadn't been born to the woman who was raising me, and a lot of my friends had been born to the mother who was raising them. The physical differences are very evident in my family and so there was a bit of difficulty in the sense of belonging. It did not get in the way of anything though. I always wondered what I would look like or how I would grow as a woman not having a future reference point. That was part of the satisfaction of meeting my birth mother.

"I call Valerie, Valerie, just as I call my stepmother by her first name. Since my oldest brother did a search for his birth mother that didn't result in a reunion, I feel very sorry about that. I feel like almost winning the lottery when I didn't even buy a ticket, since she searched for and found me, rather than the other way around.

"In the third grade we did our family tree. That was very confusing for me, as the connection of genetics was much more prioritized than it had been in our home or at church. I came home with a lot of questions and confusion about what a family really is.

I was upset and I think my parents were bothered about how the family was being presented. Still, all of our names reflect some connection in our adoptive family. It seemed that the school was challenging that in emphasizing genetics so much. I found myself feeling uncomfortable with some of the questions that I wanted to ask. It was a turning point in my understanding of how others perceived adoption. There had been some other times that I hadn't asked questions – I felt it would make my parents feel uncomfortable. I know for my brothers, marriage and having their own children has been a very meaningful experience for them – having blood relatives and seeing children who look like them.

"Because of the way my parents presented the reason I was placed for adoption, I have internalized the feeling that it was best for me. There was a person, who, at the time, had circumstances that presented difficulties. The decision for her to care for me was not an option, and I was provided a life and given to a family where I would have an opportunity to be cared for and to be loved. That was a gift – a decision made out of selflessness and love. Back then it had to be a big decision to make, and I have always respected it.

"Since my brother's search had been unsuccessful, I never really entertained the idea of doing a search. My parents thought that his doing a search was a natural progression, especially after having his own children. The element of discovery was normal for him. They were supportive and understanding if he, as an adult man, wanted to do it.

"When I first got the phone call about Valerie's search, I was shocked. It was totally unexpected but with some resolution – she was still alive and looking for me. Being on the receiving end is what works best for me. It was good to be found. It was more in tune with my life style – I'm not one to upset the apple cart. I had some fear at the time of the first call – having the answers – it took away the fantasy. I had to go through a grieving process in giving up the vision that had sustained me for almost thirty-four years. I'd had a sense of who that person was. Having the reality of the person surface was something I would not be able to fit into the scenario in my mind. It was going to be what it was. Over those thirty-four years, that person had, through fantasy, adapted to the needs I had at any given time. It was an imaginary person who had progressed throughout my life.

"My first feeling when I saw Valerie was that she was really tall. I had known of her height and it had been overwhelming. It had been very troubling for me at times in my life. In junior high I thought I was going to grow taller than all the boys in my class. My parents told me there was a possibility that I could be taller than my two older siblings or even my father. Actually, I am short to average height. But the other feeling I had was one of joy – a feeling I have as yet not been able to describe. Words just don't suffice.

"The relationship we have now is fabulous. I'm enjoying it very much. She is easygoing, supportive and wonderful to talk with. She has embraced my being a part of her life and has been open to meeting the people in my family and vice versa. She told me the name of my birth father. I know he's short and she says if he were to see me he would undoubtedly acknowledge me as his child. I look a lot like him. For now, I would just like to keep the process of the relationship with Valerie going for a while. I don't feel the need to jump into his world. As far as I know, his other children don't know that I exist. I'm not sure it's my place to get in touch with him and possibly change his world.

"As soon as I finished the call with you about Valerie searching for me, I hung up and called my family. I was bursting. I couldn't believe it was actually happening. It was pretty amazing and still is. My adoptive mother has been cautious, but wants to be supportive, knowing how important this is to me. Still she wants to give me guidance. They've met Valerie twice. My mom doesn't seem to be disturbed about the reunion, but just wants me to take it slowly and do what is best for me. You know, she has seen me develop through the years and knows me well, whereas Valerie has just begun to know me, and is coming on a turn of the curve. There is definitely a knowing sense for Valerie, but I think it is very different. I share a very strong connection with each of them. My mother had seen me through every day of my life, and she's very protective of me. She definitely has not opposed the reunion. The first meeting took me away from the family Thanksgiving celebration, but she was very aware of the importance it had for me. She's seen how much clarity it has brought – how I feel about certain things – it has given me a better sense or understanding of who I really am.

"Valerie and I have spent quite a bit of time together, and there have been a lot of wonderful things that have brought us closer. I haven't spent much time with my adoptive family recently. I have always kept in regular contact with my mom and dad. Now I involve Valerie in my call schedule, but since I am not in the same state that they are in, it does involve the phone a lot.

"My dad has just been delighted with the whole process and how it has brought more clarity to my sense of being – a typical parental hope that one would want their child to have. It has defined what is my nature and what is my nurture. My spirit is a lot like Valerie's. When you talked to me you mentioned that we sounded alike. I've met several members of her family as well as some friends, like those who are in her Tall Club. I feel close to the family members, also. I look like some of them, especially around the eyes. But I am much shorter than all of them. Valerie told me that my birth father knew about me and his parents insisted that I be adopted by a Catholic family. I've been raised Catholic.

"I am a very happy and healthy person, more so since I have had this reunion. If I had ever done a search it would have been to say, 'Thank you!'

"I am just so grateful for the CIP and what it accomplished. It has been a truly amazing gift in my life. I wish that everyone could see this aspect of adoption."

Lorraine, Shelley's adoptive mother:
"We were able to adopt after we had only been married for five years. We felt very comfortable in telling the three children about their adoption and answering any questions they had. We wanted to be sure they were familiar with the word at home before they heard it from someone else. I don't believe they really understood that they were born to another woman until they were teenagers and understood the process of conception. It was at this age that we had more detailed discussions of the adoptive process. We always conveyed the idea that the plan was made with love and concern for the child.

"We had agreed that when they turned 21 we would give them all the information the agency had provided. We then told them that if they wanted to know more about their background they would probably have to do a search for their birth mother, and we would support them. We also warned them that it may not be comfortable for the birth parent and may not be a situation that they'd care to reopen. We told them to be aware that they may be opening a Pandora's box or a kettle of worms. It could possibly be quite unpleasant. So I cautioned them, but I also gave them my blessing.

"We always felt that their curiosity was normal, as anyone would want to know about their background. The two younger ones never mentioned anything about doing a search even though Shelley had many questions. She was quite short and built solidly and always wanted to be tall and willowy and like a model. She is much more solid than I am because I am very petite and small-boned. She was the most emotional of the children and I had wondered how a search might affect her. After you called her she called me immediately to ask my advice. I told her it was her decision. I just didn't want her to get hurt. She is the most sensitive one in the family but she was also the one who really needed this to happen in her life and the timing was perfect. I knew her expectations were high and I didn't want her to be disappointed. She was always the one who wanted to know who she looked like, why she had this or that trait and she was always aware of the ways in which she was different from us.

"I feel this has been a healthy experience for Shelley. It has answered a lot of questions and provided closure for her. I have met Valerie and think she is wonderful. When the three of us get together it is like 'old girls' week'. We chat away for hours. Shelley was very nervous about the two of us meeting. Since Valerie and I are both in the same state and Shelley is in another state, I don't think Shelley will see Valerie every time she comes here, even though I suggested that she celebrate this year's birthday with Valerie. I feel that perhaps Valerie would like to play more of a motherly role than Shelley wants. Valerie has been looking for Shelley for such a long time. Shelley says I'm her mom and that will never change. Valerie is Valerie! Any contacts Valerie and I have will always be with Shelley, too. Shelley is a Pollyanna and wants to please everyone, so I hope she won't feel obligated to meet everyone's needs. Shelley is very bubbly and talkative and sensitive – Valerie is also. Shelley has been pleased to find where this comes from.

"I don't feel I have lost a thing as a result of this reunion. Shelley really knows more now about who she is and I am very pleased about that."

Courtney

"My parents always told me the adoption story about a beautiful blond princess. I was that princess. There was never any negative tone to it. I don't think there was ever one precise moment that I understood the whole concept about being born to someone else. My parents have always been my parents. My older brother is also adopted and then they had a son. They'd tried many years to have a birth child and all of a sudden it happened!

"My mom is great. She always read the pros and cons of searching in Dear Abby and has always been very supportive of my interest in finding my birth mother, but concerned about what could be the worst case scenario. I have always wanted to search. I was under the assumption that you could find your natural mother, but it's obviously not the case in Arizona. I joined Search Triad for a while and then moved to Oregon and would resume the search off and on. Finally, after I had two girls, I knew I really wanted more family history. I finally contacted you (Shirley) at thirty-three. I had actually talked with you about ten years ago when I first started my search. The search and reunion went great. You told me my birth mother was in very poor health – it was difficult to understand her speech. So it may be hard to get a good history. We weren't sure she'd even remember giving up a child in view of her mental state.

"The first one I talked with was my brother, Steve, who is the one who takes care of her. He is twenty-three. He jokes around that we could have other siblings out there, but to his knowledge we are the only ones. He told me she'd had multiple strokes and she is very hard to understand on the phone. She is severely paralyzed on her right side and is confined to a wheel chair. I went to meet both of them. I wanted him to feel comfortable before I met her and to know what I was doing – not looking for a mom, but out of curiosity and a sense of belonging and other good stuff.

"My parents were really glad about the search and seemed comfortable with it. They had some concern because they had been told that she had never told anyone about placing a child. They were concerned about my reaction and that I might be disappointed or find a totally dysfunctional family. But I was so pleased with what I found. I am very saddened that she is in the state that she is in because she is just a fun, fun lady. She has a great sense of humor and is ornery, not bad ornery, but that fiery spirit which I love. I have sent Christmas cards and things like that but that is about it. I feel it would be a lot different if she were not in poor health. Her prognosis is poor. I keep in contact with Steve. I really enjoy him. I hope to build a strong relationship with him. My last contact was about six months ago, but prior to that it was once a week.

"I think there is a bit of jealousy on my mom's part, probably normal. I have been respectful of that and kept things as low-key as possible – have not been too giddy about it, and didn't go gaga over the situation. I was very pleased, as you were able to get updated family medical history from her mother, my grandmother.

"When I met her it was hard to tell if I looked like her – her face was distorted from the illness, but Steve and I are the spitting image of each other. He is very devoted to her. He is a real gem, an incredible kid. He is really all she has, except her mother who comes into town occasionally.

"I have gained from this reunion, more of a sense of where I am in life and a lot of my questions have been answered. I know someone resembles me. I have never looked like my parents and my little girls have an Italian dad and they look just like him – dark-haired. I am blond and blue-eyed. My girlfriend who went with me to meet them was absolutely astounded at how much Steve and I show the same idiosyncrasies and similar verbiage. It is almost eerie. I would definitely do the search again, except I would have done it a lot earlier. Then I would have been able to meet her before she had any strokes. I had no idea how easy it was. She was not able to tell me who my natural father is. I am just glad she didn't deny she had ever given birth to me. Anything like that would have been hard to handle."

Courtney's adoptive mother:

"We had tried for seven years to have children and since we were approaching thirty, we decided we had better do it then or not at all. Very early on we decided to be very open about adoption. I told Courtney that she had another mother who could not keep her and she wanted her to grow up in a family with a mommy and daddy. So she gave us the greatest gift she could ever give. For a while Courtney, for some reason was referring to her space mom as being her other mom. One of her friends asked her mom if she had a space mom. Her mother told her she didn't. So I explained to Courtney that she was lucky in many respects that she had another person, but she didn't need to share all those aspects with her friends. It may make them feel envious.

"I don't really remember any specific incidents of Courtney asking questions until after high school. We told her what we knew. We had taken an adoption class and that class sponsored a panel of adoptees who told why they had wanted to search for biological parents. With that we saw a wonderful spectrum of reasons why people would want to search. So I think we were prepared.

"When Courtney was in eighth grade, we had some problems with her and she threw some alcohol in my face, left the house and went to stay with a friend who lived in the neighborhood. We talked with the parents and financially supported her while she was there. We felt she needed help as we had been involved with Tough Love with our older son. We had her sign a contract when she came home, but we continued to have some problems with her. Once she got in trouble with the police and eventually we sent her to a school in another state and that turned out to be a wonderful solution. However, I don't know of anything that would indicate that her actions were directed toward us because of being adopted. I do remember one time when she told us that she felt sure her biological mother would let her do something that we had prohibited. I told her that mother would want her to do the right thing just as we did.

"When she came home she was involved in wanting to search, but her attempts became futile. So she gave it up. It was not until her second child was born that she contacted you. We were really not for it or against it. It was entirely her decision to make. She wasn't looking for another mother. I don't think I had any pangs about it. The one thing that worried us was that she might be disillusioned by what she would find and she might encounter something that wouldn't be pleasant for her. As it turned out, we were very glad she was able to accomplish it. We are sorry that she is not really able to communicate with her birth mother. Now the important thing for her is to keep in contact with her brother there. She still would like to obtain more information about her birth father.

"When I eventually did get pregnant with our third child, we were concerned about how to tell the children. But we were able to relate it to a situation in our life at the time: we decided to plant some flower seeds in the yard and asked the children to help. We watered them daily and after about a week they did not come up and we were afraid the children would get impatient. We then decided to just pick up some blooms from the nursery and plant them on the same site. Then eventually the plants from the seeds came up. So we told the children that we planted some seeds to grow a baby, but that did not happen, and so we adopted two babies and now those seeds are beginning to grow and mommy is going to have a baby. I was about seven months along when we told them. That seemed to satisfy them. There was very little rivalry while they were growing up. I don't think they resented the way he came into the family as compared to how they did."

Shirley: I noted with them that they'd had some very serious problems with their older son and some disconcerting ones with Courtney. I wondered if they had ever had any problems with their birth son. No! Except that he doesn't have a lot of ambition. I had a brief chat with Steve, Courtney's half brother, who is very busy working full time and going to school.

Steve:
"Well, it was very odd when you contacted me. The circumstances were odd, but the news was even stranger and then I talked with my mom about it. To learn that I had a sibling out there was really kind of strange. No one but my grandma had known that she had given up a child for adoption. I was bowled over completely. I guess I would have been ready for almost any kind of news after that. It was an amazing revelation.

"Since I found out about it and we've met – everything – it's almost like a time extract. We look a lot the same, have some of the same interests, share some of the same views and kind of act similarly. We have a lot of things in common. It is interesting to see that.

"Of course, I am very glad it happened. I'm not sure what it means to Mom. It is hard to say. I think it did mean a lot, but I don't think she was amazed by it or anything like that. It is hard to tell because of her condition. She was excited. I think she was happy they met. I was an only child before and now it feels good to know that I do have a sibling. Courtney and I keep in touch. We each call the other periodically. We have only met each other once. I think we'd have seen each other again if we both didn't have such busy schedules. We will be seeing each other in the future, I'm sure."

Gordon

"Being adopted, I realized I was different from other children, but that was because I was special. My parents told me they really wanted me and chose me out of the other kids. Now I know how the process works and adoptive parents really get what they are given. They don't get to choose. But they did go to extra lengths to get me. We never talked about 'birth parents.' I never had any questions because I had a pretty good life. I wasn't concerned about it back then. I did understand that I had grown inside another woman at about the junior high school age. They said she was just a young girl who could not take care of me so love was the main part of that decision. I was raised an only child.

"I actually became curious after my son was born and we knew all about my wife's health history, but not mine. I wanted to know then so he'd have a complete health history. I told my parents I was going to search and they really pushed me in that direction. It was last year when I was thirty-three. When I got totally involved, they were 100% behind it. I learned about the CIP through an adoption agency and they told me about ISRR, too. I tried them but nothing came of it. Now I've had a reunion with my birth mother.

"Feelings at first contact were a mixture of excitement and deep inside, I wanted to know her reason for placing me for adoption. Also I was curious about the circumstances of my conception. We went out to her house and I could hear the screaming of my three half sisters. One of them – the youngest – was very excited. It was exciting but pretty strange at first. I learned that she was getting back at a boy friend and got involved with a co-worker. Then I found out what her age was. I learned that she was twenty-one years old. She wasn't a kid anymore. I had understood that she was only sixteen or seventeen. Her parents – mostly her stepmother – didn't want her to have a child. She went to a 'half-way house' or something because she didn't want to have an abortion. The fact that she was that old was a little disappointing for me. It was likely a one-night stand.

"Now our relationship is pretty good. It is a little tough, but we see them about every two or three weeks for dinner, and things. It is really great as far as my one sister is concerned. She has two children that are both around the age of my son – so he's picked up a couple of cousins along the way. I have developed a good relationship with all three of my sisters and I have a good relationship with Maxine, my birth mother. We E-mail every few days. Her husband is a real nice guy, too. He made the transition easier. I am feeling more comfortable around them. My adoptive parents are fine with it – not jealous or hurt. I don't refer to them as my adoptive parents. They are just my parents. I am definitely closer to them. I see my mom every day as she takes care of my son and I work with my dad. We are very close. I have a very good family and that is probably the reason I didn't think about it much over the years as I was growing up.

"My parents have gone with us to visit and have dinner with them a few times. My son has a T-ball game this weekend and they may all be there. There are some members of my birth family I haven't met, mostly the ones who live out of town. I've met the ones who live here, like her father and stepmother. I've a little resentment toward her stepmother since she pushed her into the adoption. But now I am glad that she gave me up for adoption in view of the life that I have had.

"I'm definitely glad that I did the search and would do it again. In my case when you have children and are facing the future with them, you really need to know the current medical history, and what problems you may have with them. I'm very glad that I got to meet my sister who is three years younger. We have grown pretty close to her and her husband. I'd never bought gifts for sisters before. It is kinda cool, but my wife had to help me out on that one. We are definitely planning to exchange presents – sure, why not?

"Negatives? I now have a lot more responsibilities to more people. When I got married, I took on a responsibility to my wife's family. Sometimes now I feel obligated to keep in contact every few days when there's really not much to say. Occasionally, there are days when I don't feel like calling. She is always pretty much talking about this being the best blessing of her life which is great, but then I have to live up to it. She says she missed thirty-three years of my life. I know that I love being a father. My son is a very smart little boy and I enjoy being involved in his activities, like T-ball, etc.

"It was great to find the other family right here close by – like a miracle. Since I grew up as an only child sometimes I wondered what it would be like to have siblings – a brother. I can imagine that would have been something very different."

Janice, Gordon's wife:

"A lot of things have changed, definitely. A lot of feelings. Gordon and Maxine talk a lot on E-mail. His mother has an idea that they keep in contact with each other, but I don't think she knows they E every day. I doubt if it would bother her even if she did know because she is great and really good about it. Gordon has not really explained to me his feelings about being adopted. He doesn't display his emotions much. He felt a bit different about being adopted, especially compared to me. I have five brothers and sisters. We are from two different worlds. At Christmas he loves it when we get together with all the siblings and the in-laws. He thought it would have been nice to have brothers and sisters. I told him that if he looked into his birth family, he might find he does have siblings. That's probably why he has taken such a strong hold on his new family. Finding out about the sisters changed him a lot. It was great to find Maxine, but he was so glad to have sisters. When you have two sets of in-laws, how do you juggle that? I am not real close to Maxine yet. She tries to get to me because she knows I can get through to Gordon on certain issues that she wants to talk about. There are things he would rather not discuss. When he found that she was twenty-one, not seventeen, he was really hurt. She should have known better by then. Even at seventeen, I wouldn't give up my own child. That's just me. Perhaps because I am so attached to my son, it is hard to think of giving up a child.

"Gordon definitely feels close to his adoptive family. I'm close to his adoptive parents, but when I'm around Maxine she looks so much like him and she just has that motherly feeling. I love the adoptive parents for who they are. I'd like to get to know Maxine better. I like her a lot, but I don't think I love her yet. Every time I look at her, I see Gordon. In Gordon finding out about some of these two things, I think it has put a bit of a wall between them. I don't think it would ever get to the point where he would call her,

'Mom.' They will likely remain friends. The point is – birth mothers need to be totally honest about their background. She was. She told him up front and he was not ready for it. He's trying. He waited a while before inviting her to our son's T-ball game as his folks and my mother were going to be there. He didn't think it was fair to his adoptive parents for her to be there. This is a problem that is happening right now. He feels a little uncomfortable when they are all together. He is very protective of his adoptive parents which means that he is definitely closer to them. When we first talked about a search, he just wanted to get health information and not have direct contact. His father has not really expressed any feelings, but his mother is happy that he found Maxine. She is the one who paid for the search. She didn't want him to feel guilty about it and didn't want him to think that she was mad. She is okay with it, she is fine.

"My mom is a very strong person. She doesn't believe in giving kids up for adoption. I mean, if you have to, you have to. But I don't think she had to. I don't think my mom is too friendly with Maxine. She is overprotective of me and all her kids and now Gordon. When we got together for the pool party, it was so weird. They were on one side and my mom and his parents were on the other side and every so often they would chat, but it was a rather tense situation. We get along with the sisters very well, especially the older one. He's glad to have three sisters. I am glad he found them even with the tension it has created because I think it will ease up. It'll take time. It will get better. It's really busy during these times, but we make a point to share. We spend Christmas Eve with my parents and Christmas Day with his parents and in-between he fits in Maxine and family. Maybe because she lives so close to my parents it is easy to slip over there last. We schedule my parents and his parents first. That is the priority. But we do fit them in. The sisters mean a lot to him. That is the motivation for the contact."

Loretta, Gordon's adoptive mother:
"We tried for eight years to start our family and finally decided to adopt. All our friends knew we had adopted and so it was a familiar subject in our home, and we included the fact that he had grown inside someone else. My husband had given me a poem that talks of, 'Not bone of my bone, nor flesh of my flesh, but

miraculously my own. You didn't grow under my heart, but in it.'
He knew that the adoption plan was made on the basis of love, not
betrayal. We occasionally told him that if he ever wanted to search
for his birth mother, we would do everything we could to help
him. His attitude was always that he didn't want to do it, and he
never asked any questions about his background. He seemed to be
comfortable with who he was and how he was doing, so we did not
press the issue. We did tell him that there were allergies in his
background and it was likely the reason he had them, too. There
was no further expressed interest until they had a son of their
own. I was glad when he told us he was going to go ahead with a
search, but I did warn him that sometimes people do not want to
know so he could be disappointed. I asked him to make sure he
did it in a very discreet way. I may have had some butterflies or
some feelings or a rush of adrenaline, but then I thought, goodness, this is what we told him we would always do. There is
always some anxiety there and some feelings of, 'Will she replace
me?' My husband felt the same way.

"He would like to know more about the natural father, but
Maxine doesn't seem to be anxious for him to move in that direction. She worked with him but it was a one-night stand, which was
very upsetting for Gordon. He feels that he doesn't want to press
her further about it. When we actually did find her and you contacted him to tell him, he called me on the phone and he was crying, sobbing – my son is emotional that way. I cried back and told
him that I was happy for him – what a wonderful thing in his life. I
wanted him to feel comfortable about my feelings. He had
expressed that to me and I think it took him a while to actually do
this as I don't think he wanted to hurt our feelings. I think he was
quite concerned about it. I kept telling him that this would be a
most wonderful thing and he should do it. Yes, I had some prickly
feelings, but nothing made me feel jealous or anything like that. I
had some curiosity. I wanted to know, too.

"We've met her and all of her family. As soon as I saw her I
knew she was his birth mother – they look very much alike. It
didn't make me feel bad or anxious. But she did have his birth
date wrong. She was two days off. I don't feel any animosity
toward this woman. When I gave her a big hug, I thanked her for
the best thing of my life. It was okay that he looked like her and
not me. I didn't feel that he had to look like me. She and I don't
have contact on our own. We have seen each other when all the
family has been involved.

"Gordon is pretty much a compulsive person and he probably got it from me. I think he is a pretty nice young man. I certainly don't think I have lost anything as a result of this reunion. He brings his son over every day for me to baby-sit because his wife has just gone back to work. I really don't feel that it's caused any problem at all. It probably has made us all a bit closer, because of all the acceptance. We have a very strong relationship. Maybe we are out of the ordinary. Further, I think it is interesting that Gordon gave his son my father's name for a middle name. My husband would be interested in finding the birth father. I think it is great that Gordon has some siblings since he did not have any growing up.

"Another thing that really upset Gordon was that Maxine got married the very next year after she gave him up. He said, 'Well, she got married right away.' I told him that was normal, that is all right. Maybe he feels bad that she didn't marry his birth father – and that she didn't keep him. But I think he's over the feeling now. He hadn't planned to search, but his father talked to him and told him that if he didn't, he would virtually regret it the rest of his life. I think he is now happy that he did. I don't know that he has contact with them every day like he has with me, but now and then he'll call to tell us he's going to dinner with them or to a birthday celebration or something. When his son has a birthday, they come, too. They are nice people and I don't resent that they are included. I don't feel threatened. The gain has been his siblings and his contact with birth relatives. It has been such a pleasant experience. I would think anyone who's adopted would wonder about them. He was delighted when he learned that she was searching for him, also.

"We hoped to have other children, but I decided that I just wanted my Gordy. I still call him that at times, but that is what we call his little boy. We now have a Gordy, Jr."

Maxine, Gordon's birth mother:
"When I was pregnant, I did not have the support of my parents (step mother and father – my mother died when I was still quite young) in keeping the baby. I was twenty, a bit older than a lot of the girls who planned adoption for their babies, but in my day and age that was really still quite young and naive and not capable of taking care of a child by myself. Years later I regretted

my decision because I did have this longing and there was a void in my life. The pregnancy was the result of a one-night stand. I contacted the father and he gave me four hundred dollars and told me to get an abortion, which I felt I could not do. He didn't participate in the adoption plan. I did it all on my own. I never was in touch with him after that. Five years before you contacted me, my brother and I had been on the Internet hoping to find Gordon. He was thirty-three when he found me. We both cried.

"When I first realized Gordon was looking for me, I felt as if my prayers had been answered and God had blessed me once again by putting him back into my life. We met as soon as we signed the necessary papers. The meeting of the whole families was the first part of December and I had been contacted November twenty second.

"Presently our relationship is wonderful. I don't see him as often as I would like, but of course he works all the time and has a family. We do live a distance from each other. Our meetings are primarily on special occasions. I have met his parents a number of times. The first time they came here and met my whole family. It was an unbelievable meeting. She thanked me very much for giving her my son who has been her son for thirty-three years, and she told me that I would never know how much he means to them. I thanked her for taking such good care of him and bringing up such a wonderful nice-looking young man. Both of us have really large noses. There are also other things in him that are like me. He is a little bit obsessive-compulsive, sometimes, a little more so than I am, but you have to love the whole person even for little things like that. We E-mail each other almost every day. We had his birthday celebration a couple of weeks ago. Our first Christmas was last year and he gave me a huge set of framed pictures from the time he was born until his senior year. Oh, that was the most wonderful gift he could have ever given me. He loved watching me open it and cry afterward. He loves to make women cry – crying runs in our family. For his birthday, I put together some pictures of the girls (I have three) and me, because they are his sisters and he loves the fact that he has sisters now. He enjoys them.

"His mother has been very open with me. She said she was glad that he found me. His parents supported him in his search endeavors. His wife is just a wonderful woman. She has always encouraged him in his contacts with us, and tells us she wants us to keep in touch with each other. She says he is a big sports fan and although there is a big game on next weekend, they are going to come to my brother's Halloween party.

"When my girls got a little older, fourteen, thirteen and nine, I told them they had a brother. They were very glad and were wondering why I hadn't told them sooner. Whenever they'd have these reunion shows on Oprah, I'd get really emotional and they couldn't understand what was going on, so I decided to tell them. They've been very pleased to meet him. My oldest was always the one who wanted an older brother and they are quite close in age.

"I don't know if it was curiosity, but I do feel the reunion satisfied everything I'd hoped and prayed for. It has given me much comfort about my adoption decision other than the fact that I wish he'd been mine. I see so much of me in him. He had such good care. I am totally impressed with the family they chose for him. They are excellent parents. My hopes and dreams have been amazingly fulfilled. I know there will be nothing but good in this relationship. I know we have many, many years left together and now that he knows he has another mom, I think he is secure in that fact. I think he feels quite comfortable around me. My husband has been very generous with his feelings and has been a great help to me in the last thirty-four years in handling the fact that he knew I had a child – somewhere and someday I'd find him or he'd find me. He has dealt with it well. Gordon's folks are like friends to me. Even though my father strongly encouraged me to place my baby for adoption, and was not in favor of my searching for him, he now seems pleased that we have a connection with Gordon."

Sharon

When I found Sharon's birth mother, she was petrified because no one knew about the child that she gave up for adoption – a 'closet' birth mother. She asked for my phone number and said she would go down the street to a pay phone and call me. She was absolutely not interested in contact at the time and gave me very little information about her medical history. She said her mother was still alive and knew nothing of the pregnancy and longevity runs in the family. She didn't want me to contact her again so Sharon was the only one I interviewed.

Sharon:
"I don't remember exactly when I became familiar with the word adoption. One of our neighbors knew and one of her children asked my mom what that was all about. Mom said the difference was that I was very wanted. She and my dad were immigrants and they had to go through a lot to adopt. I realized that adoption applied to me and I felt a bit different, but not in a negative way. I knew I didn't come from my mom and dad, but they never referred to my birth or natural parents. Still, they seemed comfortable in talking about it, but didn't belabor it. I always felt very loved. My brother was also adopted.

"I think there was some fleeting curiosity during my growing up years, but I never did anything about it for fear of hurting my parents' feelings. At college I decided to look into it. I called your agency and talked with you (Shirley). You gave me some of their history. My birth father was in advertising and my birth mother's hobby was art. I was majoring in Journalism and had an interest in art and marketing. My parents hadn't told me why she placed me for adoption, but they were not married and of different religions and from different sides of the tracks. You may have the impression that they had love as their purpose in placing me and it was the most practical thing to do. She was in college. She came to Arizona to stay with her sister – the only family member who knew about it. Abortion was not an option. I never told my parents about my talk with you, but I did tell my brother who was not curious about his birth parents. That made me feel guilty so I shelved it.

"Later I had some childbirth complications and I had concerns about my medical background. I asked Mom if she had any information. She said she didn't, but she called the agency and they sent all they had, which was very little. But Mom was supportive of my curiosity – not sure if she would've if she knew I'd want other information.

"I was forty-two when I asked you to do the search. The only thing you were able to get from my birth mother was that her mother was still alive and longevity ran in her family. She has a daughter whom she feels would love to know that she has a sister. Some people may have a burning desire to develop that type of relationship for a multitude of reasons, but I think they would be lacking for love or a connection in their own family. There has never been that void in my life. It never occurred to me that either of my birth parents would have other children that I may one day have a relationship with. I was only curious about my birth parents – medical history, life achievements, the circumstances of my conception, if there was a drinking problem, if I was conceived two weeks after they met, etc. I later learned they dated for two years, she was from a well-to-do family and he was not so they would not have accepted him into their fold. Later he put himself through Notre Dame and obtained a Master's Degree. Something happened they were not prepared for, and they made the best decision they could at the time. I felt pretty comfortable that I was from good stock. That appeased and satisfied my curiosity. Further, I was adopted by a terrific set of parents. I really wasn't hurt by her decision not to meet with me. I just know if I placed a child for adoption I would want to know how things had worked out, hopefully justifying my decision.

"Oh, I had an abortion before I was married and always thought it was such an awful thing to do, especially when my birth mother gave me the opportunity to live. I was eight weeks along and my mother didn't know. The father was a fellow I had been dating for some time. I knew I was not capable of raising a child so, with great difficulty, I made the decision as I played over and over the circumstances of my adoption. Hopefully I am over the guilt now, but no one else knows about it.

"You also contacted my successful birth father, married with four children all of whom are very successful, too. That was the first he knew of me, but didn't deny it, and didn't want contact. He referred you to his attorney for further information. I lost interest at that point. He may have thought I was after his money. That would be the last thing I would want him to think. So I said, 'That's it!'

"I have no ill will or resentment toward either of them. I just feel very appreciative of the fact that they made a good decision forty-six years ago. I'm glad I did the search even though it didn't turn out as we had hoped. For me just knowing they are intelligent, capable people was reassuring and good enough for me. I can surely understand how he felt, not knowing that I even existed and then getting that phone call. His life is likely very much like he wanted so this was like a bump in the road of his well-ordered life. I think I was more interested in contact with him than with her. She must have been in her late sixties when you talked with her. Apparently she feared the people who were a part of her life would judge her by her past mistakes. I'd have wanted to know."

The Long Wait

Here are just a few short words about a search that I did in mid-2004. I was searching for the birth mother of a young man who lives here in the Phoenix valley. It had been a long and very difficult search. The birth mother's family had moved here from a Midwestern state and so I was looking all over this area for her and eventually learned that they moved back to that state after a very short period here. I finally was able to contact her eighty-one-year-old father and he promptly gave me her number. I talked with her and she expressed willingness to sign a consent form permitting me to give her son her identifying information – name, address and telephone number. He, too, would have to sign such a form so she could have his information.

When I received both of the consents, I contacted them to let them know about each other. For weeks I kept in contact to see if they had talked with each other yet. The answer was always that they had not. Finally, about three months later, I got a call from his wife to tell me that the night before she had decided both of them were "fraidy cats" and she had grown impatient with neither of them taking the step to make contact – so she picked up the phone and called the birth mother. They had a two-hour conversation and it flowed very smoothly. During the course of the conversation, her husband came home and was shocked to find that she was talking with his birth mother. He had been out with some friends and they were going to stop by for a drink, but, for some reason or another, he felt he should come home. When she was about to terminate the call, she decided that she would turn the phone over to him. Both he and the birth mother were reluctant for it to happen but the wife just gave him the phone and told him to say hello. The woman had said that she wouldn't know what to say to him. Well, she found out – they talked for three-and-one-half hours! They were both thrilled! His wife states that they are so much alike. They use the same words and in the same manner.

They are both meticulous, both love to do yard work. She feels that he is is a completely different person today. When he got off the phone in the wee hours of the morning, he hugged his wife in gratitude for making the call.

Wally

"My parents adopted my older brother and me. They had no birth children. We grew up feeling that adoption was an okay thing. I was never really curious about my birth background until I, at eighteen, placed a baby for adoption. From that time on I thought a lot about adoption because I wanted my birth mother and father to know that I was okay since that is what I wondered about my daughter. I'm alive and well. Since the reunion, I talk with my birth mom every single day. I kind of keep my two sets of parents separate. I was a little afraid of hurting my adoptive parents' feelings, and I didn't ask them a lot of questions and assumed they didn't know a lot. Mom understood that my birth mother was a really young college student – but that turned out to be untrue. That's what she was told. I wasn't too curious about why she gave me up. I figured since she was young she wanted me to have a better family. She was motivated by love and concern, not rejection. It had not been a big deal to me until I was a birth father myself.

"I was twenty-eight when I decided to search. I had talked with my wife about it before. I didn't want to disrupt anyone's life. I wanted to do it more for their benefit than for mine. It has turned out to be a very good relationship with my birth mom. My birth father passed away when he was really young. I have a great relationship with my birth mother's husband and her son and daughter (my half-siblings) and it has been a blessing for all of us.

"When I told my parents I was going to search, they were supportive, but a little apprehensive. They didn't want me to get hurt, but they understood the reasons why. They realized it was something I needed to do – not like I was trying to replace them. I have a lot of customers in my business and when a woman came in who looked at all like me, I wondered if she could be my birth mother, especially if she was about the right age. You know, there is always the possibility. I never would have gone out on a search if it had not been for my situation.

"Once you put us in touch with each other, there were just phone calls and letters over about a month's period. The first time we talked, I felt like I had known her all my life – an immediate connection. Then she came here. I went there shortly after by myself. I've been there about ten times and my wife about four or five times. We're going back in a couple of months for my sister's wedding. She is twenty-five and my brother is twenty-one. I talk with them frequently, too. It doesn't feel like we were ever apart, like I've known them all my life. Vicky (birth mother) has no contact with my adoptive parents, but she has met them. They didn't know about the first time she came here, but the next time I had a big barbecue for my friends and Mom and Dad and they met her. It was a big get-together for her so everyone could meet her. They all got to meet each other and they talked all night. The next day both of my moms and my wife went to lunch together – I was working. They don't have any contact now. They may have exchanged a few letters and Christmas cards. I don't think they have a lot to say to each other. Vicky has expressed her gratitude to my parents for doing a good job of raising me. I didn't tell them about her first visit because there was so much going on and everything happened so fast. There were so many emotions to deal with and that would have just added to the whole thing. I've told them about every time I've gone there. My mom was a little hurt by my talking with Vicky so much. My dad was okay with it when he found out that my birth dad has passed away as he felt there was no competition for him. It was better after they met Vicky. I feel very close to both families. I have a strong connection with Vicky and my brother and sister because the age difference is not that much. Vicky just turned fifty and I am thirty-one. We are not that far apart. My dad is sixty-five and my mom is sixty-three, so we are farther apart in age. I feel a little closer to my birth family because of that. I have siblings who are younger whom I can talk with. In terms of love, my feelings are the same. I'm so thankful for all that my parents have given me and the way they raised me. They are great people.

"I didn't want to place my daughter, but the birth mother and her family had the say. It was an uphill battle. We went together for about three years and we did consider marriage. We continued seeing each other off and on, but it was really hard. She went away to school and I'd see her when she came home, but it was not serious anymore. She now lives in another state. We called each other on our baby's birthday for about the first ten years, but I don't know where she is now. She knows where I am, but I don't hear from her. My wife and I are expecting a child – eleven weeks along. This will be a child I will get to raise.

"This has all been a really good experience. I would recommend it to anyone. When my mom was a little upset about things, I told her that this is how it was going to be and there is only one thing you can do – that is, accept it and love me and know that I'm going to love you the same. You can't get mad at me or have hurt feelings about it. There's no way around it. You can either get over it so we can be as we were or you can hold a grudge and we can have a ruined relationship from here on out. She then said that she didn't want that so let's get things back to where they need to be. She understood that this was important not only to me, but to Vicky."

Jane, Wally's wife:

"Wally first talked about a search five or six years ago. His adoptive mom had always said that if he ever wanted to know about his birth background, to just let her know and she would give him the information. So I called and she gave us the name of the agency. He had me call because it was too emotional for him. He likely would never have done a search if he had not placed a child for adoption. I hope his daughter will search for him – he needs it to heal. He needs to know that she is okay and he did the right thing. He still struggles with his decision. He signed papers for the adoption, helped choose the parents, involved in the whole process, but at the same time, he was young and, in fact, does not feel that it was his decision. It was the girl's and her parents' decision. They would not have let him raise the baby on his own. If he knew then what he knows now, he would've definitely done it. He looks at the situation now and says, 'I'm 31 and have been married for ten years and there's no reason why I can't have a fourteen year old.' But obviously it is a little different when you are nineteen. I don't know what he would have done through all those years, but he is so heartbroken that he just knows he wants to be with his daughter. I really hope for him that she does find him. I think he needs it.

"It is interesting with his birth mother. She didn't tell anyone that she was pregnant and she was living with the pain all by herself all her life, a 'closet birth mother'. Even now she gets very emotional and thinks she needs to make things up to Wally since she didn't raise him. It's been so good for both of them to have the contact. Right now he is so anxious to be a father. I'm not afraid that he's going to favor his daughter over this child. I know he will be an amazing father. I don't believe that once he has contact with the child he gave up that his feelings will be affected negatively for the child he is raising. We find out in a few days the gender of the child that I am expecting. I do think it will be different in our situation because our child will know about his daughter whereas Wally's brother and sister didn't know about him before the reunion. We will raise our child to be the type of person who will be accepting of that. I think they will be happy to find her and welcome her as a sister.

"I always knew Wally was adopted. His parents talked of it openly. It is one thing to talk about knowing your birth mother and another to be in close contact with her. His mom was a little hurt at first, but after she had a chance to talk with Vicky and to see the type of person she is, she wasn't overbearing and knew she wasn't trying to take her son away from her. It made her relax and she decided it's going to be okay. I think it would be hard for most adoptive parents, and they would feel threatened. Deborah, his adoptive mother, likely does not know the frequency with which he is in touch with Vicky, but then he is in touch with Deborah four or five times a week. Their waking hours are quite different from ours. They arise and retire very early. They're both still working.

"When Wally first had contact with Vicky it was like he had just found his missing piece. He felt whole, like he belonged. There is a closeness there; it is really interesting because he never lacked that with his adoptive parents. They have a good relationship and he had a wonderful childhood. He was loved and cared for. It was not like he missed a thing. The day the three of us went to lunch was great. Once they started talking, I was the observer. It was neat to see their interaction. Deborah realized that Vicky recognized her as his mom. I don't think she felt threatened after that.

"Wally isn't as uptight now as he used to be. He has a different outlook on life. He gets upset with people who are not involved with their children's lives. He is more sensitive. He knows he'll be a very involved parent when he has the opportunity. He sends letters to his daughter's adoptive parents, but isn't sure they are getting to them. The agency director intercepted one of them and could tell that Wally was not doing well. The two of them had a meeting and that's when he got the child's name and the first names of the adoptive parents. I can't imagine what it would be like to not know my birth parents so I had to help him by filling out the papers when he started the search process. It was easy for me – I wanted to have the peace of knowing, too. It's been a very positive thing for him. It's easier for him to have a lot of contact with his birth family because of ages and schedules. I enjoy his birth family a lot. We get together with his folks for dinner and holidays. Deborah is an excellent mother-in-law. I think our contact with them will increase once the baby is born as they are really anxious to have grandchildren. They will make more of an effort to keep in close touch.

"Vicky calls me at work just to say hi and sends flowers to me all the time. I think Wally is more complete now and I think he needed that before we had kids. He wants to have this kind of relationship with his daughter so he is trying to be the son to Vicky that he would have his daughter be to him. Most adoptees would not understand their birth parents' feelings and realize all they had gone through. Even though they may be told what the circumstances were they may still think, 'Yes, but did they really want me? Have they really been thinking about me all these years? Do they really love me as much as they should?' But Wally knows how deeply he loves his daughter, so he never had to question that with his birth mom."

Vicky, the birth mom:
"I made an adoption plan because I was all alone, frightened and very unsure of what the future would hold. I regretted making the plan daily. The father of the child didn't believe it was his and was already involved with someone else. My father had a stroke and was in a nursing home at the age of forty-one and my mother was struggling. It was a difficult time for everyone, so I chose not to tell anyone. I came to Arizona. When you contacted me, I was very, very scared and it all came back. I had tried to deny it all those years and act as if it had not happened, but in hearing your voice, it was reality. Unsettling. No one in my family knew about it

but my husband and my brother who has since died. I came to Phoenix to live with him during my pregnancy. My mother has now met Wally and been to his house. She calls him from time to time and she has crocheted things for them. He is definitely part of the family now. We first met on the phone. He was at your house and you dialed the number so no identifying information would be released. I had not given my consent for that as I needed his assurance that he would be willing to just talk with me and not know the rest of the family. As soon as I met him in person, three months later, and the connection was made, I knew I was going to have to open up my life to my family and have him be a part of our family, which I wanted. After I went there the first time, I went back to Nebraska and told my family.

"My husband brought it up, but my mother knew that something was troubling me as I had lost almost twenty pounds. I was pretty emotional and weak. I had regrets all those years. I kept very busy. I work constantly. I don't just sit around so I didn't have time to think. It's just too painful. Knowing that I had to tell my family and friends was very stressful for me. I was very unstable. My husband told my mom that I needed to tell her something. We sat down and she held my hand as I told her. We cried. My brother was the one who helped me through it but essentially I went through it by myself. I was too young and too scared to ask any questions. I don't remember much counseling. They were very kind. But it wasn't like it is today where you are required to talk about it. Occasionally things come back to me. I remember sneaking down to the nursery to see if I had a boy or a girl. I told my family I was coming to Arizona to help my brother. We were a close family and no one thought anything of it.

"Now our relationship is a very healthy one. I took a walk with my children to tell them about Wally. They really enjoy Wally. They look forward to going to see him when they can afford to. It was very difficult and emotional for me to talk with them about it. They were very sad that I had found it so difficult to let them know, and that I had to go through what I did alone. They were very proud of me for doing what they felt would have been the right thing at the time. It was a very great relief although it still took some time for me to start healing. The last year has been wonderful and everybody in my community pretty much knows about it whether they are close friends or not. They have all been very supportive and happy for us. They are looking forward to meeting them all when they come for the wedding. I am grateful that you encouraged me. It was the right thing.

"It has changed me. I am definitely emotionally stronger now. I'm not consumed with what people think. I feel good about myself whereas I didn't before, even though I have a wonderful husband and we have two beautiful children. I should never have been so hard on myself. All I ever wanted to do was be a wife and a mom and when that happened to me with my high school sweetheart, I felt that there was something wrong with me, so I've spent most of my married life just doing, doing, doing and trying to be the perfect mom and wife. I was making up for that bad person I thought I was. I actually like myself now, and it's wonderful. Wally has been a big part of that and I can't even call it forgiving because he says he really has nothing to forgive me for. He thanks me for what I did. I thought I had to have his forgiveness, but that is not how he felt about it. So he has really made me feel good about myself. I have a husband and two other children who were proud of me. They didn't know all the underlying stuff for all those years. They've accepted my whole history.

"I've met Wally's parents and his mom shared a lot of childhood stories about him and thanked me for giving him to them and allowing him in their lives. That was very good for me. Wally calls me Mom and so he now has his Arizona mom and his Wisconsin mom. A lot of curiosity about his life has been satisfied. I still have my regrets about missing out on so much of it, but a lot of the pieces are filled in. I now feel that I did make a good decision at that time. I'm not sure that I will ever feel that it was the right thing to do. I don't think I could do it over again. I do know in my heart that he was given far more than I would have been able to give him. If I'd had the strength then that I have now I definitely would have kept him. However, the strength I have now has definitely come from the reunion.

"There are an amazing amount of similarities between Wally and my other son – mannerisms. They have similar anxieties, how they look at things. Very short tempered, many expressions. They have a mutual admiration society. My son and daughter are close to each other, but there is something about an older brother. My son would like to find a job in Arizona after he graduates so he could be close to Wally. Wally makes a good role model for him, so it's fun to see the relationship develop. My daughter is so glad they are coming for her wedding. My husband thinks Wally is a perfect fit for our family.

"Obviously we have to be very careful with, and respectful of, Wally's parents – I wouldn't want them to feel threatened. I hope they are fine. He loves them to death and is very grateful for everything, but he needed to know his history. We are so much alike. The way he looks at life he is just able to sense when I'm putting myself down, and he can pull me out of it. That puts things in perspective. For him to want all his friends and their parents to meet me makes me feel that he is proud of me, and that makes me feel good about myself. I have to thank him a lot for how my life is going right now. I really am different. I feel whole and complete. It can be talked about since everyone now knows all the details. In the beginning I had to explain everything to people. That was a difficult time and now it is all behind me. When he has time in his life we get to share a few moments."

Deborah, the adoptive mother:

"I came from a family of six children. I love children and always wanted children. I always felt that I would adopt. I had been having some female problems. My aunt had adopted so I knew about adoption. It didn't feel foreign to me and it didn't make any difference to me if I had a child of my own blood. Everything went very smoothly and we had a great time with the kids. I often read them the adoption book, 'The Family That Grew,' and would put their name in place of the child's name in the book. Once a little boy across the street told Wally he was adopted. He came in the house and was so mad and told us about it. His brother cracked up laughing and said, 'Well, we are adopted.' Wally responded with, 'You may be adopted, but I'm not.' For some reason he thought the word adoption was bad – so I got the book out again and read it to him. Later he said he had three moms – me, a friend Sue and that dumb lady who gave him up. I told him she gave him up because she loved him, not because she didn't want him. She wanted you to have a mother and father and a nice home. He then said he thought he would like to meet her – she sounded awfully nice. Then he had nothing more to say about it for some time.

"As a teen, he asked me what I knew about his birth mother. I gave him the papers from the adoption agency. His questions didn't bother me as I had expected him to be curious. But when the time came that he wanted to see her and then the time after he found her, there were some problems. I had not realized how painful his relinquishment of his daughter had been for him. At the time he asked me what he should do. I said I couldn't tell him, but whatever he decided, we would be behind him. The girl's parents put so much pressure on him. I told him that I wish he had told me he wanted to keep the baby because we would have done anything we could to help. He felt that there was nothing he could do, almost like an outsider. I now feel very bad about it because he's so distraught over the whole thing. I'm sure the child has a good home. It is hard on him, but likely best for the child.

"That experience changed him a lot. When he married, he didn't want to have children. His wife said she'd bug him no more – he'd have to come around to it on his own. Years went by and it seemed he was just not interested in having a child. He told his wife that it was because of the child that he gave up. That was his child as far as he was concerned. I think that changed when he met Vicky. Then he decided they should have children, but there was difficulty in conceiving. They went through a lot.

"When Wally met Vicky, there were some changes. One day I called him and asked him for a favor. He started yelling and wanted to know why people keep asking him to do stuff. I told him to never mind. I later learned that's when Vicky was here for her first visit (that I was not aware of) and she'd just told him she hadn't told her kids about him and wanted to wait until her son graduated from high school. He pointed out that he'd told everyone about his daughter so why couldn't she tell them. He wanted her to be excited and tell everyone right away. He didn't want her to hide the fact that she had a baby she gave up for adoption. When I learned about it I told him that she may have a very good reason to wait. She knew her kids and Wally didn't.

"I knew Wally was going to be with her on Mother's Day. He called me and told me not to be upset. He explained he was not going because of Mother's Day, but for her son's graduation. I thought, 'I'm not that dumb!' We argued about it. He said he had a good friend who told him that he should be with his mother on Mother's Day. I told him he had completely invalidated me at that point. It hurt a lot. When he came back, I asked him how he felt about it. He said, 'I love her just like I love you, no difference, no less, no more, get over it.' I said I was having a hard time dealing with it because his reaction to this whole thing just blew me away. He saw her again in June and September – probably six trips in the first year. I told him I had a feeling that his reaction to Vicky, as strong as it is, has a lot to do with his giving up his baby. He told me not to think for him. I told him I hoped when he finds his little girl she treats him the way he is treating Vicky, because if she doesn't, he is going to be very hurt.

"I've met Vicky and she is a sweetheart – someone I could have been friends with. Now that all this time has passed, the hurt feelings are gone. I feel that if something happens to me he has somebody. My mom just passed away and it would be kind of nice to have another mom here. I miss her. For him, he will have another family to make it easier. I don't think Wally realizes when I'm gone how hard it is going to be. I don't think he has any idea so at least he's got someone. That's a comforting feeling for me. I have told him that I want no secrets. There's nothing wrong in his going to visit Vicky for a week. It's the secrets that bother me – you know, the hiding. He went on one trip and I didn't even know he was gone. The not telling hurts more than the telling. There isn't anymore of that now – when he goes, I know. When he went the first time, I got all his pictures from birth on and gave them to him to take to her. I didn't have time to put them in an album, but she can do with them what she wants – baby pictures, childhood, baseball, gymnastics, football, everything. So she could have her own album of Wally. I have no hard feelings against her. I could surely understand that she was anxious to see Wally. I am glad that he has a positive relationship with his half brother and sister, too. His brother came to visit during the holidays. They were able to spend some one-on-one time together.

"If I have lost anything as a result of this reunion, I still feel that I have had the best years. Maybe the closeness is not quite like it used to be. We don't see Wally as much as we used to. He does call often. I think it hurts my husband the most, more than it does me. He has never said anything to Wally and I hope he never does. I don't want him to get into it with Wally. Wally is happy. I guess if he is totally up front with us, he won't hurt our feelings. He knows how it feels to lose a child. He thinks Vicky's gone through the same thing and so he's trying to make it up to her. He, of course, does not agree. He thinks it has nothing to do with it. He writes letters to his daughter and is keeping the letters for her. If they meet, all those letters will be given to her. He's living his life around it. I can't believe his daughter will react in the same way he has.

"They now know they are having a boy. I think he would indulge a girl to no end. He was thrilled that it was a boy. He came

Shirley Budd Pusey

over to show me the ultrasound pictures. Everything is okay with us now. I'm just concerned about Wally. He was a model child, never any problems. I hope his kindness is reciprocated."

One Last Story...

As a final note, I want to share this reunion story:

Faith, a birth mother, was happy, surprised, shocked, and apprehensive when I called to let her know that the baby boy she had placed for adoption twenty-nine years before was searching for her. Faith had told her husband (not the birth father) prior to their marriage about this chapter in her life, but had not told her son and daughter as she was concerned about their reaction. So for six months, she and Brent, the adoptee, shared non-identifying correspondence through me.

Faith finally decided to tell her family on her birthday. After opening her gifts, she courageously announced that she had received a very special gift earlier in the year. She then explained about my initial call to her and shared the letters and pictures that she had received from Brent. Her son's reaction? -- "I always wanted a big brother."

A reunion was soon planned for Faith and her family, Brent, his wife and his adoptive parents.

If you would like to share your adoption reunion story with the author for possible inclusion in a future volume, please send it to Shirley Budd Pusey, c/o Acacia Publishing, 1366 E. Thomas, Suite 305, Phoenix, AZ 85014.

Shirley Budd Pusey